SUMMA PUBLICATIONS, INC.

Thomas M. Hines
Publisher

William C. Carter
Editor in chief

Orders:
  P.O. Box 660725
  Birmingham, AL 35266-0725

Editorial Address:
  2530 Mountain Brook Circle
  Birmingham, AL 35223

Weaving Balzac's Web

Weaving Balzac's Web

Spinning Tales and Creating the Whole
of *La Comédie humaine*

James C. Madden

SUMMA PUBLICATIONS, INC.
Birmingham, Alabama
2003

Copyright 2003
Summa Publications, Inc.
ISBN 1-883479-41-X

Library of Congress Control Number 2003100001

Printed in the United States of America

For my parents,
Kay and Joe Madden

Contents

Contents (continued)

Acknowledgments

To study Balzac is necessarily to follow paths carved out by others, so I feel I must first acknowledge the many fine Balzacians whose work has enriched and illuminated my own readings of *La Comédie humaine*.

This book began as a doctoral thesis at the University of Illinois, and I would like to thank colleagues and friends in the French Department there for their support and encouragement over the years, especially those who had a direct influence on the development of this study. My thanks to Nicolae Popescu for the healthy skepticism he brought to his reading and our discussions about Balzac. Anna Livia Brawn read through early drafts with a keen eye, and I greatly appreciate her detailed, challenging, and encouraging comments. Emile Talbot was a constant source of support, advice and perspective not only with regard to this project—from its conception to publication—but in all aspects of my career. My debt and my gratitude are greatest to Armine Kotin Mortimer. It was she who introduced me to Balzac, and she has since been unfailingly generous with her time, talents, and counsel. Her input and encouragement were essential to the completion of this book. My sincere thanks to you all.

I would also like to thank my family for their unflagging support: My brother and sisters, Eileen, Fran, and Nancy, and above all my parents, Kay and Joe Madden, who have always encouraged my impractical career choices. For this, and for everything else, this book is dedicated to them.

—*J. C. M.*

Introduction

Stories, Told and Heard

LA COMÉDIE HUMAINE IS A STORY composed of stories. The almost one
hundred individual stories represented by the numerous titles—which are
subtitles in some sense—make up the whole, a vibrant and moving portrait
of Paris and France under the Restoration and the July Monarchy. As the
title of the whole indicates, we must always remember that *La Comédie
humaine* has a larger sense, a broader meaning; 1830s Paris is merely the
frame in which larger truths about the human condition are played out.

On a realistic, extratextual level, this story and these stories are
told to us, the readers of *La Comédie humaine,* by Balzac; they exist as
literature, within the pages of the book we have in hand. But these stories
also exist on a diegetic level, that is on the same fictional level as the characters in them, and they exist on that level as stories. The famous recurring
characters of Balzac's text often know each other, or at least of each other,
and they know each other's stories. Many of the individual stories, the
plots of the different novels and *nouvelles,* take place because one character either knows or seeks to know the story of another. Rastignac's desire
to succeed socially leads to his learning stories: that of Mme de Beauséant,
that of Mme de Nucingen, that of Vautrin, and ultimately the whole story
of *Le Père Goriot.* Rose Cormon's fortune is known to the people of
Alençon, the quest for it creates the action of *La Vieille fille.* As Léo
Mazet has pointed out, the circulation of recurring characters in *La
Comédie humaine* is only one example of the ties that bind the individual
stories into one: "La circulation de personnages de texte(s) en texte(s) ne

représente à l'évidence qu'un paradgime d'autres circulations qui affectent profondément chaque texte" [*It is evident that the circulation of characters from text(s) to text(s) merely represents a paradigm for other circulations that profoundly affect each individual text*] ("Récit(s) dans le récit," 129). Stories circulate within the text in much the same way characters do, and can be considered just as important.

Often in *La Comédie humaine* we, as readers, are allowed to witness the circulation of stories. The act of narration is an important one both in Balzac's text and within his fictional world. Balzac highly esteemed the art of the raconteur; as we see in *Autre étude de femme,* he placed it on a higher level than literature and saw the oral tradition as part of the beautiful by-gone world, swept away by the Revolution. His stories are often set in narrative frames that show us the act of narration as an interaction among his characters, and most often the characters in both the frame and the object story it presents are part of his famous system. Such narrative framing was hardly innovative; we see it in the French tradition at least as early as Marguerite de Navarre's *Heptaméron,* and that work was preceded in Europe by the *Decameron* and the *Canterbury Tales.* What is unique to Balzac's frames, I believe, is their importance to the works in which they appear, as well as to the larger work as a whole, which is itself still another frame. Balzac's frames are rarely incidental and should never be ignored. Most obviously, they serve to link individual stories to the edifice of *La Comédie humaine* as a whole; in *Sarrasine,* for example, the story of the sculptor and the castrato is told to Mme de Rochefide (*Béatrix,* et al.) by an anonymous narrator who is a friend of Mme d'Espard (*L'Interdiction,* et al.), etc. Such linkage between the object story and the work as a whole is a primary function of Balzac's frames. Yet this linkage—which is in itself often more complex than it first appears—is not the only function of the frames; in many cases, it is not even necessary. The miser Gobseck is a frequent, if often secondary, character in many works of *La Comédie humaine,* and the character has no need of Derville or the Grandlieu family to place him in the larger text. Even the Lantys, the family of the castrato's niece in *Sarrasine,* appear briefly in the larger chronicle.

In *S/Z,* his exhaustive study of Balzac's *Sarrasine,* Roland Barthes observes of the relationship between the frame and the story:

il ne peut plus être question d'établir une hiérarchie rhétorique entre les
deux parties de l'histoire, comme on le fait communément : la soirée
chez les Lanty n'est pas un simple prologue et l'aventure de Sarrasine
n'est pas l'histoire principale; le sculpteur n'est pas le héros et le nar-
rateur n'est pas un simple personnage protatique. (96)
there can no longer be any question of establishing a hierarchy be-
tween the two parts of the story, as is commonly done: the party at the
Lantys' is not simply a prologue and the adventure of Sarrasine is not
the principal story; the sculptor is not the hero and the narrator is not
merely a protatic character.

Barthes proves this point in the rest of his book with respect to *Sarrasine*.
What he does not say—it is not in the scope of *S/Z*—is that this is generally true of the framed narratives of *La Comédie humaine*. While I would
not go so far as to say that the framed stories are not in fact the principal
stories in the majority of cases, it is true that the frames are much more
than prologues. It is especially important to consider the characters in the
frames; as Barthes suggests, the narrators and narratees in these texts do
far more than serve as a pretext for communicating the story to the reader.
Those who tell Balzac's stories, as well as those who listen to them—the
latter in fact sharing the role of audience with the reader—do far more
than perform this simple function of communication. These characters,
whom readers meet before the story begins, and who are still with us when
it has ended, very often influence the readers' understanding of the object
story. The figures in the frame frequently comment on the characters or on
a given theme in the object story. Sometimes they are not so active, and it
is their mere presence in the frame that suggests a link, based on information about them given either in the frame or in another part of *La Comédie
humaine*. Balzac's narrative frames and the characters in them serve not
only to provoke what Allan Pasco called an "outward motion," from the
framed story to the larger world of *La Comédie humaine* (*Balzacian
Montage*, 103), but also an inward movement, from *La Comédie humaine*
to the frame, and from the frame into the framed story.

Obviously, as with almost any reading of Balzac's work, the system of recurring characters plays an important part in this view of the figures in the frames; however an in-depth knowledge of Balzac's *dramatis
personae* is by no means always necessary to the readers' appreciation of

the story/frame relationship. Such works as *Gobseck* and *La Messe de l'athée,* while certainly enriched by a knowledge of the larger *Comédie humaine,* can be considered self-contained, that is to say that the naive reader can appreciate the effect of the narrator and the narratee, the link between frame and story, almost as well as the experienced *Balzacien.* In each case, a careful construction gives unity to the frame/story combination, increasing the text's complexity, and the readers' interest in and enjoyment of the work. A careful analysis of the frames and the frame characters of *La Comédie humaine* strongly suggests that Balzac was conscious of this effect—of framed stories being enriched by the characters in the frames—and sought to exploit it, and that he did so with a subtlety not often recognized on the part of this author haunted by what Gérard Genette called a "démon explicatif" (*Figures II,* 79). This view of Balzac's work reveals a richness, a complexity, and an ambiguity in the interconnections and interplay of the different parts of this textual whole that are too often ignored, by readers and critics alike. Studying the narrators and narratees of *La Comédie humaine,* and studying their relationships to the stories told in the text helps us to see the complexity of Balzac's work as a whole. Characters interact with each other just as stories, attitudes, and reactions intersect and interconnect. The reader of Balzac's text(s) enters into an extremely complex equation, which is further complicated by his own knowledge of and perceptions of *La Comédie humaine.* Far from being the monolith that so many of its detractors describe, *La Comédie humaine* is an unstable text, with many openings and gaps for the reader to fill in. The world Balzac paints is in motion, as indicated by Michel Butor's analogy of *La Comédie humaine* as a *mobile romanesque* (*Répertoire,* 83). It can even be chaotic, as turbulent for the readers as the society it describes is for the characters. A first reading of *La Comédie humaine,* whether of the whole or of fragments, shows us Balzac's world as it is; who the characters are, what they do, and how they interrelate and interact with each other—all the different parts of the mobile and the connections between them. It is the rereading of the text(s) that sets the mobile in motion.

This study seeks to demonstrate that complex interconnected motion by a close examination of frame/story configurations throughout *La Comédie humaine.* As readers and rereaders, we become part of the creation of the whole of *La Comédie humaine.* The more we know about Balzac's fictional world, the more we see and appreciate the myriad threads of this enormous and intricate textual web. Our active reading enables us to understand that the recurring characters do far more in this text than simply create the *effet de réel* so important to Balzac's artistic vision. They and the other threads of meaning create the dynamic unity of this vital and vibrant text. It is hoped that this approach will further illustrate Pierre Barbéris' essential description of Balzac as a visionary realist: "réaliste parce que visionnaire, visionnaire parce que réaliste" (*Le Monde de Balzac*, 13).

The first chapter offers a close examination of the narrators, those characters that take over the act of storytelling from the authorial narrator, who for the sake of clarity is designated as the Narrator throughout this book. Two different kinds of narrator are discussed: the character-narrators, who are identifiable as part of Balzac's system of recurring characters, and the narrating *je,* anonymous, first-person narrators who, while also fictional characters, are not so easy to place in Balzac's world. Chapter 2 is a discussion of the narratees, those characters who listen to the stories told. These characters can affect our perception of an object story through active commentary, or more subtly, through the deceptively passive act of listening. Chapter 3 looks at texts in which the lines are not so clearly drawn between narrator and narratee. In these cases, the roles are shared by several characters, further complicating our task as readers. Chapter 4 is an examination of embedded narratives. I draw a distinction between framed narratives, in which the object story is the main story, and embedded narratives, where the object story is secondary, a plot element in a larger narrative construction. These cases offer an interesting opportunity to examine the motivations for and the effects of the act of narration in a more developed context. Finally the conclusion presents some general observations about the nature of reading *La Comédie humaine* that have grown out the research and writing of this book, preceded by a discussion of questions of credibility. I believe that Balzac uses the reputations that he has created for his own characters to support or (more interestingly) to undermine them in storytelling situations. With a subtlety that belies the stereotype of *le romancier qui dit tout,* Balzac destabilizes his own text, creating ambiguity and further challenging the reader. In the end, we see that, contrary to the judgment of so many readers and critics,

Balzac has not told us everything. *La Comédie humaine* is a text filled with shadowy spaces for the reader to explore.

Chapter I

Telling More Than They Say: The Narrators

BECAUSE OF THEIR HIGHLY VISIBLE AND obviously active role, Balzac's narrators offer a logical and convenient point of departure for this exploration of the text. The study of narrators in *La Comédie humaine* suggests itself, in part, because of an absence. Balzac's Narrator, the voice or entity that describes the action which takes place in *La Comédie humaine,* is such a strong presence in the text—even an aggressive one, to use Michael Lastinger's expression ("Narration et 'point de vue' dans deux romans de Balzac," 271)—that any instance in which Balzac causes this Narrator to yield to another voice, to a character, is necessarily intriguing. Many critics, most perhaps, simply assimilate this Narrator with the author himself, and there is nothing surprising in this: Balzac and his Narrator share opinions on virtually every subject, as far as we can tell. However, it is necessary to distinguish between this Narrator and the author, and not merely because this distinction serves my purposes. As Gérard Genette observed, Balzac's Narrator is someone who knows the maison Vauquer and its inhabitants in *Le Père Goriot,* and who knows Paris as it exists in *La Comédie humaine* and the characters who inhabit it; these characters are real people for that narrating voice (*Figures III,* 276). To use a more properly Balzacian analogy, we can think in the terms Balzac himself used in his *avant-propos* of 1842: "La Société française allait être l'historien, je ne devais être que le secrétaire" (1:11)[1] [*Society was to be the historian, I was to be merely the scribe*]; the Narrator is an observer, a chronicler, who shares with us the people and events in the world in which he sees (almost) all. Balzac, as author, is the creator-god of this world, of this society which is the historian, while the Narrator is merely a scribe. Balzac knows everything, the Narrator knows almost everything. "Almost," because there are riddles in *La Comédie humaine* whose answers the Narrator either does not know or chooses not to share with us. The force of the Narrator's presence in the text is such that it is easy for us to overlook what he does *not* say, what shadows Balzac has left in different parts of his world.

It is important to define exactly what, on a textual level, this Narrator is. There are certain textual indications that this entity has a masculine orientation, and so masculine pronouns are used to refer to the Narrator, but we cannot consider him to be a character like the other characters of the *Comédie humaine;* he is not "human" in the way that Goriot or the duchesse de Langeais are. There is no pretense, indeed no possibility, that the Narrator is corporeal; he is not bound by any laws of space or motion in the context of the stories of *La Comédie humaine.* He reads characters' thoughts and knows their secrets, sometimes better than they do themselves. He knows their pasts and in some cases their futures. Not even Vautrin, for all his nearly supernatural perception, sees into souls like the Narrator does; if he did, he would never be trapped by Mlle Michonneau. This superhuman vision and knowledge make it impossible for this Narrator to be considered a character like all the others. It is for this reason that I believe that the "je" who narrates so many of Balzac's shorter works must be considered as distinct from the Narrator of such works as *Le Père Goriot* and *La Cousine Bette.* These "je" are people—physical, human, and in many cases limited. The narrator of *Le Message* makes a friend and is having an affair and does not know that the countess Juliette de Montpersan is making him a gift until many months after the action of the story has taken place; the narrator of *Sarrasine* is a friend of the marquise

---

[1] All citations from the primary text refer to the *Pléiade* edition of *La Comédie humaine* (eds. P-G Castex et al.), the volume number followed by the page number. Unless otherwise indicated, all references to editorial material also refer to the *Pléiade* edition, with the author's name given in the specific reference. All translations, including any errors or infelicities, are my own.

d'Espard and does not know, when he begins telling his tale to the marquise de Rochefide, that she will ultimately break their implied contract.
Perhaps more importantly, he seems to know nothing of her career in later
texts. The several narrating "je" of the *Comédie humaine* are characters in
their own right, they have personalities, personal opinions, and experiences, etc. They are not drawn with the fullness of the named, recurring
characters, because we do not have the Narrator's God's-eye view to give
us their descriptions and histories, but we should nonetheless accord them
the same status as Rastignac or Eugénie Grandet. These first-person narrators will be discussed in more detail further on. Before discussing the
character-narrators, it is necessary to further explore the voice through
which they come to us, the voice that cedes its place to them, *qui leur
donne la parole,* as the French put it so well.

Perhaps the best place to begin a study of Balzac's Narrator is with
Le Père Goriot. There are two reasons for this, the first being that this
novel is probably the most common point of entry into Balzac's world, so
it is logical that we should begin studying the Narrator at the point where
most of us first meet him. The novel begins with the celebrated description
of the house where the action will begin, where the individual stories of
Rastignac, Vautrin, and Goriot will collide, creating the catharsis that in
turn creates the novel's central story. In addition to the traditional exposition providing the setting of time and place, the Narrator in the opening
pages of this novel directly addresses the reader, really the Narratee. This
is the second, and perhaps more important, reason for beginning a study of
the Narrator with *Le Père Goriot.* What is interesting about these passages
is not the insistence on truth of the story to be told (*"All is true!"*), which
is fairly conventional, but the tone with which the Narrator addresses the
Narratee. The Narrator is at once defiant and defensive, informing the
reader in advance that what follows will be dark and depressing, full of
"souffrances réelles" and of "joies souvent fausses" (3:50), but it is only
the truth. By insisting that he is only reporting a true story, typical of
Paris, the Narrator makes of *Le Père Goriot* not only a novel, but also an
indictment of society, including the Narratee:

> ...vous qui tenez ce livre d'une main blanche, vous qui vous enfon-
> cez dans un moelleux fauteuil en vous disant: « Peut-être ceci va-t-il
> m'amuser. » Après avoir lu les secrètes infortunes du père Goriot, vous

dînerez avec appétit en mettant votre insensibilité sur le compte de
l'auteur, en le taxant d'exagération, en l'accusant de poésie. Ah! sa-
chez-le: ce drame n'est ni une fiction, ni un roman. *All is true!* il est si
véritable, que chacun peut en reconnaître les éléments chez soi, dans
son cœur, peut-être. (3:50)
you who hold this book in a white hand, settling yourself into a soft
armchair thinking "Perhaps this will amuse me." After having read the
secret miseries of old Goriot, you will dine with a healthy appetite, all
the while blaming the author for your own insensitivity, taxing him with
exaggeration, accusing him of making poetry. Ah! Know this: this
drama is neither a fiction, nor a novel. All is true! *It is so true to life*
that each of you will recognize its essential elements in your own life,
in your own heart, perhaps.

This passage clearly shows that the Narrator wishes to be seen as a neutral
observer; any darkness, any pessimism that his story may contain is not
his fault, but the fault of a cruel and indifferent society, of which the Narratee is a part, and of which the Narrator is a mere observer. This implicit
condemnation of the Narratee shows us that the Narrator's pretention of
neutrality is a false stand; he is a judge as well as an observer, and he finds
the reader of his tale ("vous qui tenez ce livre d'une main blanche") guilty
of the same cruel indifference as the characters who will kill Goriot. In a
larger sense, since we are discussing *La Comédie humaine* and not *La
Comédie parisienne,* we can say that the reader is implicitly cast in this
role, and is thus meant to see himself as an accomplice to these crimes,
every bit as guilty as the Narratee.

These opening pages also show the great assurance of the Narrator
as he describes the setting of the story, confident that the Narratee will
recognize both what is being described and the reliability of the description. The minutiae that the Narrator gives reinforce the purely factual
aspect he wishes to give to his account, confirming again his trustworthiness. We are thus induced to trust the Narrator, to accept his authority as a
reporter. Taking this a step further, this same trustworthiness establishes
the Narrator as a judge as well: if he is only reporting the facts as an objective observer, then his condemnation must be valid. As several critics
have pointed out, the Narrator's direct interventions, his overt commentaries on the action taking place, become less significant as the novel pro-

gresses. This is best illustrated by the way in which the biography of old Goriot is revealed to the reader. The first details are provided by the Narrator, in an omniscient mode, as he describes Goriot's decline by giving details of his paradoxical ascent in the Maison Vauquer. Monsieur Goriot first occupies one of the nicer apartments on the first floor (at 1,200 francs a year), and his status declines as he moves up one floor and correspondingly lower in the opinion of Mme Vauquer and the other residents, until he finally becomes papa Goriot, up in the attic, in the room next to Rastignac and Mlle Michonneau (at 45 francs a month). Once this is established, however, Balzac allows other voices to provide necessary background information. The duchesse de Langeais tells Rastignac and Mme de Beauséant the story of Goriot and the marriages of his daughters, and what information remains to be learned is given by the Narrator, but as a synopsis of what Rastignac learned by making enquiries of Goriot's successor, M. Muret. As Pierre Barbéris pointed out, this progression shows Balzac's desire that his world should stand on its own in the readers' minds, that the Narrator's discourse should be seen as reporting rather than the writing of fiction, as observation rather than creation (*Le Monde de Balzac*, 87). The Narrator is not telling us anything about Goriot and his family that is not more or less common knowledge, albeit in different milieus, of the Paris that Narrator and Narratee both know so well.

This progressive relinquishment of control of information by the Narrator shows us another aspect of Balzac's narrative technique. Although the Narrator, as Balzac's textual alter-ego, is privy to all the information in this world, it is not always directly from his voice that we learn what is going on in a given text. There are several things that the Narrator, for different reasons, does not reveal to us. One example of this phenomenon: about halfway through *Le Père Goriot*, Delphine gives Rastignac a watch, with the following note: "Je veux que vous pensiez à moi à toute heure, *parce que*. . . –Delphine." [*I want you to think of me at all times, because. . .*] And the Narrator comments: "Ce dernier mot faisait sans doute allusion à quelque scène qui avait eu lieu entre eux, Eugène en fut attendri" [*This last word was doubtless an allusion to some scene that had taken place between them, Eugene was touched*] (198). It is not difficult for the reader to guess what sort of scene the Narrator is referring to, as the "sans doute" indicates; even without the Narrator's comment, Delphine's *parce que*. . . is in itself quite suggestive. What is most interesting about this passage is the Narrator's reticence. It is as if the Narrator, and Balzac behind him, want to afford the couple a little privacy, and to suggest that the reader is not necessarily privy to every important moment in their relationship. The affair between Delphine and Eugène is developing on its own, away from the reader's prying eyes, outside the scope of the Narrator's view. A similar moment of reticence can be found in *La Cousine Bette,* when the Narrator is describing Bette's apartment, with the exception of her bedroom: "Quant à la chambre, personne n'y avait jamais pénétré" [*As for the bedroom, no one had ever ventured so far*] (7:138). Again, the symbolism is not subtle, and surely isn't meant to be, but the Narrator's reticence says as much about the situation as a long explication could.

On a few occasions, the Narrator simply announces that he is incapable of reproducing something. One interesting case of this kind of silence can be found in *Béatrix.* Insulted in her verbal duel with Camille Maupin, Béatrix de Rochefide is provoked into a furious response:

> elle lança sur Camille un regard plein de haine [. . .] et trouva, sans les chercher, les flèches les plus acérées de son carquois. Camille écouta froidement [. . .] cette tirade furieuse qui pétilla d'injures si mordantes qu'il est impossible de la rapporter. (2:800)
> *she threw at Camille a look full of hate. . . and found without looking for them the sharpest arrows in her quiver. Camille listened to her coldly. . . this furious tirade crackled with insults so cutting that it is impossible to reproduce them.*

Béatrix has a similar explosion of anger later in the novel, "une kyrielle d'épigrammes atroces" (878), that the Narrator shrinks from reproducing for us. These tirades are interesting not only because of what they reveal to us about Béatrix, but because of what they tell us about the Narrator. A cynical explanation would be that Balzac does not trust his own skill as a writer, that he is unsure of his ability to produce "épigrammes" of the force his scenes require. Another explanation (far more plausible—Balzac did not suffer from low self-esteem) is that it is language that Balzac did not trust in these cases; Balzac quite possibly felt words were inadequate to portray the blind fury that is latent within Béatrix. The examples from *Béatrix* were chosen because they are both easily located and identified, and also because they are unusual. In itself, this reluctance to diminish emotion by putting it into words is not uncommon in *La Comédie humaine;* usually, however, these silences cover happiness rather than rage. For example, the three years of happiness that Mme de Beauséant and Gaston de Neuil spend in Switzerland occupies only a paragraph in the text of *La Femme abandonnée* (2:492). In *Splendeurs et misères des courtisanes,* one of the original chapter titles, reprinted in the Garnier-Flammarion edition (1968), is "Chapitre ennuyeux car il explique quatre ans de bonheur" [*A boring chapter as it describes four years of happiness*] (114); four pages for four years in the longest novel of *La Comédie humaine.* The irony in this chapter title aside, we see again that Balzac chose to leave in the readers' imagination these lovers' idylls that are beyond words, and to let us imagine just what verbal arrows the deceptively blond and fragile Mme de Rochefide could find in her quiver.

There are obviously many examples of reticence of one kind or another in *La Comédie humaine,* and to list and comment on them all would be an almost endless undertaking. We should note however one last type of silence in Balzac's text, the silences that are to be found, as Lucien Dällenbach put it, between the individual texts ("Du Fragment au cosmos," 426). As Balzac himself explained in his preface to *Une fille d'Eve, La Comédie humaine* resembles life in this way:

> il en est ainsi dans le monde social. Vous rencontrez au milieu d'un salon un homme que vous avez perdu de vue depuis dix ans: il est premier ministre ou capitaliste, vous l'avez connu sans redingote, sans esprit public ou privé, vous l'admirez dans sa gloire, vous vous étonnez de sa fortune ou de ses talents [etc.]. (2:265)
>
> *It is like this in society. You meet in the middle of salon a man that you lost sight of ten years ago: he is prime minister or a capitalist, you knew him without a coat, without any wit public or private, you admire him in his glory, you are astounded by his fortune or his talents. . .*

We do not always see the entire evolution of characters in *La Comédie humaine*; there are gaps. Many of these gaps are filled in, if only sketchily or by allusion, in other texts of *La Comédie humaine*, but sometimes, we are left to fill in the blanks on our own. One striking case of a character evolving between texts offers a good example of Balzacian restraint, an

animal whose very existence some find doubtful. This is the case of Anselme Popinot, a character who has two important appearances in *La
Comédie humaine*. Popinot offers an excellent example of a character
evolving outside of our perspective as readers, and this development deserves to be analyzed in some detail.

In *César Birotteau*, Anselme is a model of virtue, whose hard work
and devotion win him the hand of Césarine and set him on the road to
fortune. The end of this Horatio Alger beginning is found in *Le Cousin
Pons*, where Anselme and Césarine have become the count and countess
Popinot, Anselme being an extremely successful businessman and former
minister of Agriculture and Commerce. Popinot's appearance in *Le Cousin
Pons* is a point of intersection for many meaningful threads of *La Comédie
humaine*. This case offers a particularly rich opportunity to examine the
force and complexity of such a point of convergence. We follow different
threads away from this point to different parts of the larger text, and we
are able to read between the lines of Balzac's apparently (but deceptively)
complete text. The nuances we find illuminate the rich ambiguity of Balzac's world.

At first glance, Popinot's social progression seems nothing but
admirable, perhaps even a virtuous parallel to Rastignac's similar, if more
morally ambiguous, advancement in position, power, and title. The only
shadow we might see in this success story is the rather absurd title of
"comte Popinot," as is illustrated by a passage from *Le Cousin Pons*, in
which Popinot is referred to both as a count and as "ce héros bourgeois de
la révolution de Juillet" (500), but this says more about Louis-Philippe and
his court than about Anselme himself. Yet things are perhaps not quite as
simple as they appear. There is after all something disturbing about the
alacrity with which the good and gentle Popinot colludes with the Camusots' condemnation of Pons. The count knows all the actors in this *drame
bourgeois*, and yet he finds credible that the *bonasse* old musician would
have conspired to play a cruel trick on Cécile Camusot. There is something here that doesn't quite add up. As is so often the case with Balzac,
the most important figure in the equation is a financial one.

When Popinot meets, and then shuns, Pons in a curiosity shop after
the collapse of the marriage Pons has tried to arrange for his "petite
cousine," Popinot has already agreed to marry his son to Cécile, a match
he had previously refused. His mind has been changed not by sympathy

for the putative victim of Pons's alleged cruel trick, but by a significant increase in her dowry, the Marville property of her parents:

> la présidente fit reluire avec art l'avantage de se nommer Popinot de Marville et l'énormité de la dot. [. . .] Aucune famille raisonnable ne pouvait refuser une pareille alliance; aussi le comte Popinot et sa femme l'acceptèrent-ils; puis, en gens intéressés à l'honneur de la famille dans laquelle ils entraient, ils promirent leur concours pour expliquer la catastrophe arrivée la veille. (564)
>
> *the présidente artfully emphasised the advantages of the name Popinot de Marville and the enormity of the dowry. No reasonable family could refuse such a match; thus the count Popinot and his wife accepted it; then, as people interested in the honor of the family which they were joining, they promised their support in explaining the catastrophe of the previous evening.*

And so, for the sake of a dowry and a marriage, Pons is condemned by the bourgeois world that used to feed him. The accusation of venality might seem a bit hasty, if this were the only evidence, but Balzac has left other clues in his text that the Popinot of 1847 is quite different from the Anselme of 1818. It appears as if the ambitious but virtuous *pied-bot*[2] of *César Birotteau* has become something of an opportunist in *Le Cousin Pons*: There is a reference to Popinot as "ce coq de la droguerie, au profit de qui, selon les envieux du quartier des Lombards, la révolution de Juillet avait été faite, au moins autant qu'à celui de la branche cadette" [*this cock of the pharmaceutical business, for whose benefit, according to the envious of the rue des Lombards, the July revolution had taken place, as much as for that of the younger branch of the royal family*] (506). The charge is obviously absurd and is undermined by being attributed to the envious bourgeois who have undoubtedly been less successful than Popinot, but there is nonetheless in this passage an explicit link between Popinot's success and the régime of which his creator so heartily disapproved. Another passage throws another ambiguous light on Anselme, when we read that Popinot, "malgré sa modestie, s'était, comme on le sait, laissé faire comte.

---

[2]In *Birotteau,* the Narrator points out that the club-foot is an infirmity that Anselme shares with Lord Byron, Walter Scott, and Talleyrand (6; 82).

« A cause de mon fils », dit-il à ses nombreux amis" [*in spite of his modesty had, as everyone knows, allowed himself to be made a count. "For my son," he explained to his numerous friends*] (515). A reader who first met Anselme in *César Birotteau* would find this modesty perfectly natural and consistent with the character described in that novel, but perhaps, to a first-time reader, it might not seem an ironic comment, as if the modest count protests too much. It is for the sake of this same son, after all, that Popinot has agreed to the marriage with Cécile Camusot (de Marville), however reluctant the groom might be (the "jeune vicomte" is described as having "des yeux peu charmés" by Cécile [506]). And we can reasonably speculate that the name of Popinot will fall away under the pressure of Marville, as Camusot has for the *présidente* and her husband.

It is also interesting to note here that the Narrator has rejected any responsibility for these remarks; it is just commercial gossip, the *qu'en dira-t-on* of the rue des Lombards. Nonetheless, Balzac has included these remarks in the text, he has placed them in the reader's conciousness—they should not be dismissed or ignored. For all of these factors to come together to cast a shadow of ambiguity on Popinot, two further considerations are necessary, two threads to be followed to illuminate the role that Anselme Popinot plays in *Le Cousin Pons* and in *La Comédie humaine* as a whole. At the end of *Le Cousin Pons*, Popinot is in possession of the "héroïne" of that novel, Pons' collection (7:763). By buying it from the Camusots, he has profited from an ill-gotten fortune, and he is at least in some degree complicit in the Camusots' crimes. A defender of Popinot might point out that he had no direct knowledge of how the Camusots came to own the collection, but this is a rather lawyerly distinction. As I said before, Popinot knows the actors involved in the drama too well, and knows the circumstances of the rupture between the Camusots and their cousin; it is not credible that he should not be at least suspicious of the Camusots' hypocritical mourning of their late benefactor. What cannot be disputed is that Popinot has benefited, as much as anyone else and more than a few, in the dispossession of Pons. This situation stands out all the more to experienced readers of *La Comédie humaine,* who are familiar with this recurring Balzacian theme of the ill-gotten fortune, as in *Madame Firmiani* and *L'Interdiction*. The link with *L'Interdiction* is especially intriguing, because one of the heroes of that *nouvelle* is none other than Anselme's uncle, the charitable magistrate Popinot, a very different sort of "héros bourgeois." It is interesting that the old judge is linked with a nephew in *L'Interdiction,* but not with Anselme. Rather, Judge Popinot seems closer to Bianchon, his nephew by marriage, than to Anselme, his nephew by blood. I do not think it is going too far to suggest that there is more of a spiritual kinship between Jean-Jules Popinot and Bianchon (a fellow healer) than between the modest judge and his socially ambitious nephew. There is a coincidence that is really too fortuitous to be a coincidence in the fact that Judge Popinot's nephew, who is guilty—if to a much lesser degree—of the same crimes as the Judge's adversary, Mme d'Espard (he has maligned an innocent man and taken his treasure), ends up allied, not only socially but politically, to the magistrate whose complacent venality was used to compensate for old Popinot's virtuous rectitude, Camusot (de Marville).

The concentration of all these factors gives the experienced reader, the *habitué* of *La Comédie humaine,* a vastly different portrait of the count Popinot than the one ostensibly given in the text of *Le Cousin Pons.* The perceptions of the reader of the whole are vastly different from those of the reader of the fragment, of the novel as a unity in and of itself. Balzac has duped us by seeming to tell all. The all-knowing, all-seeing Narrator has not been all-telling; his assertive, aggressive *bavardage* has perhaps obscured a certain selective reticence. The consideration of such factors as recurring themes or of (seemingly) contradictory aspects of the "biography" of a given Balzacian character do much to enhance our reading of *La Comédie humaine.* They complexify the text and challenge the reader; they challenge not only our memories, but our judgment as well. For if Balzac leaves little to the imagination when he describes the plots or characters of individual novels, the *Comédie humaine* as a whole is rich with ambiguities, with questions that it is up to the reader not only to answer, but to discover as well. These questions are often left unanswered altogether, and the ambiguities remain just that, because it is relatively rare, and certainly more rare than is generally acknowledged, that Balzac paints a character who is purely 'good' or purely 'evil'—even the definitions of those words are not as clear, within *La Comédie humaine,* as is commonly believed.

La Comédie humaine is an enormously complicated text, and reading it is an enormously complicated process. Each text is connected to so many others, in so many different ways, that when we read a given fragment, a novel or *nouvelle,* we are always reading a part of a larger whole. The perceptions of each reader change according to his or her own personal Balzacian baggage, according to which themes or motifs have seemed important, according to what characters and characteristics have stood out to us through our own reading and rereadings. In the case just outlined, it is Popinot's brusque rejection of Pons that makes us wonder, that sets in motion the Balzacian mobile; *Le Cousin Pons* is connected to *César Birotteau* and to *L'Interdiction* just as much as to *La Cousine Bette,* *Le Père Goriot,* and so on and back again through the seemingly endless connections and interconnections of Balzac's unbelievably complex world and even more complex text. This complexity, these interconnections destabilize the authority of the Narrator. The reader who understands these connections (or at least is aware of their presence, which is sometimes the best we can hope for) can go beyond the Narrator, over his head, to meet with Balzac in the text to become that ideal Barthesian reader, the one who is not just a consumer but also a producer of text (*S/Z,* 10). What, if indeed anything, has happened to Anselme Popinot between 1819 and 1847? how and why has he changed or not changed between *César Birotteau* and *Le Cousin Pons?* It is up to the reader to decide. The supposedly omniscient Narrator's authority is limited: we can go beyond it. Through careful analysis of different parts of the Balzacian mobile, the (re)reader of *La Comédie humaine* can become—at least to some degree—independent of the Narrator.

Section I: The Character-Narrators

If this degree of independence can exist with regard to the Narrator, who is so forceful a presence as to be often mistaken for Balzac himself, the reader can presume an even greater degree of autonomy with regard to the character-narrators, those storytellers who are part of Balzac's reappearing cast of thousands. Because they are both characters and narrators, there is still another degree of separation between us readers and these storytellers, because the Narrator has told us their stories. We know enough about them as characters and have enough distance from them, to be able to make judgments about them as storytellers; we can consider their motivation(s) for telling their story, and we can judge their credibility as well. That the act of storytelling is not innocent in *La Comédie humaine* is generally recognized, at least in one well-known case. It is universally acknowledged, I believe, that the narrator of *Sarrasine* tells his story in an attempt to seduce Mme de Rochefide. There are several other cases where the act of storytelling has a deeper motive than mere entertainment: in *Gobseck,* Derville's goal initially is to arrange a marriage, and there remains in the text as we know it today remnants of the didactic intent of *Les dangers de l'inconduite;* Maurice de L'Hostal, in *Honorine,* is seeking to absolve women—one woman, at least—of the blame for failed marriages and infidelity, even if the circumstances of his narration do have a strong social setting; in *Autre étude de femme,* entertainment, the art of the raconteur and conversation is specifically given as the reason for the stories being told, and even within that *nouvelle,* deeper motivations can be discerned for many of the stories and remarks presented. Not only can our knowledge about the storytellers give us many clues about the story told, in many cases, the story—what is narrated and how the act of narration is performed—is very often revealing as well; these factors can often tell us a lot about the character doing the telling and/or the circumstances in which the story is told. For an example of this, we again turn to *Le Père Goriot.*

I have already mentioned the duchesse de Langeais's role in revealing the story of Goriot and his family. Although not what is usually thought of as a framed narrative, this case does show us how Balzac used character-narrators and the act of narration to tell us about his world, above and beyond what is told in the story. The duchess's story is told from a distinct point of view, one that Balzac determines for us before she begins to tell. Mme de Langeais has already been established as being of the faubourg Saint-Germain, the highest stratum of Balzacian aristocracy, and there is just enough *aigreur* in the portrait given of her to cast her in the role of Arsinoé in the *duel de salon* between herself and Mme de Beauséant. She has also established her contempt for Mme de Restaud, "[l]a fille d'un vermicellier," [*the daughter of a grain merchant*] before she begins to tell the story of the *vermicellier* himself. Mme de Langeais is filled with contempt for the man whose name she refuses to pronounce correctly (Foriot, Moriot, Doriot, etc.). It is clear that this mispronunciation is an affectation; both of these noble ladies know a great deal about Goriot and his daughters, but to acknowledge this knowledge would be to give these grasping *bourgeois* an importance they do not deserve. Balzac shows us this not only with Mme de Langeais's name game, but with another technique. When Goriot's two daughters are mentioned, Mme de Beauséant shows a certain hesitant familiarity with the situation:

> La seconde n'est-elle pas, dit la vicomtesse en regardant madame de Langeais, mariée à un banquier dont le nom est allemand, un baron de Nucingen? Ne se nomme-t-elle pas Delphine? N'est-ce pas une blonde qui a une loge de côté à l'Opéra, qui vient aussi aux Bouffons, et rit très-haut pour se faire remarquer? (3:112)
>
> *"Isn't the younger daughter," said the vicomtesse looking at Mme de Langeais, "married to a banker with a German name, a certain baron de Nucingen? Isn't her name Delphine? Isn't she a blonde who has a side box at the Opera, who also goes to the Bouffons, and laughs too loudly to make herself noticed?"*

It seems to us, by the time the vicomtesse has finished asking her questions, that she knows a few too many details to really have to ask them. This impression is confirmed for us by Mme de Langeais: "La duchesse sourit en disant: —Mais, ma chère, je vous admire. Pourquoi vous occupez-vous donc tant de ces gens-là?" [*The duchess smiled and said: "But my dear, how I admire you. Why do you pay so much attention to such people?"*]. This gratuitous dig at her (so-called) best friend tells us a lot about Mme de Langeais, her friendship with Mme de Beauséant, and the world in which they live. It also tells a lot about the snobbish hypocrisy of the duchess; as we learn quite quickly, she herself is exceedingly well-informed about *ces gens-là*, and it is she who tells virtually the whole story of the Goriot family.

By using the duchess as his narrator, Balzac succeeds in communicating to us not only the story of Goriot and his abandonment by his daughters, but also the social position of those ambitious daughters and the state of the *monde* that they, and Rastignac, aspire to break into. Along with this specifically textual situation, Balzac also paints an important aspect of the sociohistoric situation of Paris in 1819. Pushing their way to the top of the social ladder, crowding in on and sharply resented by the aristocrats, are the bourgeois represented not only by the *filles Goriot,* but by Delphine's husband, the German banker. Throughout *La Comédie humaine,* we can often find similar clues, similar details, embedded in the act of narration, that enrich both the story we are reading and the text as a whole. Sometimes these clues are found in the text we are reading, sometimes they are to be found in another text that we have read or will read, and sometimes, perhaps most rarely but also most interestingly, these clues are to be found between the texts, in those spaces that only the experienced Balzacian can find, much less explore. The rereader of *La Comédie humaine* evaluates all these clues in order to independently judge the credibility of a particular character as a narrator, as a witness, so to speak, and to determine the true meaning of his or her story.

Men in Black: Privileged Observers and Narrators in *La Comédie humaine*

Balzac's narrators, like his Narrator, like Balzac himself, are observers, who relate their observations to others. It is not surprising that Balzac strongly favors as narrators those characters whose social roles both require a special talent for observation and give them ample opportunities to observe. One of the most famous passages in *La Comédie humaine* comes from *Le Colonel Chabert,* where the lawyer Derville talks about the horrors he has seen in his practice, what Pierre Barbéris calls Derville's "j'ai vu":

> J'ai vu mourir un père dans un grenier, sans sou ni maille, abandonné
> par deux filles auxquelles il avait donné quarante mille livres de rente!

J'ai vu brûler des testaments; j'ai vu des mères dépouillant leurs en-
fants, des maris volant leurs femmes, des femmes tuant leurs maris en
se servant de l'amour qu'elles leur inspiraient pour les rendre fous ou
imbéciles, afin de vivre en paix avec un amant. J'ai vu des femmes
donnant à l'enfant d'un premier lit des goûts qui devaient amener sa
mort, afin d'enrichir l'enfant de l'amour. Je ne puis vous dire tout ce
que j'ai vu, car j'ai vu des crimes contre lesquels la justice est impuis-
sante. Enfin, toutes les horreurs que les romanciers croient inventer
sont toujours au-dessous de la vérité. (3:373)

*I have seen a father dying in an attic, without a cent, abandoned by his
two daughters whom he had given incomes of forty thousand pounds a
year! I've seen wills burned, I've seen mothers rob their children, husbands stealing from wives, wives killing their husbands using the love
they inspire to render their husbands mad or stupid, so that they can
live in peace with a lover. I've seen women giving their legitimate children habits which will lead to death, in order to enrich a child born of
love. I cannot tell you all that I've seen, for I have seen crimes in the
face of which justice is helpless. All the horrors that novelists think they
invent always pale in the face of reality.*

This passage shows us a fairly brazen tactic used by Balzac—Derville at-
testing to Balzac's authenticity—while at the same time giving us an idea
of what secrets lawyers are privy to. Whatever shocking stories we may
find in *La Comédie humaine*, and many of them we will recognize as
events witnessed by Derville, they only scratch the surface of those things
a Parisian lawyer has seen. And it is not just lawyers who have their "j'ai
vu"; as Derville indicates in this same speech, there are other men who
bear the same dubious privilege as observers, the men who wear black
robes:

Savez-vous [. . .] qu'il existe dans notre société trois hommes, le Prêtre,
le Médecin et l'Homme de justice, qui ne peuvent pas estimer le
monde. Ils ont des robes noires, peut-être parce qu'ils portent le deuil
de toutes les vertus, de toutes les illusions.

*Do you know that there are in our society three men, the Priest, the
Physician and the Man of Law, who cannot respect this world. They*

wear black robes, perhaps because they are in mourning for all virtues,
for every illusion.

Each of the three types named has an especially advantageous position as
narrator, because his profession inspires a certain amount of confidence,
especially in the bourgeois-dominated world of *La Comédie humaine*. This
serves them doubly: As observers, they are trusted by those they talk to,
from whom they learn their stories; and as storytellers, they are judged to
be more credible by their audience. This confidence operates both within
the text and outside of it. We, like the characters in the text we are reading,
are inclined to trust a doctor (or a priest or a lawyer) because, however
sophisticated we may be as readers, on some level we perceive a degree of
trust placed in these characters by the author, who wants us to pay attention to what they say, and to believe them.

Derville is the only significant member of the bar in Balzac's
world who illustrates this point. As for doctors, one thinks immediately of
Bianchon. As Barbéris pointed out, Bianchon too has his "j'ai vu" (*Le
Monde de Balzac,* 379). Desplein, who trained Bianchon, also has his
moment of observation, in which he can also be observed. Which brings
us to an interesting absence among Balzac's character-narrators, the Priest.
The first of Derville's black-robed men is absent from the list of Balzac's
character-narrators.

A Striking Silence: On the Absence of Priests as Narrators

Given the proclaimed importance of the church in Balzac's work
("j'écris à la lumiere de deux Vérités éternelles: la Religion, [et] la Monarchie" [*Avant-propos*; 1:13] *I write by the light of two eternal Truths, Religion and the Monarchy*), it is surprising how few priests are important
characters in *La Comédie humaine*. Perhaps more surprising, and definitely more relevant to the purposes of this study, is the lack of any priest
as a narrator, given the generally recognized importance of Derville and
Bianchon, representing the other two parts of Balzac's black-robed trinity.
Several reasons can be given for this absence. The first is social. In *La
Comédie humaine*, storytelling is a worldly activity, it takes place in the
monde, whether *grand* (*Gobseck, Honorine, Autre étude de femme*) or
demi (*Un homme d'affaires, Un prince de la bohème*). These are reso-

lutely secular spaces. Priests have almost no place in Balzac's social world, at least in Paris. With *La Comédie humaine*, we are no longer in the eighteenth century with its *abbés mondains*. The only one of this species we see is the priest, and later bishop, de Maronis, the "bon diable violet" [*good old purple devil*] who provides his pupille de Marsay with a very non-Catholic education, and he dies in 1812 after having unleashed on Restoration Paris a pupil as worthy of Laclos as of Talleyrand. Those priests we do see playing some social role are relegated to the provincial cities, such as Birotteau in Tours, Duret in Sancerre, and Grancey in Besançon. Priests do not, as a rule, tell stories in *La Comédie humaine* quite simply because they do not go to those places where stories are told.

Whether this absence of priests in the *grand monde* is peculiar to Balzac or more generally true of nineteenth century society is debatable. Certainly this is not true of all contemporary literature. In *Le Rouge et le noir*, for instance, priests and high prelates play a much greater role in society than they do in Balzac's oeuvre and they seem to be on much more intimate terms with aristocrats, as is evidenced by the friendship of the abbé Chélan and the marquis de La Mole. The marquis's nephew, the youthful bishop of Agde, who has the exquisite manners of the Parisian nobility, seems exclusively concerned with the ceremonial and superficial aspects of the ceremony at Verrières. His ceremonial robes are a uniform, even a costume in a social pageant. Stendhal's clergymen are also far more active politically than Balzac's. The *Congrégation*, which plays such an important role in *Le Rouge et le noir*, is mentioned only in passing in *La Comédie humaine*, in *Le Curé de Tours*, and in *Les Employés*. Even in what de Marsay derisively refers to as "le parti prêtre," there are many dukes, but no priests or bishops are specifically named, only "la Grande Aumônerie" (*Le Contrat de mariage*, 3:647). Mme de Fervaques, with whom Julien Sorel has a brief epistolary flirtation, plays among the high clergy a role similar to the one Mme d'Espard plays among the high officials of Balzac's magistrature. Even the provincial clergy seems more sophisticated in Stendhal's world. The Besançon of *Le Rouge et le noir*, with its literate and epicurean bishop, hardly seems like the same town as the Besançon of *Albert Savarus*, where society is dominated by the somewhat absurd Mme de Watteville. Indeed, Balzac's Besançon seems more like Verrières. And the scheming grand vicar de Frilaire, with his political intrigues and his desire to seduce Mathilde, has more in common with the cardinal de Retz than with the rather modest, if far more admirable, abbé de Grancey, his counterpart in Balzac's Besançon.

The other reason for the lack of tale-telling priests is more subtle. Not only do priests, as a rule, not go where stories are told, the stories told in *La Comédie humaine* are the result of observations, of secrets confessed or uncovered. Obviously, those secrets that a priest would learn or observe would usually be learned in the confessional, or in circumstances that would prevent the priest from sharing what he had learned. Balzac displays a marked respect for the confessional in *La Comédie humaine;* it is one of those places from which the Narrator is held back. In *Le Curé du village*, for example, Véronique Graslin's secret is only hinted at until the public confession of her sins, and this public confession is hotly debated between Véronique's confessor and his archbishop. Obviously, this restraint and this public confession have much to do with basic narrative technique—Balzac is trying to build drama in his novel—but there is a certain mystery maintained about the sacrament. In *Un Drame au bord de la mer,* Balzac goes to some lengths to maintain this sacred secrecy. Cambremer, having killed his spoiled son for stealing from his mother, confesses his sin to a parish priest, who refuses to give absolution until Cambremer has made a confession to "un homme de justice" (10:1171). This second, secular confession was overheard by the mother of the poor fisherman who serves as guide and storyteller to Louis Lambert and Pauline. There is no mention in the *nouvelle* of any legal consequences of this second confession, its only function seems to be to communicate Cambremer's confession without violating the confessional. We can attribute this to Balzac's personal ethics or to his authorial scruples: a good *bretonne* peasant would surely not have eavesdropped on her *curé.* Finally, there is a somewhat similar case in *Albert Savarus.* When Rosalie de Watteville, having ruined Albert's life with her meddling, is so overcome by guilt as to need to reveal her "affreuses combinaisons" to de Grancey, we learn with the vicar general about the letters that Rosalie intercepted and answered through forgery. However, while this is a confession, it is not a sacrament; de Grancey declares to Rosalie: "je ne suis pas ici le grand-pénitencier, vous n'êtes pas agénouillée aux pieds de Dieu, je suis un ami terrifié par l'appréhension de vos châtiments [*I am not here to sit in judgment on you as a priest, you are not kneeling at the feet of God, I am a friend terrified at the thought of the punishments that await you*]"

confession will come later, so what we have witnessed need not be hidden
from us in the same way that Véronique's and Cambremer's confessions
were.

There is at least one case in *La Comédie humaine* in which a story
told originates in the confessional. In *Une double famille,* old Madame
Crochard—fearing for her soul after having, for all intents and purposes,
prostituted her only daughter, Caroline—makes a deathbed confession to a
priest, which priest happens to be the unscrupulous abbé Fontanon, confessor of the *dévote* Mme de Granville. Fontanon, more concerned with
increasing his power over Angélique than with his sacramental duties, informs his penitent of her husband's second family, ultimately destroying
both the legitimate and illegitimate sides of Granville's double family. We
do not see the confession of Caroline's mother; we have a general idea of
what is said, but we do not witness the confession itself. We do however
see Fontanon violating the sanctity of the confessional, informing Angélique of her husband's infidelity. The Narrator respects what the priest
does not. This act of narration is not social, it is malevolent, and its consequences are disastrous. This example of a bad priest would lend some support to a third possible explanation for the lack of priests in Balzac's text,
that, despite Balzac's frequent pious nods to the Catholic church, he quite
simply had very little use for priests.

Diagnosticians of *le corps social*: Doctors as Narrators

It is not surprising that Balzac should assign the role of storyteller
to doctors. There are fairly frequent allusions to either the author or the
Narrator as some kind of doctor; for example, in the dedication of *Les
Parents pauvres,* Balzac refers to himself as a "docteur en médecine so-
ciale, le vétérinaire de maux incurables" of the social animal (7:53). Doctors are among those privileged observers for whom, according to
Derville, there are no secrets. I have already alluded to Bianchon's several
"j'ai vu"; they are found in a passage of *L'Interdiction,* where Bianchon
informs his supposedly more sophisticated friend Rastignac of Mme
d'Espard's true age, along with a few other facts about the world. The
doctor educates the dandy about how society women appear when they do
not know they are being seen. Once again we see that doctors in general
and Bianchon in particular are among those who see beyond appearance,

who see into that *troisième dessous* that so fascinated Balzac, and that makes Balzac's writing so fascinating. It is in *La Messe de l'athée* that we see Bianchon in the process of becoming an observer. He learns this, as he learns so much, from the brilliant Desplein: "Desplein ne manquait pas d'emmener Bianchon pour se faire assister par lui dans les maisons opulentes où [. . .] se révélaient insensiblement au provincial les mystères de la vie parisienne" [*Desplein did not fail to take Bianchon along in those opulent houses where all the mysteries of Parisian life were slowly revealed to the provincial youth*]. Rastignac's initiation took place at the balls and in the boudoirs where people (women) were prepared to be observed; Bianchon's takes place in necessarily unguarded moments, when defenses are down and the truth is revealed.

Both of the significant doctor-characters in *La Comédie humaine*, Bianchon and Desplein, are also storytellers. Desplein tells his own story in *La Messe de l'athée* [*The Atheist's Mass*]; allusions to Bianchon as a skilled raconteur are fairly frequent, although he has only one significant act of narration—that is, one that we can see—in *Autre étude de femme*. Both cases offer excellent examples of how Balzac used the representation of the act of narration and narrative frames within *La Comédie humaine*. Interestingly, neither Desplein's nor Bianchon's story has much to do with the narrator's profession. Each one may have more credibility as a narrator because we know what their profession is, but nothing in the stories themselves indicates any special knowledge of medicine, or any confidences gained from the doctor-patient relationship.

La Messe de l'athée is among the less discussed of Balzac's texts, even though it contains, in my opinion, one of Balzac's most interesting characters, the brusque and gifted surgeon Desplein, and one of *La Comédie humaine*'s most interesting riddles: is Desplein, who professes nonbelief and who has founded a regular mass in memory of a benefactor, really an atheist? Many critics have seen this *nouvelle* as simply a refutation of atheism by the Catholic and conservative Balzac. A careful reading of the text and the character (both *personnage* and *caractère*) of Desplein reveals both text and character to be far more subtle and complex than is generally believed. This is also an excellent example of what I call a self-contained text. It is not really necessary that the reader have a broad or deep knowledge of *La Comédie humaine* in order to interpret or understand the characters and the story that they are involved in. In fact, this text offers a far more complete description of Desplein than we have any-where else in *La Comédie humaine;* without *La messe,* Desplein would be a decidedly minor and frankly rather uninteresting character: a brilliant surgeon who was Bianchon's teacher and mentor, *voilà tout.* In *La Messe de l'athée,* we meet an original and fascinating character: a brilliant healer who despises humanity, an aggressive social climber who gives free medi-cal care to the Auvergnat water-bearers of Paris, the untouchables of the many-casted society of *La Comédie humaine.* The most interesting ambi-guity of all is the way in which Balzac qualifies Desplein as a genius, and yet places limits on that genius. Desplein, an empiricist in medicine as in all things, takes all his talent and glory with him when he dies, leaving nothing behind to make him remembered as a great doctor. All these con-tradictions create an ambiguous character, and this ambiguity further com-plicates the central enigma of the *nouvelle,* the one implied by the title.

The reader learns in the opening pages that Desplein professes a complete and unquestioning atheism, and a Voltairean contempt for the Catholic church. Our surprise, then, is as great as Bianchon's, through whose point of view the Narrator gives the exposition of the story, when Desplein is seen attending mass, a perpetual mass, we later learn, which the purported atheist has founded. We learn that this mass has been estab-lished in memory of an Auvergnat water-carrier who served as Desplein's foster father during the great surgeon's studies. The poor and lonely older man having sacrificed to protect, as meagerly as his means permitted, the young medical student, the successful surgeon honors his late benefactor's memory in two ways: by founding the quadrennial mass, and by treating, *gratis,* the poor water-carriers of Paris. Critics focus on the mass—as Bal-zac intended, having made it part of the title—seeing it as an unresolvable contradiction in the character of Desplein. They interpret it as evidence that, in Balzac's view, even atheists really believe in God. What is less remarked upon is the other half of the twin contradiction, that this social climbing and slightly avaricious surgeon should give the benefits of his skills to those who cannot return any favors materially or socially. Both of these acts are perfectly compatible with a Christian lifestyle, such as the one led by the *frères de la consolation* in *L'Envers de l'histoire contempo-raine,* but that does not necessarily mean they cannot indicate any other philosophy.

Once again, clues in the text can help us see both sides of the question more clearly, if not actually to resolve it. In the opening part of the frame, the Narrator describes to us Desplein's belief, or lack thereof:

> Desplein n'était pas dans le doute, il affirmait. Son athéisme pur et franc ressemblait à celui de beaucoup de savants, les meilleures gens du monde, mais invinciblement athées, athées comme les gens religieux n'admettent pas qu'il puisse y avoir d'athées. (3:386)
>
> *Desplein did not doubt, he was sure. His pure and frank atheism was like that of many scientists, the finest people in the world, but invincibly atheist, atheists of the kind that religious people cannot admit exist.*

The passage is interesting not only because of its unequivocal nature, but also and especially because of the last sentence. The attitude of these *gens religieux* who don't even want to admit that pure atheists such as Desplein can exist would seem quite close to the one that most readers and critics of this *nouvelle* impute to Balzac, the arch-conservative who wrote the *avant-propos* of 1842. Later in the opening part of the frame, we see this same attitude again: "Cet homme mourut, dit-on, dans l'impénitence finale où meurent malheureusement beaucoup de beaux génies, à qui Dieu puisse pardonner" [*This man died, it is said, in the final impenitence in which unfortunately many glorious geniuses do, may God have mercy on them*] (387). This sentence clearly shows us that the Narrator is in the Catholic camp, but the report on Desplein's death is somewhat removed from the Narrator by the "dit-on"; the Narrator is distancing himself from the story, reporting what is known and said, and no longer what he may have "seen." This is important, because we find a similar report toward the end of the nouvelle, in the closing part of the frame:

> Bianchon, qui soigna Desplein dans sa dernière maladie, n'ose pas affirmer aujourd'hui que l'illustre chirurgien soit mort athée. Des croyants n'aimeront-ils pas à penser que l'humble Auvergnat sera venu lui ouvrir la porte du ciel. (401)
>
> *Bianchon, who cared for Desplein in his last illness, does not dare affirm that the illustrious surgeon died an atheist. Wouldn't believers like to think that the humble Auvergnat came to open the gates of heaven to him?*

Again we see a certain narrative distance; it is not the Narrator but Bianchon who refuses to confirm that Desplein died an atheist.[3] The second part of the paragraph is also interesting for its hesitancy. What believers will enjoy thinking is not necessarily what the Narrator thinks, and it certainly gives no indication of Desplein's own thoughts on his deathbed. In the frame of this tale, we see the riddle posed, and a deceptively straightforward answer given. For further clues, we must turn to the tale itself.

After having told Bianchon the story of Bourgeat, the water-carrier who served him as a "second père," Desplein tells of his benefactor's religious faith and last wishes:

> Catholique ardent, il ne m'avait jamais dit un mot sur mon irréligion. Quand il fut en danger, il me pria de ne rien ménager pour qu'il eût les secours de l'Eglise[. . .] Quand j'eus mis en terre mon unique bienfaiteur, je cherchai comment m'acquitter envers lui [. . .] il avait une conviction religieuse, avais-je le droit de la discuter? Il m'avait timidement parlé des messes dites pour le repos des morts, il ne voulait pas m'imposer ce devoir, en pensant que ce serait faire payer ses services. Aussitôt que j'ai pu établir une fondation, j'ai donné à Saint-Sulpice la somme nécesaire pour y faire dire quatre messes par an. (400-01)
>
> *An ardent Catholic, he had never said a word to me about my lack of faith. When his life was in danger, he asked me to spare no effort to procure for him the rites of the Church. When I had buried my lone benefactor, I sought a way to repay my debt to him ... he had a deep religious faith, did I have the right to challenge it? He had timidly spoken to me of masses said for the benefit of the dead, he didn't wish to impose this duty on me, thinking that would be paying him for his kindness. As soon as I was able to establish a foundation, I gave the church of Saint-Sulpice the sum necessary for four masses each year.*

Clearly, the masses are meant as a tribute to Bourgeat, not to God. Desplein continues: "le jour où se dit cette messe, j'y vais *en son nom*, et je

---

[3] The shift to the present tense is another interesting aspect of this passage, and one that occurs in other works of *La Comédie humaine*. It confers upon Balzac's world an eternal quality, suggesting that the characters' lives continue after we have closed the book, that they continue to evolve outside of our field of vision.

récite *pour lui* les prières voulues" [*on the day of this mass, I go* in his name, *and I recite* for him *the required prayers*] (401, emphasis mine). A sentence from the frame supports the idea that Desplein's church-going is an act of duty, and not of faith. When Bianchon first sees him in the church, Desplein is on his knees before the alter, "en restant sérieux comme s'il fût agi d'une opération" [*remaining as serious as if engaged in an operation*] (391); he is always the scientist, even in church. And if any doubt remains, Desplein adds a last unequivocal and extremely interesting comment on the matter: "je donnerais ma fortune pour que la croyance de Bourgeat pût m'entrer dans la cervelle" [*I would give my entire fortune if Bougeat's belief could enter my brain*] (401). Desplein's atheism is not an intellectual pose, he may even regret it, but his scientific intellect will allow him no other belief. The most we can say is that Desplein has reversed Pascal's wager to arrive at a stance he can live with: "Dieu doit être un bon diable, il ne saurait m'en vouloir" [*God must be a good old devil, he won't hold it against me*] (401). In spite of the doubts raised by the Narrator, it seems more likely that Desplein did indeed die outside of a state of grace. The fact that this atheist leads one of the more admirable and interesting lives of all the characters in *La Comédie humaine*, almost as admirable as Jean-Jules Popinot, destabilizes the text by subverting the traditional view of Balzac as an staunch conservative, a inflexible supporter of Throne and Altar.

Desplein's story obviously has more to do with his personal history rather than with his professional activities. His profession may influence our impression of him or his credibility, and his scientific bent is certainly tied into his atheism, but he is not sharing with us anything learned through the practice of medecine, any of those secrets that Bianchon hints at in *L'Interdiction*. The same is true of Bianchon. His reputation as a raconteur is firmly established in *La Comédie humaine*; in *La Muse du département*, Lousteau indicates to the provincial audience gathered at Dinah de La Baudraye's chateau that Bianchon has his "petite réputation de conteur" in Paris. The story that Bianchon tells in *La Muse* is *La Grande Bretèche*, the same one he tells in *Autre étude de femme*, but it is only in *Autre étude* that we see the act of narration itself, that we can read the story as Bianchon tells it. In both cases, the reaction of Bianchon's listeners confirms for us that his reputation is merited. In *La Muse*, his story is followed by "un moment de silence assez flatteur" (688); in *Autre étude*,

we can see in the attitude of the assembled listeners the great appreciation
that people have for Bianchon as a storyteller. After Bianchon has told one
story, he is complimented, and quickly pressed to tell another:

> —Les histoires que conte le docteur, dit le duc de Rhétoré, font des
> impressions bien profondes.
> —Mais douces, reprit Mlle des Touches.
> —Ah! madame, repliqua le docteur, j'ai des histoires terribles dans
> mon répertoire; mais chaque récit a son heure dans une conversation,
> [. . .]
> —Mais il est deux heures du matin . . . dit la maîtresse de la
> maison.
> —Dites, monsieur Bianchon!. . . . » demanda-t-on de tous côtés.
> A un geste du complaisant docteur, le silence régna. (3:710)
> *"The stories the doctor tells," said the Duke de Rhétoré, "make deep*
> *impressions."*
> *"But sweet ones," added Mlle des Touches.*
> *"Ah! Madame," replied the doctor, "I have some terrible stories in*
> *my repertoire; but every tale has its moment in a conversation [. . .]"*
> *"But it's two o'clock in the morning. . ." said the mistress of the*
> *house.*
> *"Tell it, monsieur Bianchon!" was the cry from all sides.*
> *After a gesture from the agreeable doctor, silence reigned.*

This anticipation, coming as it does from the most elite figures of Balzac's
Parisian society, including from the writer Félicité des Touches, herself a
storyteller of genius, is surely more flattering than the silence of the provincials. The end of Bianchon's story will again cause a reflective silence
among his listeners; this silence is in itself interesting, as we will see later.
What is important here is that we see that Bianchon's stories are known
and appreciated in the world of *La Comédie humaine*. Also interesting is
the allusion to the secrets Bianchon knows, those *histoires terribles* that
we don't hear him tell. There is an echo here of Derville's speech from *Le
Colonel Chabert*, of those *horreurs* that surpass anything that novelists
think they invent.

     However, those stories learned through the practice of medicine
remain privileged information; this is hidden from us, like those stories

that come from the confessional. The story that Bianchon shares, *La Grande Bretèche,* is not one he learned from his professional functions; Bianchon learned the story of Mme de Merret as a traveler, not a doctor. It is quite possible to argue that his social and professional status helped to loosen the tongues of the *notaire* Regnault and the *aubergiste* Mme Lepas, who provide him with the first two-thirds of the story, but he learns the key to the enigma from the chambermaid Rosalie, who is induced to speak not to a doctor, but to a lover. What Bianchon is, as he tells his story to his elite Parisian friends, is a Parisian elitist. In Bianchon's narration, we see quite plainly that Bianchon is a creature of a specific place, time, and culture; the young doctor who learns the tragic story of Mme de Merret and her Spanish lover is a Parisian dandy with romantic and literary sensibilities. These qualities are discernible at different points in the story. The romantic can be seen in the opening pages, in the long paragraph in which Bianchon describes the mysterious property that gives his story its name. Fascinated by the mysteriously deserted house and its overgrown garden, and having nothing better to do, the young doctor imagines "délicieux romans" and "un drame assez noir" to explain to himself the cause of the mystery (713); as he gradually penetrates the enigma, through the explanations given to him by his three narrators, he declares himself entangled in a "roman à la Radcliffe" (718). Bianchon's urban elitism can be seen in a couple of glancing references to "petites villes" such as Angoulême (708)—even though, as we know, Bianchon comes from Sancerre—and more importantly from the dismissive and condescending way with which he describes his interlocutors, especially the provincial lawyer Regnault. Bianchon's outsider status may also have some importance in causing Regnault and the landlady to tell their stories, although, as Bianchon observes, they seem to have told their stories before. Only Rosalie has kept the secret of the events she witnessed at la Grande Bretèche, and she is persuaded to speak, literally seduced into speaking, by an elegant young dandy from Paris. And even she is not spared Bianchon's mocking condescension when described to the brilliant assembly in Félicité des Touches's dining room.

Bianchon's mockery of his provincial informants does nothing to lessen the effect of the story; this is a reflection of his—and, of course, Balzac's—skill as a storyteller. The preamble to the story in the narrative frame, and Bianchon's reluctance to tell the story, prepare us for a shocking, perhaps even grotesque story. The light tone with which the narrator describes the near ruin of la Grande Bretèche and his own youthful and perhaps excessively romantic musings about it make us forget his warnings, to some degree. Then there is a marked and interesting difference between the tone that Bianchon uses to describe Monsieur Regnault and the small-town lawyer's story, the haunting description of the skeletal Mme de Merret on her deathbed. This discrepancy in tone reintroduces suspense in the story, which is augmented by the classic detective story structure of the tale, as we learn the end first, and then the events that led to that end. The suspense builds as Mme Lepas then gives the beginning of the story, the marriage of M. and Mme de Merret, and the arrival of the Spanish nobleman Férédia as a prisoner of war in Angoulême. The comic tone of Bianchon's narration continues as he describes his seduction of Rosalie, but all comic overtones disappear as Bianchon gives the dénouement of the story in his own voice:

> Mais s'il fallait reproduire fidèlement la diffuse éloquence de Rosalie, un volume entier suffirait à peine. Or, comme l'événement dont elle me donna la confuse connaissance se trouve placé, entre le bavardage du notaire et celui de Mme Lepas [. . .] je n'ai plus qu'à vous le dire en peu de mots. J'abrège donc. (724)
>
> *But if I were obliged to faithfully reproduce Rosalie's diffuse eloquence, an entire volume would hardly suffice. So, since the events that she recounted to me so confusedly come between the lawyer's gossip and that of Mme Lepas, I need only relate it to you in a few words. Let me summarize.*

This shift in voice is accompanied by another shift in tone, focusing on the drama of the events of the Merrets, and letting the comic aspect of his provincial romance fall away, accelerating the pace of the narration. The attention of the readers (and, we must imagine, Bianchon's listeners) is likewise focused, the suspense heightened for the horrible dénouement. It becomes clear to us at this point where Bianchon's reputation comes from; Balzac has lent his character his own storytelling talents, and the silence that follows is deafening.

Derville: Gobseck's Mouthpiece

If priests and doctors keep the secrets of their professions, Derville's story comes directly from his legal practice, and he is acting as a lawyer even as he tells the story in the Grandlieu's salon. Derville is, again, the only significant lawyer-narrator in *La Comédie humaine;* this fact is more than a little surprising, given that this profession is the one most closely associated with the all-important transactions that determine the transfer of wealth, such as marriage contracts and wills, that produce so many of Balzac's stories. I insist on the fact that this is Derville's only act of narration, because in his introduction to *Gobseck* in the Pléiade edition, Pierre Citron names Derville, with Bianchon, as one of the two "conteur[s] de talent" in *La Comédie humaine* (2:947). Derville's reputation is due not to the number of the stories he tells, but to the force of this one story. There is no breach of confidence or ethics when Derville tells the story of Gobseck and the Restaud family, because he is acting as Gobseck's lawyer, and as the agent of Ernest de Restaud's dead father. The count had arranged with the usurer for the latter to protect the Restaud children and their fortune from the lust-inspired greed of their mother. By telling his story to the vicomtesse de Grandlieu, Derville is seeking to arrange a suitable marriage for Ernest, fulfilling Gobseck's obligation to the count in this last act as a distant, even hidden, foster father. This fusion of the *mondaine* activity of storytelling with professional duty is wholly consistent with the character (again, *personnage* and *caractère*) of Derville. As Barbéris pointed out, Derville is a somewhat marginal presence in *La Comédie humaine,* in the sense that he has one foot in the *grand monde,* and the other in a domestic retreat with his wife, the former Fanny Malvaut (*Le Monde de Balzac,* 362), who is glimpsed only fleetingly in *Gobseck.* The Narrator hints at this trait in the opening part of the frame, where we learn that with the exception of the occasional evening spent at the hôtel de Grandlieu, Derville "n'allait dans le monde que pour entretenir ses relations" [*only went out into society to maintain his professional relationships*] (964). Derville does not socialize, he networks. This is consistent with the image of Derville given in *Le Colonel Chabert,* where we learn that Derville's habit is to work after returning from a ball in the early hours of the morning.

Derville's story goes well beyond what Mme de Grandlieu wants
or needs to know, to give the fantastic ending of Gobseck's life. Of course,
this is the story that Balzac wants to tell, but Derville, carried away by the
force of his own story, is compelled to go farther than the interest of his
textual narratee requires him to do.

Gobseck is also interesting because it offers a striking example of a
narrative technique that Balzac used fairly frequently, the narration within
the narration. We have seen an example of this in *La Grande Bretèche,* in
which Bianchon collects his story from his three provincial interlocutors.
Derville is not the only narrator in *Gobseck;* within the story that the lawyer tells Mme de Grandlieu and her brother, Gobseck himself tells a story
to Derville, his own autobiography. Some critics have seen as incongruous
that the famously secretive and taciturn moneylender should suddenly become loquacious and confiding, but Jean-Luc Seylaz makes an interesting
comparison between Gobseck's confession and Mme de Merteuil's autobiographical letter to Valmont in *Les Liaisons dangereuses* ("Réflexions
sur *Gobseck,*" 303). These are two characters of uncommon intelligence
and power, and they owe their power to the fact that they operate in secret,
albeit in quite different ways. They also have in common what Seylaz
calls an "orgueil luciférien" (302), so it is not so surprising that neither of
them are above wanting to boast a little of their power, if only to one selected confidant, whom they trust both to understand the extent of their
gifts and to be sufficiently impressed with their stories.

Gobseck's metadiegetic narration is also interesting because of its
links to the diegetic narratees, Mme de Grandlieu and her brother. In this
relationship, we see that the complexity of Balzac's narrative configurations are not due solely to their construction. In Gobseck's narration, we
can sense the powerful hatred that this deceptively small man has for the
great of the world, the joy that he takes from having them under his power.
As he relates his visit to the Restauds' hotel, he speaks in terms that
clearly show his resentment. Sent away by Mme de Restaud, who owes
him money, Gobseck dirties the carpet, seemingly out of pure spite: "Et je
m'en vais en signant ma présence sur le tapis qui couvrait les dalles de
l'escalier. J'aime à crotter les tapis de l'homme riche, non par petitesse,
mais pour leur faire sentir la griffe de la Nécessité" [*"And so I left, mark-
ing my presence on the carpet which covered the stones of the stairs. I like
to muck up a rich man's carpets, not out of pettiness, but to make him feel*

the claws of Necessity"] (2:971). When he finally sees the countess, there is an almost palpable hatred in the thoughts that Anastasie de Restaud inspires in him, which he shares with Derville:

> . . .en moi-même je me disais: 'paie ton luxe, paie ton nom, paie ton bonheur, paie le monopole dont tu jouis. Pour se garantir leurs biens, les riches ont inventé des tribunaux, des juges, et cette guillotine [. . .] Mais, pour vous [. . .] il est des remords, des grincements de dents cachés sous un sourire, et des gueules de lions fantastiques qui vous donnent un coup de dent au cœur.' (973)
>
> *. . .to myself I said: Pay for your luxury, pay for your name, pay for your happiness, pay for the monopoly you enjoy. To ensure their wealth, the rich have invented courts, judges, and that guillotine. . . But for you, there is remorse, the gnashing of teeth hidden behind a smile, and the fangs of otherworldly lions to slash at your heart.*

And finally, as he leaves the hotel:

> Je trouvai dans la cour une nuée de valets qui brossaient leurs livrées, ciraient leurs bottes ou nettoyaient de somptueux équipages. 'Voilà, me dis-je, ce qui amène ces gens-là chez moi. Voilà ce qui les pousse à voler décemment des millions, à trahir leur patrie. Pour ne pas se crotter en allant à pied, le grand seigneur, ou celui qui le singe, prend une bonne fois un bain de boue!' (974)
>
> *I found in the court a swarm of valets brushing their liveries, polishing their boots and cleaning sumptuous carriages. "This," I said to myself, "is what leads these people to me. This is what pushes them to genteelly steal millions, to betray their country. In order not to get muddy walking on foot, the great lord, and those who ape him, take one good bath in the muck!*

These passages are interesting in and of themselves, first for their overtly political, proto-marxist tone of class resentment, even warfare, as Gobseck silently combats the great of his world with their own greed. Also interesting is the way they suggest that Gobseck might be more engaged in this world than he chooses to admit; the anger in these sentences is a bit strong for the man who boasts that "le monde n'a pas la moindre prise sur moi"

[*The world doesn't have even the slightest hold on me*] (970). Yet to find
the real interest of these passages, we should consider them in the larger
context of *La Comédie humaine*. For example, when Gobseck seethes
"paie ton nom" while he negotiates with the comtesse de Restaud, readers
familiar with *Le Père Goriot* will remember that Anastasie did just that
when she married the comte de Restaud.

Returning to the relationship of these passages to their ultimate
textual *destinataire*, we should never forget that, as we read these words,
they are being transmitted by Derville to the vicomtesse de Grandlieu,
member of one of the most influential noble families of Balzac's stable.
This link between the miser and the *grande dame* becomes clearer and
more direct when we consider Derville in light of his professional status.
He is a lawyer, he is paid to speak for others, and as he tells his story, he is
acting as Gobseck's lawyer, as his mouthpiece, to put it crudely. In this
point of view, Derville becomes neutral, a direct conduit to the vicomtesse
for Gobseck's hate-filled tirade. This functional neutrality is textually emphasized by the absence, pointed out by Pierre Citron,[4] of any physical
description of the character, either in *Gobseck,* or anywhere else in *La
Comédie humaine*. The same phrase that resonates with readers of *Le Père
Goriot*—"paie ton nom"—has a textual echo in the frame of *Gobseck*, and
in this sense is aimed directly at Mme de Grandlieu. To a certain degree,
the *vicomtesse* can be said to think that Ernest de Restaud must pay for the
right to ally himself with the name of Grandlieu. If her primary stated objection to the marriage of her daughter Camille to the grandson of old Goriot is the scandalous conduct of Ernest's mother, it seems that other
considerations might outweigh the danger of a *mésalliance:* "M. Ernest
doit être bien riche pour faire accepter sa mère par une famille comme la
nôtre" [*M. Ernest will have to be very rich indeed to make his mother acceptable to a family like ours*] (1013). This central truth of *La Comédie
humaine* rings true again: money is the great leveler, even among the already rich.

It is also in light of this direct narrator-narratee relationship between Gobseck and the vicomtesse that the political aspects of Gobseck's
discourse become truly interesting, as we can consider them within the

---

[4] Interestingly, Derville shares this unusual distinction with "son autre conteur de talent,
Bianchon" (intro., éd. Pléiade; 2: 947)

context of the larger *Comédie humaine,* without referring to any extra-textual historical or political situations. The nobles of the faubourg Saint-Germain are politically powerful in Balzac's world, and the Grandlieus are one of the first, if not the first, families of the faubourg. We can go beyond this generalization, as there are several indications in the text that Mme de Grandlieu herself has considerable influence. Her protection would have guaranteed Derville a rapid advancement in the magistrature, had he chosen to pursue that career; and the fact that she only returned to France with Louis XVIII, and was for a time supported by the civil list (962-63), suggests a close relationship between this woman and the royal family.[5] This indicates that the vicomtesse is an active member of the ruling class that, according to Gobseck, invented the courts and the guillotine not to protect society, but to maintain the social order and their own wealth. Also interesting is the charge that the rich steal decently and betray their government for wealth. This is a major Balzacian theme, that behind every great fortune lies a great crime (cf. *L'Interdiction, Madame Firmiani, Le Cousin Pons,* etc.). But again, there is no need to look outside of *Gobseck* for a point of reference. We have pertinent information about the vicomtesse's fortune in the *nouvelle.* She seems to have profited quite well from political events. Her friendship with Derville is based on his having recovered a number of confiscated *biens nationaux* in the early days of the Restoration; through Derville's efforts, the family recovered a fortune worth about 60,000 francs a year, which suggests a capital of two million francs, plus their Parisian hotel. This is before the indemnity law, the famous *milliard des émigrés,* from which she gained "des sommes énormes" (962). There is something troubling about this doubly restored fortune, especially given the proximity of this financial data to Gobseck's invective. From a certain political point of view, one that Gobseck seems to hold, the Grandlieu family could be seen as profiteers at the expense of the state.

This is not to suggest that Balzac was condemning the Grandlieus outright. Obviously, if the Narrator cannot be equated with Balzac, we should certainly refrain from making that equation with characters. Balzac specifically warns us against doing so in the *avant-propos* of 1842: "Aussi, quand on voudra m'opposer à moi-même, se trouvera-t-il qu'on

---

[5] The action of *Gobseck* takes place in the winter of 1829-30, so we are still under the Bourbons.

aura mal interprété quelque ironie, ou bien l'on rétorquera mal à propos
contre moi le discours d'un de mes personnages" [*And so, whenever
someone wants to challenge me with my own words, they will have misin-
terpreted some irony, or perhaps they will have mistakenly turned against
me the words of one of my characters*] (1:12). What we see is rather a version of Balzac's own opinion, exaggerated to the point of deformation.
However, as great a mistake as it would be to try to read Balzac's opinion
in (or into) those of every character, it would be just as great a mistake to
dismiss characters' opinions because they differ too much from what we
presume to know about Balzac's personal political and social ideology.
This case illustrates why such dogmatism would be dangerous, as *Gobseck*
was begun in 1830, long before Balzac placed himself in the legitimist
camp. Nearly contemporary to the early versions of *Gobseck* is *Le Bal de
Sceaux,* where the great nobility is presented in a distinctly unflattering
light, and where Louis XVIII himself is portrayed complaining about
parasitism on the part of the old nobility as represented by the comte de
Fontaine and his family, each of whom profits in some way from the
count's relationship to the king. The case of the comte de Fontaine and his
family can be directly and unfavorably compared to that of the du Guénic
family in *Béatrix*. Like the count, the old baron du Guénic is a former
Chouan, who continued to *chouanner* even in 1832. Du Guénic refuses to
seek compensation for his services to the Bourbons: "On croirait que j'ai
servi le roi par intérêt" [*People will think I served the king out of self-
interest*] (2:653). The evolution of Balzac's personal opinions, and the
doubts that have been raised about what those opinions were or may have
been at any given point in time, further complicate our task as readers. We
are forced to turn back to the text, which can be just as hard to pin down as
Balzac himself.

A final point to be made here about the frame/story relationship in
Gobseck is the self-contained nature of this *nouvelle;* that is to say that this
work is virtually independent of the rest of *La Comédie humaine* as far as
the understanding of its characters. While a reading of other texts, especially *Le Père Goriot,* would give the reader a more complete understanding of *Gobseck*, its characters and its nuances, the essentials can all
be found by a careful reading of the text as given. This is not to say,
however, that *Gobseck* is somehow shut off from the rest of *La Comédie
humaine*. Indeed, *Gobseck* is an excellent illustration of exactly how

effective the system of recurring characters can be. In the other texts in which he appears, Gobseck is a miser and a moneylender, and little more; he has his brothers in other texts of *la Comédie humaine* (Grandet, Gigonnet, G. Rigou, etc.) and in the larger European literary tradition (Shylock, Harpagon, Scrooge, Dostoyevsky's pawnbroker, etc.). But in this *nouvelle* we learn the extent and the basis of Gobseck's power. He is not merely obsessed with gold like Grandet, he does not crave power in the conventional sense like Nucingen. Gobseck's power is based in psychology and philosophy; he lives apart from the world, while still exercising great power in it. Once we have read *Gobseck,* the name, when we see it in other texts, signifies far more than a simple debt. We know that any character who goes to see "papa Gobseck" has surrendered to the monster known as Paris.

Speaking to Persuade: The Statesman and the Diplomat

There are two other character-narrators whose profession casts a different light on their role as narrator. The first is Maurice de l'Hostal, who tells the story of Honorine in the *nouvelle* of the same name. Maurice is trained as a lawyer, but I do not place him in the same category as Derville, because he works and, I believe, speaks as a diplomat. The act of narration in *Honorine* is chiefly interesting because of its narratees, and will be more thoroughly discussed in the next chapter, but the narrator does deserve some mention. The second is Henri de Marsay, in *Autre étude de femme* and *Une Ténébreuse affaire.* While not specifically trained in the law, as far as we know, de Marsay has had a parallel career to many of Balzac's law students, having moved from the purely social scene to triumph in politics. De Marsay dies prime minister, and it is as a successful and politician that we see him tell his stores.

Ambassador to a Court of Love: Maurice de l'Hostal in *Honorine*

In mid May of 1836, at the home of the French consul general in Genoa, a brilliant company, including the celebrated writer Camille Maupin (alias Félicité des Touches), the critic Claude Vignon, and the painter Léon de Lora, has gathered for dinner. Included with these recurring characters, all associated with Balzac's art world, are two Italians whose sophistication makes them "deux Français déguisés en Génois" (2: 527), and the Byronian consul himself, Maurice de l'Hostal. The wives of several guests are also present, including Mme de l'Hostal who will play a small but significant role in the *nouvelle*. After dinner, on the terrace, the conversation turns to literature and "l'éternel fonds de boutique de la ré-publique de lettres: la faute de la femme!" [*the eternal subject matter in the republic of letters: the fault of woman!*]. The women present, including Mlle des Touches and Mme de l'Hostal, are "impitoyables" [*pitiless*] for their less virtuous sisters, while the men take up the cause of the weaker members of the weaker sex (531). The subject and the setting—outdoors in springtime—and above all the company—only the noblest of men and women are present—all combine to suggest a nineteenth-century version of the medieval courts of love, presided over not by a queen, but by one of the most unusual and highly respected woman of *La Comédie humaine,* Félicité des Touches. The word court (*cour*) can mean either a royal or a legal court, so Maurice's double role of lawyer and diplomat is especially relevant here. Like Derville, he uses his voice to serve another by telling a story, that of Honorine, the estranged wife of Maurice's benefactor, who is named only "le comte Octave."

Maurice succeeds as a storyteller and thus as an advocate, as a diplomat. When his story is finished, Mlle des Touches is no longer *impi-toyable,* rather she clearly shows her sympathy for Honorine by finding Octave responsible for his wife's death. Her judgment is terse and une-quivocal: "Connaissait-il sa position d'assassin?" [*Was he aware of his role of assassin?*] (595). If it is not surprising to us that Félicité has found Honorine innocent—we more or less expect a story of this kind to be ef-fective—the harshness with which she judges Octave is surprising, even somewhat disconcerting. The sudden and complete about-face might make us suspect Balzac of pushing too hard to make Maurice's story seem ef-fective, but an analysis of Félicité des Touches's own story—which will be given in the next chapter—demonstrates that this reaction is completely consistent with her character.

As a judge of Maurice's story, we should consider Mlle des Touches's social role as well as her personal history. For if Félicité is the most important member of Maurice's audience, she is not the only one. The other members of the company who are recurring characters, Claude Vignon and Léon de Lora, are, as already mentioned, both members of

Balzac's artistic world; the lawyer is speaking before a jury of artists. This point underlines the importance of Balzac's physical description of Maurice, of the fact that the consul resembles Byron. What might at first seem to be only a cliché, used to suggest a romantic, melancholic temperament, has another purpose as well; Maurice's resemblance to Byron is relevant not only to his role in his own story—that is, as the romantic hero—but also to his role as narrator. The comparison strongly implies to us that this diplomat is not the cold calculator that stereotype might suggest (Talleyrand and Metternich outside *La Comédie humaine,* Charles de Vandenesse or Canalis within). He is poetic, if not actually a poet (2:528), and his story is not a cold factual summary that could only appeal to the mind, but a poetic tale—if not actually a poem—that speaks to the heart and to the soul. The sensitive reader will be touched by this story, as are the artists who listen to it.

Les Dernières armes d'un lion: Henri de Marsay as Storyteller

Like *Honorine, Autre étude de femme* is a text complicated by Balzac's revisions and rewriting. It is complicated not only for critics, but for more casual readers as well. Because of a number of contradictions, some difficult and some frankly impossible to resolve, *Autre étude* is often described and even dismissed as a flawed text; I prefer to think of it as flawed because unfinished, and far too interesting to be dismissed. These flaws and what I believe are possible explanations for them will, again, be more thoroughly discussed in a later chapter. For now, I will only discuss a part of the text that is relatively unscarred by the flaws of the larger text, the first internal narration by de Marsay. At the same gathering of illustrious Parisians where Bianchon tells the story of *La Grande Bretèche,* Henri de Marsay, the former "roi [des] dandies" (*IP;* 5:389) who has become prime minister, tells the story of how a woman helped shape him both as a *lion* and as a politician. This story of education and initiation was published separately in an 1845 edition of *La Comédie humaine,* under the title *Premières armes d'un lion.* It is de Marsay's recounting of an early love affair, in which he was first the dupe and then the deceiver of a duchess known only as Charlotte, a beautiful widow six years his senior. Head over heels in love, Henri discovers that his beloved is concealing from him her engagement to another man, a rich, older duke. The story illustrates de

Marsay's grace under pressure, as he turns the tables on Charlotte, and, more importantly, learns with this first and last love never to let emotion overtake reason. It was this worldly experience of social politics that forged the man who would become the king of the dandies under the Restoration and prime minister under the July Monarchy.

This story causes some consternation among critics of *La Comédie humaine* because, since what we see here is purported to be the story of de Marsay's first love, it would seem that Balzac (and/or de Marsay) has forgotten the unforgettable Paquita Valdès, the girl with the golden eyes, who was the object of de Marsay's violent passion in the *nouvelle* of the same name. Another problem concerns the internal chronology of *La Comédie humaine*, which is famously and undeniably, if understandably, flawed. According to information given in *La Fille aux yeux d'or*, de Marsay's age at the time of his affair with Paquita, which takes place during the Hundred Days, would have been 22 or 23; in *Autre étude*, he gives his age at the time of his affair with Charlotte, which takes place just after Waterloo ("la Restauration allait se raffermir," 3:678) as 17. Again, it seems that Balzac has forgotten some details. There is however a brief passage in *Autre étude* which suggests that *La Fille aux yeux d'or* was not far from Balzac's mind when he wrote this part of *Autre étude*. Before beginning his story, de Marsay says that only his friend Ronquerolles knew of his affair with Charlotte and that he would have feared his friend's smile during his story, "mais il est parti" (678). The remark seems perfectly insignificant on the surface, but Ronquerolles' absence in *Autre étude* is significant because of his presence in *La Fille aux yeux d'or*. In the latter text, Ronquerolles appears, very briefly, at the beginning of the story, when he and de Marsay, fellow members of the *Treize*, share a silent communication (5:1058). Ronquerolles shared not only the secret of Charlotte, but, as a member of the *Treize*, the far more scandalous secret of the love(s) and death of Paquita. This somewhat tenuous link is reinforced by a suppressed passage from an early (1834) version of *L'Histoire des Treize*. As Anthony Pugh noted (*Balzac's Recurring Characters*, 44), at the end of an early version of *La Duchesse de Langeais*, after the failed attempt to kidnap Antoinette from her convent, de Marsay suggests that Ronquerolles console General Montriveau by telling the story of Paquita Valdès. The variant is given in the *Pléiade* edition:

Ta duchesse!. . . je l'ai connue. Elle ne valait pas *ma fille aux yeux d'or*. [. . .] Tu n'étais pas encore des nôtres! —Ronquerolles, dit-il en se tournant vers le marquis, conte-lui donc cette affaire-là pour le distraire; tu sais mieux que moi en faire valoir les détails. (5:1526, var. c)

Your duchess!. . . I knew her. She was no match for my girl with the golden eyes. You weren't one of us yet! Ronquerolles," he said, turning to the marquis, "tell him that story; you know how to bring out the details better than I."

This passage confirms the idea that Ronquerolles knew the story of Paquita, while the fact that it was supressed, and that Montriveau was not yet a member of the *Treize* in 1815, would mean that de Marsay need not fear the general's smile when he tells the story of Charlotte, since Montriveau, also present at Félicité des Touches's *souper,* probably does not know about Paquita.

The relevance of this admittedly rather complicated exegesis is that it suggests, not necessarily an oversight on Balzac's part, but that de Marsay is dissembling. For his own reasons, he has chosen to conceal a part of the truth. It is obvious why he does so: not only is the story of Paquita, de Marsay, and his half-sister, Margarita de San-Réal, particularly sordid, it also involves the secret affairs of the *Treize.* None of this is part of de Marsay's public image. Throughout *La Comédie humaine,* de Marsay has a double nature; the public side is the polished, almost effeminate dandy whose acts of violence are purely social, as when he ostentatiously disdains Lucien de Rubempré and Mme de Bargeton at the opera in *Illusions perdues* ("Quoiqu'à deux pas du nouveau venu, de Marsay prit son lorgnon pour le voir" [*Although only two steps away from the newcomer, de Marsay used his opera glasses to look at him*] 5:277-78). The secret side is the cruel and violent member of the *Treize,* who is not only prepared to murder Paquita, but is also very probably the rapist of Lydie Peyrade, exacting a particularly brutal vengeance on behalf of Vautrin (*SMC;* 6:661, 678). I have always thought that de Marsay's double nature was a deliberately exaggerated metaphor for Balzac's society, especially the Parisian aristocracy: cruelty hidden under elegance and manners like brass claws sheathed in a velvet glove. It is when this dual nature is synthesized into one that de Marsay becomes prime minister, combining ambition, ruthlessness, and power with the tact and diplomacy required by parliamentary politics. It is not surprising that, as a narrator, de Marsay reveals a secret, but not his secret self.

If we accept that de Marsay is at the very least shading the truth, we necessarily must ask ouselves why. De Marsay is a parliamentary politician, but he is hardly campaigning for votes in an elegant dining room at two o'clock in the morning. I think the reason has to do with de Marsay, the aging lion. Among the company at Mlle des Touches's *souper* are many of his fellow veterans of the social battles of the Restoration, including former lovers (Mme de Cadignan, Delphine de Nucingen, and very probably his step-mother, Lady Dudley), romantic rivals (Rastignac, Félix de Vandenesse), and in general people whom de Marsay might like to impress (Nucingen, a foreign ambassador, Mme d'Espard). The story he tells is that of his first social skirmish and victory; his act of narration can be seen as a last victory, a final demonstration of superiority for a man whose end is near. Just as Gobseck was moved to confide in Derville, whom he trusted to appreciate his story, de Marsay is seeking to impress those he sees as his peers, and to affirm his place as first among equals. This desire to impress may explain the discrepancy in de Marsay's age. De Marsay in 1833 mocks his own youthful exaltation of 1815: "Je gardais *ses* vieux gants, je buvais en infusion les fleurs qu'*elle* avait portées, je me relevais la nuit pour aller voir *ses* fenêtres" [*I kept* her *old gloves, I drank a brew made from the flowers* she *had carried, I got out of bed at night to go and look at* her *windows*] (3:678); along these same lines are the hairs (*her* hairs) de Marsay has sewn into his hankerchiefs, the clue which eventually leads Henri to the truth, that his true love is a *coquette*. What might seem to be a charming naïveté in a seventeen-year-old boy would seem a bit ridiculous in the twenty-three-year-old de Marsay actually was, especially to someone who knows, as does Ronquerolles, what de Marsay was at twenty-three. But only Ronquerolles or a very sharp-eared listener would have noticed the inconsistency; only readers have the luxury of cross-referencing. If lying about his age serves de Marsay as a face-saver, it serves him in another way as well. Not only is romantic excess more excusable in a seventeen-year-old, he is also more impressive as the cool manipulator who tricks Charlotte. By shaving six years off his own age (the same difference he gives between his own age and Charlotte's—were they actually the same age?), de Marsay paints himself as a prodigy in social gamesmanship, which eventually leads him to statesmanship.

This discrepancy in age might seem a minor point, especially considering how common this particular sort of mistake is in *La Comédie humaine,* but we should never be too quick to dismiss such inconsistencies as mistakes that Balzac has made. These faults can often serve as openings, creating that distance between the narrator(s) and the reader, those blank spaces that we can exploit to interpret the text, to analyze other discrepancies more closely. Another such breach is, perhaps, de Marsay's pretense that his duchess is both unknown and unrecognizable to the assembled company. It strains our credibility that none of the nearly thirty guests present—some of whom have been in the *monde* as long as de Marsay—would be able to recognize the lady described, especially considering the clues that de Marsay gives, a title and a first name. Balzac seems to have recognized this at some point, as is revealed by yet another suppressed passage, an exchange between two other guests, both very familiar with Balzac's *monde* and to the reader: "Comme il n'y a que trente duchesses en France, dit la princesse de Cadignan à la marquise d'Espard, nous finirons par la deviner. . ." (*"Since there are only thirty duchesses in France,"* *said the princesse de Cadignan to the marquise d'Espard, "we'll figure* *out who it is in the end,"* 3:1497, var. a). Perhaps to preserve some sense of mystery, inside and outside of the text, Balzac suppressed this very logical passage, which makes me wonder if de Marsay did not change the names to protect the not so innocent. If he did, there is nonetheless one guest who recognizes Charlotte:

> Vous êtes tous disposés à condamner cette femme, dit lady Dudley, eh bien, je comprends comment elle ne considérait pas son mariage comme une inconstance! Les hommes ne veulent jamais distinguer entre la constance et la fidélité. Je connais la femme de qui M. de Marsay nous a conté l'histoire, et c'est une de vos dernières grandes dames!. . . (689)
>
> *"You're all ready to condemn this woman," said Lady Dudley, "well, I* *understand why she didn't consider her marriage to be an inconstancy!* *Men are never willing to distinguish between constancy and fidelity. I* *know the woman whose story M. de Marsay has told us, and she is one* *of the last of your great ladies!"*

It is surprising that Lady Dudley should come to the defense of anyone, much less of another woman. This apparent inconsistency may offer the chance for another interpretation. Perhaps de Marsay has changed not only the name but the circumstances of his story, perhaps *Premières armes d'un lion* is a disguised telling of the story of Henri and his step-mother. In *Le Lys dans la vallée,* there is a suggestion that the two have a quasi-incestuous relationship, which is perfectly consistent with the curious mores of the Dudley family. The timing of the affair with Charlotte also roughly corresponds to the time of his affair with Lady Dudley. Furthermore, everything we know about Lady Dudley herself makes it plausible that her remarks should be self-defense rather than the defense of another woman, and that her words are a veiled riposte to de Marsay's similarly disguised thrust. This may seem a very bold interpretation, but as I will attempt to demonstrate further on, the verbal interplay among the many recurring characters of *Autre étude de femme* is filled with such hidden meanings, and Balzac, uncharacteristically does very little to help us see them.

In his final appearance on the stage of *La Comédie humaine,* at the end of *Une Ténébreuse affaire,* de Marsay tells one last story. In the epilogue to what is probably the most complexly plotted of Balzac's novels, de Marsay tells the story that sheds a retroactive light on the shadowy business of the abduction of the imperial count and senator Malin de Gondreville and the trial of the Simeuse brothers under Napoleon's reign, in 1806. The storytelling is prompted when, in 1833, the novel's extraordinary heroine, Laurence de Cinq-Cygne, suddenly leaves the house of the princesse de Cadignan when Malin, her arch-enemy, is announced. The fanatically legitimist Laurence holds Malin responsible, with some justification, for the death of her Simeuse cousins and also for the destruction of her own noble house. Laurence's hatred for Malin is well known in Balzac's *monde,* and Diane de Cadignan tells de Marsay that he may have foiled her plans to marry her son to Laurence's daughter. De Marsay seeks to repair the damage by revealing to Diane the secrets of state that underlie the mystery of Malin de Gondreville's abduction[6] and the trial of the

---

[6] Balzac based this story on the factual but still mysterious abduction of the imperial senator Clément de Ris, the model for Malin de Gondreville.

Simeuse brothers. Diane can then reveal the truth to Laurence and cement the alliance between Georges de Maufrigneuse and Berthe de Cing-Cygne.

Once again, the company is a well-chosen audience for a tale of political intrigue; many of Balzac's politically connected characters are present, not only Diane and de Marsay, but also Rastignac, the marquise d'Espard, Vandenesse, the powerful dukes de Lenoncourt and de Navarreins, two famous orators from the *chambre des pairs,* and a pair of anonymous ambassadors. De Marsay tells his story with confidence that this well-connected elite will be able to follow the threads of his narration, recognizing the players and understanding the nuances of their words and actions. The story goes back to 1800, several years before the abduction of Malin. De Marsay describes a remarkable meeting between Talleyrand, Fouché, Sièyes, and Carnot. The four men are plotting to overthrow First Counsul Bonaparte in the event of his defeat at the hands of the Austrians. The opportunistic Malin, who has hidden himself in a shadowy corner, is included in the plot because the others want to keep him quiet. The five will form a new Directory in the event of the collapse of the consular régime. In order to ensure Malin's silence, Fouché, who considers this fifth conspirator especially untrustworthy, forces him to print up the initial proclamations and directives of their shadow government, and to hide them at his recently acquired estate of Gondreville, the ancestral home of the Simeuse family, seized and sold as a *bien national.* Later, when Napoleon seems firmly established as Emperor, Fouché arranges the abduction of Malin, by men resembling the Simeuses and their friends, in order to find and destroy the lethally incriminating documents hidden at Gondreville. Fouché also hopes, de Marsay tells us, to find proof of the correspondance that the double-dealing senator had carried on, through the Terror and the Empire, with the exiled Louis XVIII. The Simeuse twins get caught in this game of cross and double-cross, they are arrested and eventually pardonned, but the valiant and loyal family retainer Michu is sacrificed for *raisons d'état.*

De Marsay's narration most obviously serves as the necessary clarification of the extremely obscure plot, but it fulfills other functions as well. De Marsay is in his last days. If the story of Charlotte was a social swansong, the boast of a fading lion, this story has its roots specifically in de Marsay's political career. The text implies that is de Marsay's last important act: "comme les lampes près de s'éteindre, [il] brillait d'un dernier

éclat" [*he shone with a final brilliance, like a lamp about to burn out*] and
we are told that this evening will mark the last time Diane de Cadignan
will see her former lover (8:686). De Marsay tells the story not only to
save Diane's marital project, but also because he alone—with the exception of the now ancient Talleyrand— knows it (689). The tale represents
something of a last will and testament. An important but secret episode in
French history is now preserved, but only orally; it can be passed on, but
only to the select few. As Owen Heathcote put it, de Marsay's imminent
demise gives his words added weight, "an almost posthumous conviction
of an apocalyptic 'memoir from beyond the grave.' [...] De Marsay be-
queathes to posterity and to history *Une Ténébreuse affaire*" ("Balzac at
the Crossroads," 133).

On another level, the revelations in de Marsay's story blur the lines
between fiction and history by bringing Balzac's fictional characters together with the great historical figures of his time. This frequent Balzacian
ploy is used with exceptional boldness in *Une Ténébreuse affaire,* where
Talleyrand and Napoleon are not merely shadows or points of reference,
but actors in the fiction; it is on the advice of Talleyrand that Laurence
obtains her cousins' pardon in a dramatic interview with Napoleon on the
eve of the battle of Iéna. De Marsay's story not only reinforces that *effet
du réel,* it also places Balzac's characters on an equal plane with the historical figures. Malin was a peer, if only through opportunistic stealth, of
Talleyrand and Fouché. De Marsay must also be placed on that high level,
since he knows not only the details of the plot of that gang of five of 1800,
he can relate word-for-word the conversation that launched their machinations. Necessarily, one of those five shared the secret with him.

It is probably not Malin, as de Marsay waits for the old count to
leave Diane's before revealing the secret—it seems he does not want
Malin to know what he knows. Our first instinct is that Talleyrand informed de Marsay: Balzac's prime minister is lavish in his praise of "le
prince, que j'admire comme un des hommes les plus remarquables de
notre temps" [*the prince, whom I admire and consider one of the most remarkable men of our time*] (869); beyond this novel, it is suggested in *Le
Contrat de mariage* that the "prince qui n'est manchot que du pied" [*that
prince whose lameness is only physical*] was an ally, perhaps even a mentor to de Marsay when the dandy turned his attention to politics (*CM*, 3:
647). However, de Marsay is remarkably well informed about the actions

and thoughts of Fouché. He tells his listeners in detail what the chief of Bonaparte's secret police did and why. The implication is that de Marsay was in the confidence of Fouché as well as Talleyrand. It is entirely fitting that the *roi des dandies,* leader of the *Treize* and of Louis-Philippe's government is the political heir to the two very different *éminences grises* of the Empire and Restoration. Once again we see how the differing facets of de Marsay's character come together to form the whole. These associations also make de Marsay more than just a fictional character; he is inserted into history by his creator, a keeper and revealer of the great secrets that slip away from historians, the facts that only a writer of fiction can reveal.

This is the real importance of de Marsay's narration. It confers upon this remarkable story the imprimatur of truth. Balzac firmly believed his version of the Clément de Ris abduction to be the truth, only the names were changed. It may never be officially recognized, but the truth is preserved by those who, in the real world, correspond to Henri de Marsay, to Diane de Cadignan. Those anonymous ambassadors and orators are, in this conceit, conduits back to the real world, just as Talleyrand and Napoleon represent the real world brought into fiction. In an exceptionally dramatic way, this reflects the way Balzac saw his entire work, as the history of that Society of which he was the mere scribe. *Une Ténébreuse affaire* is one of the most porous points of the barrier that separated the world Balzac observed from the the one he created.

Writers Blocked

There is one remaining professional category that needs to be mentioned in relation to narration and storytelling: writers. There are a number of significant writer-characters in *La Comédie humaine*: Daniel d'Arthez and Camille Maupin belong at the top of the list, as both are qualified as authors of genius; Raoul Nathan and Lucien de Rubempré seem to have real talent, even if the latter eventually lowers himself to journalism; Balzac has less respect for Lousteau and his lover, Dinah de La Baudraye, and the vaudevillian Du Bruel probably figures near the bottom of the list as well; finally, we should not forget the poet Canalis, the critic Claude Vignon, and the journalist Blondet. Albert Savarus publishes his one *nouvelle, L'Ambitieux par amour,* and is thus a priori a

writer, but he is a lawyer and a politician by profession, and a writer
somewhat by chance. What Savarus is first and foremost is a lover, and all
three of these professions are subordinated to this most important role in
his life. It is surprising, given this rather long list and the importance of so
many of these characters in the plots of the various texts in which they appear, to note how little of their output we as readers see. We cannot read
their writing, we do not even know the titles of any of d'Arthez or Camille
Maupin's work. Balzac does reproduce (so to speak) a number of poems,
but usually only so he can mock them, their authors, and verse in general.
Like the sanctity of the confessional and the professional discretion of the
doctors, this is another curious silence in *La Comédie humaine.*

Of all the writers of fiction in *La Comédie humaine,* we see only
two act as storytellers, and they tell the same story: in *Un prince de la Bohème,* Dinah de La Baudraye reads aloud the written version of the story
she heard from the writer Raoul Nathan; the story of La Palférine and
Tullia will be published, after Dinah has changed the names. *Albert Savarus* does contain an internal narration, but not the act of the *raconteur,* the
oral communication that is so important to Balzac. *L'Ambitieux par amour*
is published, and we read it, along with Rosalie de Watteville, as a written
text. What is most interesting about these internal metafictions is that they
are both false fictions. The stories related in these two examples are both
true; they really happened on the same diegetic level where the characters
who write them live. La Palférine and Tullia inhabit the same Parisian Bohemia as Dinah and Nathan; and in spite of the changed names, Savarus's
story is every bit as autodiegetic, or autobiographical, as de Marsay's or
Maurice de l'Hostal's. Like the substitution of recurring characters for real
people, like the use of his own characters as metaphors or points of reference within the text, this absence of true metafictions within *La Comédie
humaine* contributes to the illusion of self-sufficiency and wholeness.
There may be lies and half-truths, there may be shading and spinning and
shifting perspectives on different stories, but there is nothing false within
La Comédie humaine. All is true!

Section II
Je est plusieurs autres: The First-Person Narrators

The use of a first person narrator is fairly frequent in *La Comédie humaine,* especially in the earlier texts. In many cases, Balzac later altered these texts so that the narrating *je* became one of the recurring characters. For instance, in both *Etude de femme* and *Autre étude de femme, je* became Bianchon. It is important to note that the several narrating *je* are different from the Narrator. As stated earlier, the Narrator is a noncorporeal entity; that is, there can be no pretense that he is a person in the sense that most fictional characters are. On the other hand, there can be no pretense that the narrating *je* are not people, for they interact with other characters, sometimes recurring characters, in a way that the Narrator does not. Perhaps even more importantly, the narrating *je* do not have the privileged knowledge that is the most important defining characteristic of the Narrator. The *je* exist on the same diegetic level as the other character-narrators, at one remove from the Narrator. That said, I have chosen to discuss these narrators separately because, even though they interact with recurring characters, they do not fit in to Balzac's system: Mme de Rochefide talks about traveling through Italy in *Béatrix,* but never mentions the man who told the strange story of a sculptor and a Roman castrato; and no one ever tells of meeting an old Venetian who claimed to be able to sense gold through walls, although the name Facino Cane is mentioned in *Massimila Doni.* We as readers have less information about these *je* than we have about a character-narrator such as Bianchon or Derville. We react to them differently, both because of the lack of information we have about them, and also because of the lack of distance we have from them. In the *je-*narrated stories, the Narrator is not present, acting as intermediary and guide. In these cases, we are dealing directly with a narrator, and our confidence in him is taken for granted, our trust is assumed. Once we have read his tale, we can step back and judge him (the *je* are all men), and make certain judgments about credibility or motivation, but even then, we have only *je*'s words to guide us.

This discussion is limited to those first-person narratives that contain some kind of frame/story relationship, in which the *je* acts as either narrator or narratee of an object story in addition to being the primary diegetic narrator. Included in this list are *Sarrasine, Un drame au bord de la mer, L'Auberge rouge, Facino Cane,* and *Une Passion dans le désert.* The narrators of *Louis Lambert* or *Le Message* will not be discussed, since these two texts contain no framed story. I will include two texts in which the narrating *je* is eventually identified as a character who can be connected to the system of recurring characters: *Un Drame au bord de la mer* and *Z. Marcas.* I feel that these works can be included in this section because the two narrators concerned—Louis Lambert and Charles Rabourdin, respectively—play relatively small roles in the network of recurring characters. Moreover, in both cases, the identity of the narrator is revealed only at the end of the story, so the naïve reader's experience with the narrator in these cases is similar to that in *Sarrasine* or *Facino Cane.* Finally, discussion of *La Maison Nucingen* will be reserved for a later chapter, for in that text the first-person narrator is part of an extremely complex narrative structure that deserves, even demands, to be examined thoroughly and separately.

A Triple Play by the Sea: Louis Lambert as Narrator and Narratee in *Un Drame au bord de la mer*

Un Drame au bord de la mer takes the form of a letter, but the reader does not learn this until the end of the text. As the story opens, we are faced with what seems to be a fairly ordinary first-person narration: an anonymous *je* recounts to an unspecified audience an adventure that he has had while vacationing in Brittany. It is only after several pages that the narratee is specified, and we learn that the narrator is telling his story to his uncle. We are not yet enlightened as to the context of this narration, but we do know we are witnessing a private communication. It is only in the final paragraphs of the text that we learn who the narrator is, and that what we are reading is in fact a letter from someone identified only as "Louis." The naïve reader of this *nouvelle* cannot go much farther in identifying the narrator, but the informed reader of *La Comédie humaine* recognizes in our narrator Louis Lambert, one of Balzac's most prominent and remarkable characters and the protagonist of a short novel that bears his name. In the novel *Louis Lambert,* we learn of the life and death of a brilliant young thinker, whose mental powers are so strong that they can only be described as supernatural. Lambert's imagination is in fact a "seconde vue," he does not merely imagine places and events, he "sees"

them, actualizes them in his mind. Lambert's mental capactities eventually
escape his control, driving him mad and, ultimately, to his death. Readers
of *Louis Lambert* also recognize Pauline, the traveling companion of *Un
Drame,* as Pauline de Villenoix, Lambert's spiritual wife, and the uncle to
whom Louis' letter is addressed as Lambert's second father, a priest who
watches over his gifted, doomed nephew. The case of *Un Drame au bord
de la mer* and *Louis Lambert* offers yet another illustration of the complexity and richness of the experience of reading *La Comédie humaine.*
The *nouvelle* stands alone to the naïve reader, but is vastly enriched by a
familiarity with the novel. For those who are able to identify Louis with
Lambert, the sense of the title takes on a new meaning, and the link between frame and story is made stronger by the addition of another layer of
meaning.

The frame presents us with Louis, a tourist in Brittany who, in the
course of his travels, learns a strange story. This well-worn device is used
to present us with the story of Cambremer, a hermit living in a cave on the
desolate Breton coast. As Louis and Pauline learn from the poor fisherman
who acts as their guide, Cambremer's solitary life is an act of perpetual
penance for having killed his own son, a spoiled adolescent who had become a dangerous thief, threatening his mother and dishonoring his family. The influence of Mérimée's *Mateo Falcone* is evident and universally
acknowledged; in fact this resemblance is often emphasized to the detri-
ment of the essential difference between the two stories, which is the
theme of remorse and repentance, unique to Balzac. Mérimée's inflexible
Corsican executes his son and immediately sends for his son-in-law as a
replacement; his *sang-froid* is brutal and constant. Balzac's Cambremer,
having executed his son for similar reasons, loses his beloved wife to grief
and offers the rest of his existence as repentance. There are thus two dramas in *Un Drame au bord de la mer:* the first is within the object story,
the infanticide required by a savage code of honor; the second is found in
the frame, the hermit perched on his rock, forever looking out to sea, the
scene of his crime.

Louis and Pauline, both clearly portrayed as people of an extreme
sensibility, are both profoundly affected by the story of Cambremer: "La
disposition de nos âmes était changée. Nous étions tous deux plongés en
de funestes réflexions, attristés par ce drame" [*The state of our souls had
changed. We were both plunged in dark reflections, saddened by this*

drama] (10:1176). The wild country around them has lost its terrible beauty and become barren and unhospitable:

> Pauline était [. . .] triste, et moi je ressentais déjà les approches de cette flamme qui me brûle le cerveau. J'étais si cruellement tourmenté par les visions que j'avais de ces trois existences, qu'elle me dit: « Louis, écris cela, tu donneras le change à la nature de cette fièvre ».
>
> Je vous ai donc écrit cette aventure, mon cher oncle; mais elle m'a déjà fait perdre le calme que je devais à mes bains et à notre séjour ici. (1177-78)
>
> *Pauline was saddened, and for myself I could already feel the approach of the flame that burns my brain. I was so cruelly tormented by the visions I was having of these three existences, that Pauline said to me: "Louis, write this down, you'll change the nature of this fever."*
>
> *And so I wrote you this adventure, my dear uncle, but it has already caused me to lose that calm that had come with the waters and my stay here.*

The closing part of the frame shows us clearly the effect of the story, as does the reaction of Félicité des Touches in *Honorine*. The reaction of the textual narratees prolongs the effect of the framed story, while at the same time guiding the readers in their reaction to it. Like a fade-out at the end of the movie, this epilogue leads us out of the narrative illusion, out of our suspension of disbelief, without abrubtly erasing the illusion.

Still another link between frame and story becomes visible when *Un Drame* is considered in light of *Louis Lambert*. Both texts are part of the *Etudes philosophiques,* the "grand principe inspirateur" of which is, according to Moïse Le Youanc, "le thème du pouvoir déstructeur de la pensée" [*the great inspiring principle is the theme of the destructive power of thought*] (intro., ed *Pléiade;* 10:1149). It is only in the final paragraphs that the reader recognizes Louis Lambert, and with that recognition, certain words in the closing part of the frame become much richer in meaning. We recognize the threatening flame as Lambert's too powerful intellect, and we can only imagine how vivid his tormenting visions must be, because Lambert, no doubt, *sees* in his mind this *drama* that we have only read, that Pauline has only heard. For readers of the whole, there is thus a third drama in this story: Lambert slipping back into madness, perhaps for the last time. The story told has driven one of its hearers insane. *Louis Lambert* shows us the total arc of Lambert's life, his intellectual development and eventual descent into madness; *Un Drame au bord de la mer* shows a small scene, possibly a crucial one, from the larger drama. We see up close how Lambert's own thoughts take hold of him, how even the comparatively small events of his life, like a vacation, are destined to lead him to madness. Gaëtan Picon has suggested still another link between story and frame in *Un Drame* by brilliantly studying how the theme of paternity runs fom the story of Cambremer out to the frame. According to Picon, this *nouvelle* contains "l'expression mythique des hantises du créateur (un père tue sons fils, le créateur et la créature s'entredévorent)" [*The mythical expression of the obsessions of the creator, (a father kills his son, creator and created destroy each other)*] (*Balzac par lui-même*, 92). Like Frankenstein and his monster, Cambremer is destroyed by his own creation, the son he molded in such a way that the final drama of their life became inevitable and fatal for both. Lambert, too, will eventually be destroyed by his own creation, by his thoughts, after attempting to destroy them. With his supernatural vision, surely Lambert saw himself in Cambremer, saw himself in the man who has doomed himself to a catatonic state, not unlike Lambert's own at the end of his life. Listening to the story of Cambremer allows visions of his own end to enter Louis Lambert's mind, and to drive him mad. Not for the last time, we see how the act of storytelling can have lethal consequences in *La Comédie humaine*.

Martyr to Bureaucracy: Telling the Story of *Z. Marcas*

Like *Un Drame au bord de la mer, Z. Marcas* is a somewhat deceptive text, because what we think is an anonymous narrating *je* is in fact a character who can be directly linked to Balzac's larger fictional world. Also, *Z. Marcas* is unique among Balzac's framed narratives in that it is only half-framed; only at the end of the story does the reader learn that what we thought was a direct first-person narration by the young law student who witnessed the final months of Marcas's life is actually the relation, by a truly anonymous *je*, of Charles Rabourdin's act of storytelling. This is not revealed until the end of the *nouvelle*, when Charles's voice is interrupted for the first time:

> Ici Charles se tut, il parut oppressé par ses souvenirs.
> « Eh bien, lui cria-t-on, qu'est-il arrivé? » (8:853)
> *And Charles was silent, he seemed oppressed by his memories.*
> *Well, we cried, what happened to him?*

It is only now that we see that the young law student's name is Charles, and he is not a primary but a metadiegetic narrator. The use of the verb *paraître* reveals that this is an eye-witness account, not of the life and death of Marcas, but of Charles Rabourdin's storytelling. This unusual structure has a double effect. First, the initial impression of a first-person narration increases the impact of Charles's story, there is no visible intermediary to blunt the effect of the portrait; the reader is drawn that much closer to the events by the illusion of an eye-witness account. Second, we are able to see, in the final paragraph, the effect that Charles's story has on his listeners, presumably his friends and peers, the "nous" of which the true diegetic narrator (*je*) is a part:

> Nous nous regardâmes tous tristement en écoutant ce récit, le dernier de ceux que nous fit Charles Rabourdin, la veille du jour où il s'embarqua sur un brick, au Havre, pour les îles de la Malaisie, car nous connaissions plus d'un Marcas, plus d'une victime de ce dévouement politique, récompensé par la trahison ou par l'oubli. (854)
> *We all looked at each other sadly listening to this tale, the last that Charles Rabourdin ever told us, the night before he embarked from Le Havre for the islands of Malaysia, because we all knew more than one Marcas, more than one victim of this political devotion, rewarded with betrayal and oblivion.*

This last paragraph shows us the immediate effect of the tale. As we will see, the story has repercussions within the world portrayed by *La Comédie humaine;* Charles's story has a ripple effect, spreading beyond the immediate time and place of the narration.

Z. Marcas is a *scène de la vie politique,* one of the few that Balzac actually finished in his lifetime. It is the story of two impoverished students living in the Latin Quarter in 1836, where they befriend an older man who lives in the same poor hotel. Charles Rabourdin is studying law, and his friend, identified only as Juste, is studying medecine. Their older neighbor, Zéphérin Marcas, is living in poverty and obscurity after a successful career in politics was cut short by the self-interested betrayal of a politician who owed his success and power largely to Marcas. The politician, in trouble, returns to ask for Marcas's help, only to betray him once more. The blow is fatal for Marcas, who is cared for in his final days by the two young students. The parallels to *Le Père Goriot* are obvious. If the old man in the pension Vauquer is the Christ of Paternity (3:231), then Marcas is crucified on the cross of "l'administration," by the incompetence and hypocrisy of the gerontocracy that Balzac despised. Marcas is killed by the minister who owes him everything, just as Goriot is killed by the daughters to whom he could never give enough.

There are of course significant differences between the two texts as well, some of which are quite revealing. First of all, Goriot is an old man, Marcas, while no longer a *jeune homme*, is still an *homme jeune*, to borrow a distinction Balzac created somewhere. Secondly, Goriot's obsessive love for his daughters is madness, a passionate *monomanie*, while Marcas's fatal flaw is an admirable, even heroic, devotion to his country. Marcas's death is both more absurd and more tragic than Goriot's, both because of his relative youth, and more importantly because of the loss to the *patrie* of this brilliant and dedicated servant.

If the circumstances of Marcas's life and especially his death recall Goriot, there are also in this almost forgotten hero characteristics that recall Vautrin. Marcas, obviously, does not cast a shadow like Vautrin's, which spreads across the whole *Comédie humaine,* but both his role in the *nouvelle* and certain aspects of his description remind us of Vautrin. Both men are described as possessing a certain physical power; Vautrin is all muscle and force—"Il avait les épaules larges, le buste bien développé, les muscles apparents," etc. [*He had broad shoulders, a well-developed torso, large muscles*] (*PG,* 2:60)—while Marcas's strength can be seen, significantly, in his head: "Sa tête, grosse et forte . . . était comme chargée de pensées" [*His head, large and strong, seemed charged with thoughts*] (834). There is also a certain similarity in their eyes, their *regard*. In *Illusions Perdues,* Carlos Herrera is said to have a "regard terrible" (5:705); and in *Le Père Goriot,* Vautrin is described as having the penetrating eye of a judge (3:60). Marcas's eyes are like lights in his face, but "ces yeux étaient humiliés. Marcas avait peur de regarder, moins pour lui que pour ceux sur lesquels il allait arrêter son regard fascinateur" [*those eyes were humiliated. Marcas was afraid to look at people, less for himself than for those on whom he would fix his hypnotizing gaze*] (835). Both portraits suggest latent power, but whereas Vautrin's forces are at once hidden and constantly engaged in his perpetual revolt against society, Marcas's power is restrained by his philosophical resignation: "il possédait une puissance, et ne voulait pas l'exercer" [*He posedded a power, and was reluctant to exercise it*] (835). Marcas has surrendered, Vautrin never does, and never can. A final Vautrin-esque element to Marcas's makeup is his cynicism. Certainly Marcas is not possessed of (or by) the same overwhelming and philosophical cynicism as Vautrin, but he is not completely devoid of pragmatism, either. Marcas is frankly and honestly ambitious, and it is this quality, Charles informs us, that prevents him from joining either the Legitimist or Republican factions in his battle against his former protector and the system he represents. However much Marcas may hate the government he served, he does not want to see the July Monarchy overthrown: "« Les ambitieux aiment l'actualité », nous dit-il en souriant" [*"The ambitious prefer the status quo," he said to us with a smile*] (844).

These similarities between *Le Père Goriot* and *Z. Marcas* are especially important because they help us to understand both Charles's role as narrator and the place of the *nouvelle* in *La Comédie humaine.* Charles Rabourdin resembles a latter-day Rastignac in this story. Not only do we see him nursing a dying, abandoned neighbor, but also receiving the counsel of an older, cynical initiator who has already studied the world that awaits the younger man. Whereas Vautrin gives Rastignac invaluable advice on the world the ambitious young provincial has already resolved to conquer, Marcas completes the disenchantment of his two young acolytes, who had already lost most of their illusions before befriending Marcas. Forced into their respective fields of study by their families, Charles and Juste see very little future in them, and put very little effort into them. They are aware of the futility of their studies, but theirs is a joyful resignation:

> Nous ne pensions qu'à nous amuser. La raison de nos désordres était
> une raison prise dans ce que la politique actuelle a de plus sérieux.
> Juste et moi, nous n'apercevions aucune place à prendre dans les deux
> professions que nos parents nous forçaient d'embrasser. Il y a cent avo-
> cats, cents médecins pour un. (831)

We only thought of amusing ourselves. The logic of our disorderly life was a reason found by serious examination of the present state of affairs. Juste and I saw no possibilities in the professions our parents were forcing us to pursue. For every doctor, for every lawyer needed, there are a hundred trained.

Youthful idealism is quickly rekindled, however, when the two students believe that their hero Marcas can rise again, and that he can make a difference. They encourage Marcas to join with his former protector a third time, only to see him fail. Exhausted by work, Marcas returns to die— forgotten by his patron—and only the two students follow his funeral procession, not to Père Lachaise this time, but to the paupers' grave at Montparnasse. It is this sad spectacle that drives first Juste and then Charles to desert their country, but not before Charles has shared the story with friends, and encouraged them to follow his example: "je déserte la France [. . .] Imitez-moi mes amis, je vais là où l'on dirige à son gré sa destinée" [*I am deserting France. . . Follow my example my friends, I am going where a man can take charge of his own destiny*] (833). Those who listen to Charles's last story, the diegetic narrator and (presumably) other friends, are left to contemplate the cautionary tale of *Z. Marcas*, which they recognize as typical of their time, "car nous connaissions plus d'un Marcas" [*for we all knew more than one Marcas*] (854).

   Z. Marcas is not the only work where Balzac expressed his comtempt for the July Monarchy in general and the gerontocracy in particular. *Un Prince de la Bohème* contains similar reflections on the wasted youth of France. However, the particular narrative strategies used in *Z. Marcas* illustrate not just the diagnosis, but progression of the disease, the promising youth of France driven to abandon *la patrie*, and Charles does not leave without infecting his friends. It is *Z. Marcas* that demonstrates that the suppression of youthful talents in France is not merely a deplorable status quo, it is also the cause of an even more harmful effect, what we would call brain drain today. This tale of thwarted ambition, set in 1836, invites comparison to Rastignac's successful ambitions, born in 1819. Charles Rabourdin goes from Montparnasse to Le Havre to the colonies, and we can presume he never looks back. Rastignac leaves Père Lachaise for the house of Nucingen, and then goes on to spectacular success. If Rastignac's success is morally tainted, we cannot say the same for

Bianchon, who is equally successful. Although written only five years apart, the two texts reflect Balzac's views on two different generations. While both examples reveal an extremely negative point of view, there is nonetheless a difference in tone. The Paris where Rastignac arrives in 1819, and in which we watch his success, is a world painted by a cynic, where vice and avarice are rewarded. The Paris that Charles and Juste flee is painted in even starker terms; not only is talent unappreciated, it is exterminated. If success is morally ambiguous in Rastignac's world, it is utterly impossible in Marcas's. The cynicism of *Le Père Goriot* has become absolute pessimism in *Z. Marcas.*

A Matter of Trust: *Je* and the Balzacian Fantastic

Etude de femme is a quite short and, I think it is safe to say, relatively unimportant text in relation to *La Comédie humaine* as a whole—a small comic piece about a somewhat flighty Parisian marquise. What is interesting is that Balzac took the time to alter this relatively uninteresting text to fit it into the web of recurring characters, including in it some of the most important names of his fictional world: Bianchon, Rastignac and Delphine de Nucingen, and Mme de Listomère, née Vandenesse (the names are important in Balzac's world, if not this particular character). This example is one of many that show the lengths to which Balzac went in his efforts to connect the disparate parts of his work into one single text. In the case of the *je*-narrated stories, the narrators, even while interacting with characters who are integral (*Sarrasine, L'Auberge Rouge*) or tangential (*Facino Cane*) parts of the great Balzacian mosaic, remain anonymous and problematic. Problematic, because we are unable to place these *je* as characters, to say anything specific about their pasts or anything at all about their futures. We do not know what other balls the narrator of *Sarrasine* may attend, or if the *je* of *L'Auberge Rouge* ever marries, or what finally happens to Facino Cane's interlocutor. Obviously, a possible explanation for this is that Balzac wished to give the illusion that the narrator was the author, that he *knew* Mme de Rochefide, that he *saw* the guilt in Taillefer's face, etc. However, another explanation is just as plausible and just as important. All three of these stories are marked to a certain extent by the supernatural, they deal with what I qualify as the Balzacian fantastic, that is to say a fantastic heavily marked with realism. This double strand can be seen clearly in the two novels in which Balzac dealt extensively with the fantastic, *La Peau de Chagrin* and *La Recherche de l'absolu*. In the latter, which has been called one of the first works of science fiction in French literature, Balthazar Claës uses science as a point of departure into the supernatural. Raphaël de Valentin, in *La Peau de chagrin*, brings his magic skin into a head-to-head conflict with the most upto-date scientific methods his creator was aware of; in one of the rare cases where Balzac clearly crosses Todorov's line between the fantastic and the marvelous, science is beaten back by the supernatural.

Among Balzac's shorter fiction, *Sarrasine* offers perhaps the best example of this peculiar variety of the fantastic. In the opening pages of the text, Balzac does all he can to create an atmosphere of supernatural romanticism, to create a fantastic aura around the old man and his secrets, from the central mystery surrounding the Lanty's fortune to the cold air that some claim emanates from the old man (6:1047), whom Mme de Rochefide describes as a ghost (1054), and who reeks of the cemetery (1053). The narrator assures us that although some extravagant people, "amis du fantatisque" [*friends of the fantastic*], describe the old man as a ghoul and a vampire, and spread other ridiculous stories about him, he is "simplement un *vieillard*" [*simply an* old man] (1047). The tension in the story is maintained through the somewhat devious use of this first-person narrator; even as *je* assures us that those who insist the old man and his fortune have some sort of fantastic, or at least romantic, origin, are extravagant people, Balzac has left in the text those hints that maintain us in the belief that these origins are fantastic. When the truth is finally revealed, it is not only realistic, it is horribly, violently, and surgically realistic. In *Sarrasine* and the other short texts marked by this Balzacian fantastic, the use of first-person narration advances the reading contract by forcing a certain amount of credibility on the reader. This presumption of trust encourages the reader's increased suspension of disbelief. The relationship between the author and the reader is advanced one step even before the story has really begun, as we put our faith in this narrating *je*.

Since the publication of Barthes's *S/Z* and the voluminous commentary on or inspired by it, few aspects of *Sarrasine* have been left unanalyzed. The relationship between frame and story is generally recognized: the narrator is telling the story of Sarrasine and La Zambinella in an attempt to seduce Mme de Rochefide, exchanging story for sex. In the end, this exchange is not consumated, and it is an open question which party violated the terms of the contract: Mme de Rochefide for rejecting the narrator, or the narrator for telling such a bizarre and troubling story. The fame of *Sarrasine* makes it a useful starting point for the discussion of the narrating *je*. We know that the narrator is a Parisian, both worldly and contemplative, as he reflects on the contrast between the lively ball taking place in the Lantys' hôtel and the wintry garden outside. Familiars of *La Comédie humaine* recognize that he moves in the same social circles as Rastignac and other major characters of Balzac's Paris: the comte de Lanty bought his house from the maréchal de Carigliano; the narrator himself speaks of Mme d'Espard as if he is a regular guest in her salon, and we later learn that he is Mme de Rochefide's escort in one of her first forays into the *monde*. We recognize in the narrator the traits that make the best storytellers: he is an observer and, we are soon to learn, he knows a secret—he is in possession of that most privileged of Balzacian information: the origin of a fortune. These are traits that he and his fellow narrators (Derville, Bianchon, and the other *je*) have in common with the Narrator, although, and I think it is worth insisting on this point, he does not have the same breadth and depth of knowledge as the Narrator, as is evidenced by the fact that he does not know that Mme de Rochefide will not give him the implied reward for his act of storytelling. The narrating *je* of *La Comédie humaine* all share, to some degree, these two traits: acute powers of observation and unique, if limited, knowledge.

A Killer('s) Story: Narration and Its After-Effects in *L'Auberge rouge*

There is a certain temptation to seek a common thread among the several narrating *je,* to see them as one nameless, shadowy storyteller who floats through Balzac's Paris, refusing to be identified. As tempting as this may be, I do not believe the argument can be sustained. The differences between the narrators of *Sarrasine* and *L'Auberge rouge* suggest that in these two texts, at least, we are hearing two different voices tell their stories. The act of narration in *Sarrasine* seems to take place around 1830, as Mme de Rochefide—born around 1808, according to *Béatrix* (2:712)—is said to be twenty-two years old (6:1050); she is naïve and somewhat awkward in society and has not yet gained her reputation as a *coquette*.

L'Auberge rouge must take place in or soon after 1830, as Taillefer is still alive in *La Peau de Chagrin*.[7] If the action of the two *nouvelles* is very nearly contemporaneous, they take place in markedly different social settings. The Lanty family of *Sarrasine* is noble, even if they probably do not move in the highest stratum of Parisian society, the circle of the Grandlieu and the Navarreins families. Nonetheless, the marquise de Rochefide (*née* Casteran) has attended their ball, and, again, the narrator seems to be on social terms with the very aristocratic marquise d'Espard. The story of *L'Auberge rouge* is told in a distinctly bourgeois milieu, the world of bankers, and the narrator seems quite at home there. The ball in *Sarrasine* is a place of formality and manners—a major plot point is Mme de Rochefide's *faux pas* and subsequent flight into the boudoir that contains the portrait of Endymion. The after-dinner atmosphere of *L'Auberge rouge* is warm and relaxed, filled with pipe smoke and "cordialité allemande" (11:89). Certainly, it is not uncommon for Balzac's characters, at least the masculine ones, to move in different social circles, but the tone of each narrator strikes me as distinct from the other's. While both are reflective, even philosophical, the narrator of *L'Auberge rouge* seems more socially conscious, more concerned with larger questions of right and wrong and with social hypocrisy. The narrator of *Sarrasine* is also concerned with hypocrisy, but only as it affects his relationship with Mme de Rochefide.

In *Sarrasine,* the anonymous *je* serves as both diegetic and metadiegetic narrator; in *L'Auberge rouge,* these roles are shared by a *je* and by "monsieur Hermann," a German banker. The text is divided into two main parts, preceded by an expository preamble. In the first part, *L'Idée et le fait,* we find the object story, told by Hermann, the tale of a brutal murder and of the innocent man executed for it; the second half, entitled *Les Deux justices,* relates the consequences of the act of narration, including Taillefer's death and the narrator's dilemma as he struggles with his own conscience. He has fallen in love with Victorine Taillefer, the beautiful, rich, and innocent daughter of the man actually guilty of the murder in

---

[7] *L'Auberge rouge* offers yet another example of the problematic chronology of *La Comédie humaine*. Victorine Taillefer, probably 17 or 18 in 1819, according to *Le Père Goriot*, is still an unmarried *jeune fille* in *L'Auberge rouge.*

Hermann's story.[8] The narrator can neither abandon Victorine, nor resolve himself to marrying her and enjoying her considerable but ill-gotten fortune. It is in the preamble that the narrating *je* sets the scene for the telling of the tale, and also establishes himself as a storyteller in his own right. The opening paragraphs of the text show us that he is an observer and that he has a talent for relating what he observes, as he describes the after-dinner scene that is so appropriate to storytelling. He describes himself as a "chercheur de tableaux" (*a seeker of tableaux*, 11:91), as someone who habitually seeks out the remarkable and the picturesque in real life. He also has a unique gift which makes him especially qualified as an observer and especially interesting as a narrator; the *je* of *L'Auberge rouge* possesses a "science divinatoire" [*gift for divination*] (92). He can, it seems, read into people's souls—or at least he thinks he can. We learn this as the narrator becomes intrigued by the anguished face of a fellow dinner guest; the narrator expresses his shame at wasting this precious gift "*in anima vili* d'un épais financier" [*on the common soul of a dull banker*]. As the reader learns, this dull banker is in fact Frédéric Taillefer, whose soul is anything but common, even if it may be vile. The narrator will use his gift to "read" Taillefer's mind as we are reading Hermann's story, which is also the story of Taillefer, the murderer described in the framed story. It is not after all as narrator, but as a narratee that we will see the narrating *je* use his gift. He will share the role of narratee with the subject of his examination, Taillefer, and the story the two characters hear will have significant consequences for each of them.

There is also a second narrator of *L'Auberge rouge,* the German banker Hermann. Hermann fits the romantic image of the German, well-fed and contented. This image may seems surprising in a world inhabited by Nucingen, but we should not forget d'Aldrigger, who is also a German banker, and is also a decent and benevolent man. Nucingen, appropriately enough, is the exception in Balzac, not the rule. Hermann's affability, combined with his profession, give him a certain amount of credibility as a narrator. Furthermore, he is described as being an "homme de goût et

---

[8] Dorothy Kelly very persuasively argued in "Balzac's *L'Auberge rouge:* On Reading an Ambiguous Text" that Taillefer's guilt is not, in fact, a certainty. The reason for my ultimate disagreement with Kelly on this point is offered in the conclusion of this study (pp. 223-24).

d'érudition" [*a man of taste and erudition*] (89); he is not merely a dull bourgeois who just happens to know a story, he is someone we can trust and whose opinions we should respect. Finally, Hermann's nationality is not indifferent to his role as narrator either; there is a brief reference to Hoffmann in the opening part of the frame-story:

> « Avant de nous quitter, monsieur Hermann va nous raconter en-core, je l'espere, une histoire allemande qui nous fasse bien peur. »
>
> Ces paroles furent prononcées au dessert par une jeune personne . . . qui, sans doute, avait lu les contes d'Hoffmann et les romans de Walter Scott. (90)
>
> *"Before leaving us, I hope that monsieur Hermann will tell us an-other of those German stories that scare us so."*
>
> *Theses words were spoken at dessert by a young person . . . who, no doubt, had read the tales of Hoffmann and the novels of Walter Scott.*

The two authors named are romantic points of reference, and the reference to Hoffmann specifically suggests the fantastic, and the *jeune personne*'s request implies that German stories are especially and delightfully fright-ening. Furthermore, the "encore" in this passage suggests to us that Hermann knows and tells lots of these stories, and that he has told them before. If these keywords set the tone, they also highlight a certain contra-diction. Hermann's story is not a gothic tale, a story of the supernatural *à la* Hoffmann; it is a story of violence and greed—it is a story by Balzac. Briefly, Hermann's tale is a murder mystery. While in a German prison for having led a revolt against the occupying Republican army, Hermann met a young Frenchman, Prosper Magnan, who was accused of killing and robbing a fellow traveler at an inn near Bonn. Prosper maintains that he is innocent of the murder, but had contemplated it, going so far as to raise his arm to slash the throat of the victim. Prosper stops himself, falls asleep, and wakes up to find the traveler dead and his money gone, along with Prosper's best friend, known only as Frédéric. There are no ghosts or vampires or Rhennish castles in this German tale. Even the quasi-supernatural element of the story, the suggestion that thoughts can kill, is uniquely Balzacian, more *philosophique* than *fantastique*. That the story is perhaps not quite what the reader—especially the reader who was Balzac's contemporary—was expecting is confirmed in the text: As Hermann nears the end of his story, just as Prosper is about to be executed for the murder Taillefer committed, the same young person who asked that Hermann tell a story asks that he leave his story unfinished:

> « Oh! n'achevez pas! s'écria la jeune persone qui avait demandé cette histoire, et qui interrompit alors brusquement le Nurembourgeois. Je veux demeurer dans l'incertitude et croire qu'il a été sauvé. (108)
>
> *"Oh! Don't finish!" cried the young woman who had asked for this story, and who now brusquely interrupted the Nuremburger. "I would rather remain uncertain and believe that he was saved."*

As with Mme de Rochefide in *Sarrasine,* a young woman, doubtless an *amie du fantastique,* finds Balzac's version of the fantastic to be too realistic for her tastes.

A final point to be made about Hermann as narrator is that he serves as a link between the frame and the story. He is not the only link; as *L'Auberge rouge* is an *étude philosophique,* the central idea is the material power of thought, more specifically the destructive power of thought. This plays in the framed story as Prosper feels that he is in part guilty because he conceived the thought of the murder (*l'idée*), he even took steps toward executing it, and these steps eventually help Taillefer get away with murder (*le fait*). In the frame, the theme is more strongly expressed, as Taillefer is killed (*le fait*) by the memories of his deed (*l'idée*), memories sharpened by Hermann's storytelling. This point illustrates a textual link, which is subtly intertwined with the conceptual one. While in prison, Hermann watched as Prosper was led away to his fatal trial:

> Lorsque le jeune homme traversa la cour, il jeta les yeux sur moi. Jamais je n'oublierai ce regard plein de pensées [. . .] Ce fut une espèce de testament silencieux et intelligible par lequel un ami léguait sa vie perdue à son dernier ami. (108)
>
> *When the young man was crossing the courtyard, he cast his eyes upon me. I will never forget that look so full of thoughts . . . It was a sort of silent but intelligible will, by which a friend was bequeathing his lost life to his last friend.*

Just as Derville acts as Gobseck's agent by telling his story to Mme de Grandlieu—thus arranging a marriage for Gobseck's ward, Ernest de Restaud—Hermann, as narrator, acts as Prosper's executor. Prosper had explicitly asked Hermann to seek out his mother, to assure her of her son's innocence in the murder at the inn; the German cannot fulfill this last request, as Mme Magnan dies before Hermann can find her. But Hermann does eventually manage to serve his friend, to execute this visually transmitted will, even if he does so unconsciously. By telling his story, which is fatal for Taillefer, Hermann avenges Prosper's death.

A Recurring *Je?* From *L'Auberge rouge* to *Facino Cane*

While the *je* of *Sarrasine* seems to be a different character than the *je* of *L'Auberge rouge,* it is quite possible that the first-person narrator of *Facino Cane* is an earlier incarnation of the *je* of *L'Auberge rouge.* The act of narration and its aftermath in *L'Auberge rouge* take place, as I pointed out, after 1830; the story of Facino Cane is told to the narrator in 1820, when the narrator was twenty years old. As a young man, this *je* lived in a poor quarter of Paris, the rue Lesdiguières, specifically. He has a concern for and an interest in the lower classes that correspond to the highly developed social conscience of the *je* of *L'Auberge rouge.* More importantly, the *je* of *Facino Cane* claims to have a gift for reading in people's souls, a gift that very much resembles the "science divinatoire" of the narrator of *L'Auberge rouge:*

> Chez moi l'observation était devenue intuitive, elle pénétrait l'âme sans négliger le corps [. . .] elle me donnait la faculté de vivre de la vie de l'individu sur laquelle elle s'excerçait, en me permettant de me sub- stituer à lui comme le derviche des *Mille et Une Nuits* prenait le corps et l'âme des personnes sur lesquelles il prononçait certaines paroles. (6:1019)
>
> *In my mind observation had become intuitive, it penetrated the soul without neglecting the body. . . it gave me the power to live the life of the individual upon whom I exercised it, by allowing me to place myself within him like the dervish of* The Arabian Nights *took the soul and the body of those upon whom he spoke certain words.*

Along with this special gift for observation, this narrator, like his counterpart in *L'Auberge rouge* who is a "chercheur de tableaux," seems to be a
collector of scenes and events that make interesting stories. The *je* of
Facino Cane speaks to (or in some way communicates with) a narratee
that we cannot see, and suggests that there are many other stories to tell,
and perhaps many stories that have been told:

> Je ne sais pas comment j'ai si longtemps gardé sans la dire l'histoire
> que je vais vous raconter, elle fait partie de ces curieux récits restés
> dans le sac d'où la mémoire les tire capricieusement [. . .] j'en ai bien
> d'autres, aussi singuliers que celui-ci, également enfouis; mais ils
> auront leur tour, croyez-le. (1020-21)
>
> *I do not know how I have managed to go so long without telling the*
> *story that I'm going to tell you, it's one of those curious tales that has*
> *stayed in the sack from which memory draws them so capriciously . . . I*
> *have many others, as remarkable as this one, buried just as deep; their*
> *turn will come, believe me.*

Many critics have seen in this narrating *je* simply a self-portrait by
Balzac. This opinion is based primarily on two points: on the proclaimed
gift of observation, which Balzac obviously shared and which is reflected
in his writing; and on the fact that this narrator, like Balzac, lived a life of
studious poverty in humble quarters in the rue Lesdiguières. Several go so
far as to make this identification without qualification; some take the assumption a step further, using Balzac's traits to describe the narrator. André Lorant, for example, in his introduction to the *Pléiade* edition of
Facino Cane, describes the narrator as "un jeune auteur parisien à ses dé-
buts" [*a young Parisian author just starting out*] (1009); however, nothing
in the text itself suggests that the storyteller is necessarily a writer. He
specifically uses verbs with an oral connotation—"dire" and "raconter"—
to describe his narration, and when he describes his studies at the Arsenal
library, he refers to his love of "science" (1019). This last term is vague
enough to suggest almost any field of study, so we have no reason to assume that the young man of the rue Lesdiguières in the *nouvelle* followed
the same career path as the man who wrote it. It is not at all unusual to
find characters in *La Comédie humaine* who have physical, biographical,
or psychological traits in common with their creator; this is as true for the

named characters (Félix de Vandenesse, Raphaël de Valentin, Louis Lambert) as for the other anonymous narrating *je* (of *Le Message,* of *Louis Lambert,* of *Sarrasine*). Such similarities do not mean we should always draw a simple line between these characters and Balzac; in fact, to do so is often to start down a false path.

Furthermore, this narrating *je*, as a character, is different from his creator in one important way: in his concern for and interest in the working class. The narrator illustrates his gift to his interlocutor(s) by describing his observation of a working class couple returning home from the theatre:

> En entendant ces gens, je pouvais épouser leur vie, je me sentais leurs guenilles sur le dos, je marchais les pieds dans leurs souliers percés; leurs désirs, leurs besoins, tout passait dans mon âme, ou mon âme passait dans la leur.
>
> *Listening to these people, I was able to adopt their lives, I felt their rags on my back, I walked with my feet in their torn shoes; their desires, their needs, everything passed into my soul, or my soul passed into theirs.*

This psychic connection leads to a definite sympathy, which is expressed in overtly political tones:

> Je m'échauffais avec eux contre les chefs d'atelier qui les tyrannisaient, ou contre les mauvaises pratiques qui les faisaient revenir plusieurs fois sans les payer [. . .] dès ce temps, j'avais décomposé les éléments de cette masse hétérogène nommée le peuple [. . .] je l'avais analysée de manière à pouvoir évaluer ses qualités bonnes ou mauvaises. Je savais déjà de quelle utilité pourrait être ce faubourg, ce séminaire de révolutions qui renferme des héros, des inventeurs, des savants pratiques, des coquins, des scélérats, des vertus, et des vices, tous comprimés par la misère, étouffés par la nécessité, noyés dans le vin, usés par les liqueurs fortes. Vous ne sauriez imaginer combien d'aventures perdues, combien de drames oubliés dans cette ville de douleur! Combien d'horribles et belles choses! L'imagination n'atteindra jamais au vrai qui s'y cache et que personne ne peut aller découvrir; il faut descendre

trop bas pour trouver ces admirables scènes ou tragiques ou comiques,
chefs-d'œuvre enfantés par le hasard. (1020)

I shared their anger against foremen who tyrannised them or against
bad customers who made them come back again and again without
paying . . . From that time on, I had deconstrutcted the elements of that
heterogeneous mass known as the working classes. I had analyzed them
in order to be able to evaluate their good and bad qualities. I could al-
ready see the potential of this neighborhood, this seminary of revolu-
tions which contained heroes, inventors, crafty players, crooks, scoun-
drels, virtues and vices, all beaten down by misery, suffocated by need,
drowned in wine, wasted by strong drink. You will never be able to
imagine how many lost adventures, how many forgotten dramas in that
city of suffering! How many horrible and beautiful things! Our imagi-
nation will never reach the truth of what is hidden there, that no one
will ever be able to discover; one must descend too low to find these
admirable scenes, some tragic and some comic, masterpieces born of
chance.

This last observation about the inadequacy of imagination again recalls
Derville's comments on the things seen by the men in black. Specific to
this narrator is his sympathy for the people he observes, as opposed to
Derville's indignation at the *grand monde.* Sympathy rather than empathy,
for it is clear throughout *Facino Cane* that the narrator is quite conscious
of the social distance between himself and his neighbors. However sympathetic, his is the voice of an observer, almost of an anthropologist, certainly not that of a revolutionary. A very similar passage is to be found in
the opening of *La Fille aux yeux d'or,* as the Narrator describes the lowest
circle of the Parisian Inferno, but this is a far darker, far more pessimistic
portrait of the "laide et forte nation" [*strong and ugly nation*] (*FYO,*
5:1042) than the one found in *Facino Cane.* The narrating *je* may be
somewhat detached, but he is at least concerned with his social inferiors;
the Narrator barely notices this class.

These sympathies are what lead the narrating *je* to become a narratee. Asked to honor a humble wedding banquet with his presence, the
narrator agrees to attend, in order to "[se] blottir dans la joie de ces
pauvres gens" [*lose himself in the poor people*] (1021). At the party, he
meets an old, blind musician, and becomes fascinated by the man's

striking appearance. The face of the blind clarinetist, which resembles "le masque en plâtre de Dante" (1022), sparks the narrator's *seconde vue*. Intrigued, he listens to the old man's story. The impoverished musician claims to be a noble Venetian, the last descendant of one of the oldest families of the ancient republic. Even more amazing is the old man's claim that he possesses the power to sense gold, to smell the metal through walls and across distances. The old man, who calls himself Facino Cane, says that he needs only a willing pair of eyes to guide him back to Venice, where his gift for finding gold will lead him to the lost treasure of the Doge. Only he can find this hoard, and he promises the narrator indescribable wealth if he will help the old man return home. The narrator at first suspects that the old man is insane, "mais il y avait dans sa voix une puissance à laquelle j'obéis" [*but there was in his voice a power that I obeyed*] (1025). At the end of the story, carried away perhaps by its force, the narrator agrees to make the journey. But Facino Cane dies before the pair can set out in search of their treasure.

This story is one that approaches Todorov's line between the fantastic and the marvelous; but Facino Cane dies before we can ever learn if we have crossed that line. The only claim to credibility the old man has is lent to him by the narrator. If this man, well educated, from a higher social class, and possessed of a gift for understanding human nature, believes the story, then we are inclined to do so as well. This is certainly the impression given when *je* cries: "Nous irons à Venise" [*We will go to Venice*] (1031), but this impression is undermined by the ending of the *nouvelle*. Balzac is known for a style of slow development followed by a rapid dénouement (Dällenbach, *Le Tout en morceaux*, 158), and *Facino Cane* offers an exemplary case of this pattern. After agreeing to leave with the old man as soon as they can raise the money for the trip, the narrator ends his tale abruptly: "Facino Cane mourut pendant l'hiver après avoir langui deux mois. Le pauvre homme avait un catarrhe" [*Facino Cane died during that winter after having languished for two months. The poor man had a catarrh*] (1032). *Je* offers no regrets for the immense fortune that was so close if the old man was telling the truth; nor does he express any rueful memories of the night he allowed atmospherics and a taste for a good story to overwhelm his common sense. We, as readers, do not know what to think of the story because we don't know if the narrator, in the end, believed the old man or not. The ending offers no commentary that would help us to determine if the story we have just read, to borrow Todorov's terminology again, is fantastic or marvelous.

A Strange Story from a Faraway Land: *Une Passion dans le désert*

Given Balzac's widespread reputation for realism, it is somewhat surprising to note how strong a presence the fantastic is within *La Comédie humaine;* yet even with that in mind, the very short *nouvelle Une Passion dans le désert* is a remarkable text. Set far from Paris or any kind of human society, this is the tale of a French soldier lost in the Egyptian desert and his love for a leopard. The shock of this bizarre story is softened by its frame, which if vague has at least some very familiar elements. A Parisian couple, having just visited a famous menagerie, discuss the skill with which the animal trainer handles his big cats. The man tells the woman that he knows a story that might well explain the trainer's hold on his animal, and we are thus presented with the story of the soldier lost in the desert during Bonaparte's Egyptian campaign and the strange bond he forms with the "panthère" he names "Mignonne" (8:1228). The object story itself is obviously intriguing and challenging for the critic, but I will concern myself only with the frame and the relationship between narrator and narratee.

In truth, very little can be said about these two characters with any certainty; they are perhaps the most "ectoplasmique[s]"—to borrow a term from Patrick Berthier (intro, ed. *Pléiade*; 8:1216)—of all the characters of *La Comédie humaine.* We can say less about this narrating *je* than about any of his brethren, and his *interlocutrice* is just as difficult to identify. What we can say about them is: that they are Parisians; that they are unmarried, as they seem to live apart; that they have a certain economic comfort, as they have the leisure time both to visit the menagerie and to talk about it at length afterwards; that they are probably romantically involved. This last point is what makes their relationship as narrator and narratee most interesting. The man seems reluctant to tell the story to his *amie;* he does so only after having been subjected to "tant d'agaceries, tant de promesses, que je consentis à lui rédiger" [*so much teasing, so many promises, that I consented to write it down for her*] a version of his story, which he had learned from an imposing old soldier on a previous visit to that same menagerie (1220). The word "promesses" is especially of interest; it seems that a deal has been struck, an exchange between a man and a woman, sex for a story. Also in this passage, we see a departure from the norm for Balzac's storytelling scenes: this story will be written, there will be no face-to-face telling of the tale here. No reason is given for this, perhaps the narrator needed time to remember his story, perhaps he wanted to be able to tell the tale without interruption, without any protestations of disbelief from his audience (Balzac's narratees have a habit of interrupting). Whatever the reason, the story is written out; we can presume that we are reading the same text as the narratee. Another curiosity is that this text is incomplete, the narrator/author has left the ending out of his written tale. Again, we can only speculate as to the reasons for this; very likely he wanted to be present to deliver the final portion of the story—the end of the passion and the death of Mignonne—and to collect his promised reward.

The similarity to *Sarrasine* is unmistakable. In an attempt to seduce a woman, a man has offered a strangely erotic story against the promise of sex. There is also one essential difference: we do not learn if the promises made are fulfilled, if the story has been successful. Certainly the narratee of *Une Passion* seems much calmer than Mme de Rochefide. Having read the written part of the story, she says only: "Eh bien . . . j'ai lu votre plaidoyer en faveur des bêtes; mais comment deux personnes si bien faites pour se comprendre ont-elles fini?" [*Well, I've read your plea on behalf of beasts; but how did two people so well made to understand each other end up?*] (1231). The calm irony in her words implies that she is not grievously offended by the bestiality hinted at in the story, while at the same time suggesting that she has detected in the narrator's story an effort to compare women (unfavorably) to panthers and vice-versa, just as some critics have seen similarities between Balzac's descriptions of Mignonne and Paquita Valdès (Berthier; 8:1216-17). Perhaps this detachment is the effect of the story having been written; she has had time to think and to compose herself before the narrator seeks her reaction or his reward. Or perhaps this woman is simply more sophisticated and more sure of herself than the twenty-two-year-old Mme de Rochefide. We are never exactly sure, because this nouvelle is open-ended. The narrator answers the woman's question, and then begins again to talk of the old soldier who told him the story and who is—we learn for certain only now—the same soldier who loved Mignonne. The story of the soldier and the leopard is complete, but we do not know if it has been successful. The *nouvelle* ends with a reflection on the nature of the desert ("c'est Dieu sans les hommes," *It's God without men* 1232), and we never learn if the strange tale of seduction in the desert facilitated a seduction in Paris.

The act of narration is rarely innocent in *La Comédie humaine.* Stories are told primarily in order to advance the plots of different works, but this is seldom the only effect. If our immediate concern as readers of, for example, *Le Père Goriot* is to learn how the bourgeois Goriot came to be the father-in-law of two titled men, the duchesse de Langeais's explanation teaches us many other things as well, about the duchess and about the world the characters live in. Narrators play an important role in our interpretation of the stories they tell, sometimes obviously, sometimes very subtly. What we know about a given narrator can reinforce or undermine his or (less often) her credibility, can make us question the intent of either a particular narrator or, underneath all of them, Balzac. The narrators who take over the task of narration from the Narrator are farther away from us, allowing us to judge, to interpret, and to question the narrators and their stories. Balzac was not unique in using character-narrators in this way. With different motivations, with different methods, and to different degrees, Mérimée, Barbey d'Aurevilley, and Maupassant—to cite only a few contemporary examples—all used their narrators to affect their readers' perceptions of their stories. What makes Balzac's work unique, in this as in so many other respects, is the system of recurring characters. It is not only in the individual works that we find information that affects us as readers, but in the whole text of *La Comédie humaine,* including those challenging but irresistible spaces between those texts. The individual texts we read inform us about the larger text of *La Comédie humaine,* while at the same time, the whole informs us about the fragment. Reading and rereading expands our knowledge about Balzac's created world, while the churning *chaosmos* of that world—to borrow a very apt phrase from Lucien Dällenbach ("Le tout en morceaux," 165)—destabilizes text and reader. Narrators are only a few among the many moving parts of the Balzacian mobile. This same movement and instability often draws our attention to another part of the mobile: the Narratee and the narratees.

Chapter II

Actively Listening: The Narratees

IF BALZAC WAS NOT ALONE IN USING narrators to influence readers' perceptions of his stories, the extensive and intricate use of narratees is, I believe, a quality unique to *La Comédie humaine*. As Marcia Thompson pointed out, "there is nothing passive about the narratees' role" in Balzac's internal narrations; they are "active and demanding" listeners (*Narrators and Narratees,* 19). Like their more obviously active counterparts, narratees can have a significant influence on our interpretation of an object story, and consequently on the frame/story text as a whole. The discussion of the first-person narrators in *L'Auberge rouge* and *Facino Cane,* where the *je* serve as both diegetic narrators and metadiegtic narratees, shows the importance of the listener in Balzac's storytelling. Thompson makes a comparison that is particularly pertinent given the frequency of storytelling as a means of seduction in Balzac's oeuvre: "In a successful seduction, as in a successful narration, both parties influence the outcome" (59-60). In most cases, those narratees that are linked to the system of recurring characters have the greatest impact on storytelling situations. Because such narrative structures tend to put the spotlight on the storyteller, the narratee plays a more understated role in the transmission of an object story; thus information about the narratee that we, as readers, bring to storytelling situation often provides the keys necessary to decode the narratee's role in the interpretation of the text.

In some cases, character-narratees overtly guide our reaction to a story, through their reaction to or commentary on the story they have heard; in other cases, their influence can be so subtle that we are unaware of it as we read. The mere presence of a given character can sometimes subtly alter a storytelling situation and so shade our perception of the story told. As readers, we can often perceive an effect of a narratee that the characters in the frame story are unaware of, because we have, through the voice of the Narrator and the system of recurring characters, privileged knowledge; we know more about these fictional persons, and their histories, than they know about each other. Sometimes, we even know more than they know about themselves; we might know their futures or have some other information about them that they themselves are not (yet) privy to. As with the narrators, the importance of the narratees in the construction of Balzac's frames shows a great care and deliberation on the part of the author, and further illustrates the incredible complexity of texts that are sometimes wrongly seen as being somewhat hastily and haphazardly put together. In *La Comédie humaine,* it is the exception rather than the rule that narratees are merely functional, passive figures in the frame.

Just as it was necessary to study the Narrator before studying the narrators, so must we consider the Narratee before the narratees. Gerald Prince has thoroughly examined the many different types of narratees and some of the different ways they can effect the relationship between reader and text in his "Introduction à l'étude du narrataire." Prince's work provides a vocabulary and a broad framework for the discussion of narratees and reader response. While I will use several of his terms, I will not use all of them, only those that I believe apply to Balzac's text(s). Prince's study begins with perhaps the most basic and important point: that we must distinguish the narratee from the reader; the narratee relates to the narrator, as the reader relates to the author. Prince makes further distinctions between: (1) the implied reader, the "audience presupposed by a text" (*Dictionary of Narratology,* 43); (2) the ideal reader, "celui qui comprendrait parfaitement et approuverait entièrement le moindre de ses mots, la plus subtile de ses intentions" [*who would completely understand and entirely approve the least word, the subtlest of the author's intentions*] ("Introduction," 180); and (3) the actual reader ("le lecteur réel"), the person physically holding and reading a given text.[1] In the case of *La Comédie humaine*, I believe that the Narratee can often—although not always—be equated with the implied reader. This may seem a conclusion too obvious to even mention, but I do not think it is always the case that the narratee and the implied reader are the same. In *Jacques le fataliste et son maître,* for example, one of the ways in which Diderot plays with the reader is by using his narrator to respond to questions, assumptions, and objections that quite possibly never occurred to the reader. In fact, Diderot begins his novel— or anti-novel—in this way, signaling immediately to the reader that the game has begun:

> Comment s'étaient-ils rencontrés? Par hasard, comme tout le monde. Comment s'appelaient-ils? Que vous importe? D'où venaient-ils? Du lieu le plus prochain. (25)
>
> *How had they met? By chance, like everyone. What were their names? What's that to you? Where did they come from? From the nearest place.*

In this one-sided dialogue, the narrator is responding to the narratee, an entity invented by the author every bit as much as was the narrator. The actual reader can be, at first, quite unsettled by the narrator's brusque questions and rude answers, and by his refusal to give us information that would be, in a more traditional narrative, central to plot. The reader of *Jacques le fataliste* is forced into the role of the narratee by the narrator's aggressive play, but it is not a settled, predictable role. We have no idea what will come next in Diderot's text; we can only discover our role of narratee in the way we learn about the narrator's role, by reading. If we refuse to play that role, we cannot continue to read the book.

Balzac's Narrator—a fairly assertive entity as well—also forces us into the role of the Narratee, but it is a less jarring transition for the reader than in *Jacques le fataliste*. The Narrator/Narratee relationship in *La Comédie humaine* is very traditional. Turning again to *Le Père Goriot,* we find in the opening pages of the novel an excellent example of how Balzac creates his Narratee. As I stated earlier, the reader, by choosing to read the

---

[1]In this chapter and throughout this book, when I use the term reader without qualification, I am referring to the actual reader.

novel, chooses to accept the role of the "vous qui tenez ce livre d'une main blanche" [*you who hold this book in a white hand*] to whom the Narrator addresses himself. However, the reader of the text does maintain some liberty, some distance from the Narratee. Consider the Narrator's accusation of insensitivity in this same passage of *Le Père Goriot,* in which a number of assumptions are made about the Narratee's psychology and eventual reaction to the horrors to be depicted in the novel: "Vous dînerez avec appétit en mettant votre insensibilité sur le compte de l'auteur, en le taxant d'exagération, en l'accusant de poésie" [*You will dine with a hearty appetite in blaming your insensitivity on the author, taxing him for exaggeration, accusing him of making poetry*] (2:50). This assumed reaction is one instance in which the Narratee and the implied reader react differently; this indifference is almost certainly the exact opposite of the effect Balzac (the author) hoped to inspire on the part of his readers—implied, real, and ideal. If we readers are sensitive—and intelligent—people, we will not react like this Narratee; rather we will recognize that all is true, and we will sympathize with the secret misfortunes of old Goriot. Even as the reader accepts the role of "vous," s/he does so without losing sight of the fact that this "vous" is someone else.

This portion of *Le Père Goriot* also offers an excellent occasion to study some of the central assumptions made about the Narratee— assumptions that would often apply to the implied and to the ideal reader, as well.[2] This selection is convenient, but virtually any extract of a few pages' length from *La Comédie humaine* is rich with those signs that are typically indicative of the narratee. The first sentence of the novel informs us that Mme Vauquer runs a "pension bourgeoise," situated "rue Neuve-Sainte-Geneviève, entre le quartier latin et le faubourg Saint-Marceau" [*a middle-class boarding house, between the Latin Quarter and the working-class district*] (2:49). The Narrator assumes that his Narratee will know what a "pension bourgeoise" is, and that he will recognize the street and neighborhood named. The assumption that the Narratee is Parisian, or at least someone familiar with Paris is continued further on, in even more explicit terms:

---

[2] Prince uses this same fragment extensively as an illustration of the narratee in his "Introduction," and what follows draws heavily on his interpretation.

l'œuvre [. . .] [s]era-t-elle comprise au-delà de Paris? le doute est permis. Les particularités de cette scène pleine d'observations et de couleurs locales ne peuvent être appréciées qu'entre les buttes de Montmartre et les hauteurs de Montrouge. (49)

Will this work be understood outside of Paris? Some doubt is permissable. The peculiarities of this scene full of observations and local color could only be appreciated between the hills of Montmartre and the heights of Montrouge.

Obviously, *Le Père Goriot* has been read and appreciated outside of these confines, just as it has been read by readers who did not hold the book in a white hand (Prince, 180). As I said earlier, the title of the whole text, *La Comédie humaine,* gives lie to the idea that Balzac was writing for a restrained public. This passage is meant not to exclude non-Parisian readers, but rather to insist upon the fact, for Parisians and for all readers, that all is true. Readers are reassured, rather than excluded, by this insistence on local color and accuracy. Through his manic explications, Balzac will enlighten the reader as to what, exactly, a "pension bourgeoise" is: we will see the Maison Vauquer, as well as its inhabitants, up close and in some detail, right down to the rates the landlady charges for different rooms and meals. The Latin Quarter, as well as the faubourg Saint-Germain and the Chaussée d'Antin—as Balzac understood them and as he felt the reader needed to know them—will become familiar. By simultaneously assuming knowledge on the part of the Narratee, and explaining to the reader exactly what he considered to be essential in his stories, Balzac enlarges his audience, beyond the Narratee and the implied reader to actual readers outside of the time and place represented in his work.

Place names and other frequent references to what Barthes called the cultural code (*S/Z*, 27) are only one way in which Balzac creates his Narratee. As Prince pointed out, the second-person subject pronoun is one of the most explicit ways in which an author can construct a narratee ("Introduction," 184). Balzac's Narrator uses *vous* quite frequently. A typical example comes from *Le Cousin Pons:* describing Pons at the beginning of the book, the Narrator notes that Pons's smile seems out of place on his sad face:

Si vous eussiez été là, vous vous seriez demandé pourquoi le sourire animait cette figure grotesque [. . .] vous l'auriez soupçonné d'avoir retrouvé quelque chose d'équivalent au bichon d'une marquise et de l'apporter triomphalement (486-87)

Had you been there, you would have asked yourself why a smile was animating this grotesque face. . . you would have suspected him of having found something like the lapdog of a marquise and now triumphantly returning it to her.

Since we—*vous*, the Narratee and the reader—were not there, did not and cannot see either Pons's face or his smile, except through the words the Narrator uses to describe them, we must take the Narrator at his word. Furthermore, we must accept that we would, in fact, have asked ourselves why he was smiling, and we would have indeed suspected him of having found a marquise's lapdog, even if the metaphor only makes sense in the context the narrator has given to us.[3] Such examples of the Narrator telling us what we would have thought—if we had seen the things the Narrator describes—are quite numerous in *La Comédie humaine*. Accepting the accuracy of the Narrator's description and of our hypothetical reaction is part of our obligation as readers; we must agree that we would have done these things if we are going to continue to read Balzac's text.

Prince gives another example of a device Balzac uses frequently to advance the reading contract. A very common syntactic construction in *La Comédie humaine* is the phrase: "un(e) de ces . . . qui . . ." [one of those . . . that . . .] This phrase shows a great deal of confidence on the part of the Narrator that his Narratee understands him perfectly. The example that Prince chooses comes from the end of *Le Père Goriot*, as Rastignac stands beside the old man's grave: ". . . Il regarda la tombe et y ensevelit sa dernière larme de jeune homme [. . .] une de ces larmes qui, de la terre où elles tombent, rejaillissent jusque dans les cieux" [*He looked at the grave and there buried his last young man's tear. . . one of those tears which, from the earth where they fall, splash into the heavens*] (290). As Prince observes:

---

[3] Pons is described as having been something of a low-grade courtesan, someone who would in fact have been very happy to fetch a lady's lost dog, and happy that a marquise would deign to ask him such a favor.

D'après ces quelques lignes, le narrataire du *Père Goriot* reconnaît le
genre de larmes que Rastignac enterre. Il en a certainement entendu
parler, il en a vu sans doute, il en a peut-être versé quelques-unes lui-
même! ("Introduction," 185)
According to these few lines, the narratee of Le Père Goriot *recognizes
the kind of tears that Rastignac is burying. He has certainly heard of
them, he has surely seen them, perhaps he has even shed a few himself!*

In this case, and in the myriad others where this "un(e) de ces . . ." construction is used, the Narratee is acting as an ideal reader, understanding
and approving exactly the sense that Balzac wants these words to have.
The real reader might not have shed some of these tears, might not know
exactly what kind of tears the Narrator is talking about; we must interpret
what kind of tears they are from the context—the tears falling into the
grave and splashing up into heaven represent the death of Rastignac the
naive provincial boy, who makes way for Rastignac the Parisian *lion* who
goes to dine with the dead man's daughter. We trust the Narrator, and—
following our chosen role as Narratee—we accept the description and
continue reading. The only alternative is to break the reading contract,
to close the book and walk away, and never learn what becomes of
Rastignac.

This somewhat presumptuous construction is one of the many reasons that lead me to conclude that Balzac's ideal reader is in fact an impossible reader. Not only are these constructions sometimes unclear, I
suspect that their sense is too personal to Balzac for anyone else to completely understand them. There are also far more practical reasons for this
impossibility. Many of the elements of the cultural code that Balzac uses
to realize his fictional world are quite simply gone: no modern reader can
eat at Le Rocher de Cancale or "chez Véry"; Mlle Mars, Talma, and
Frédéric Lemaître are dead, and the theaters where they performed are
mostly gone; Balzac's Paris would be even stranger to a modern Parisian
than it was to Chabert returned from the grave. Balzac's Paris may have
seemed a bit peculiar, even to his contemporaries; for example, Rose Fortassier has maintained that Balzac's faubourg Saint-Germain was even
more aloof, even more closed off than the real thing (*Les Mondains de
"La Comédie humaine,"* 55-56). Many types of characters common to
Balzac's world were unique to Balzac's way of thinking: people with yel-

low eyes like Mme Cibot in *Le Cousin Pons* and exotic *Juives* such as
Esther and Josépha. Added to these idiosyncratic complications, which are
of course to be found in the work of any author, are those that result from
the system of recurring characters. In spite of rereading, of character in-
dexes and notes, it would require a superhuman memory to take into account every feature of every recurring character, every detail of their
biographies, as we encounter them in our rereading. So much in this world
is unfamiliar or unknowable to us for so many different reasons, that I
think it is safe to say that only Balzac could have met the requirements for
the ideal reader of *La Comédie humaine*. This does not mean that Balzac's
world is closed off from us. Quite the opposite, the impossibility of the
ideal reader means that the space behind the Narratee is wide open, acces-
sible to anyone who is able to read Balzac's text. The detail and explanation that so many people mock make it possible for us (with some help, it
is true, from the introductions and notes of critical editions) to enter into,
and to immerse ourselves in, Balzac's created world. The Narratee's place
offers the reader the best possible vantage point for watching *La Comédie
humaine* unfold.

As regards the frame stories and their narratees, this space allows
us to be so close to the storytelling situation that we can appreciate, judge,
and interpret the story from virtually the same perspective as the characters who listen to it. At the same time, we maintain enough distance that
we are also able to evaluate the narratees and their reactions to the stories.
Sometimes we can make these judgments by considering only the individual work—as in *Gobseck* and *La messe de l'athée*—but more often than
not, we must step back and consider the larger text to appreciate the narratees' reactions to the stories they hear. To fully appreciate the complexity of Balzac's frame/story constructions requires a type of reader not
specified by Prince, a type of reader unique, as far as I know, to *La
Comédie humaine* that I call the *lecteur initié*. This reader has read if not
all at least a very significant portion of *La Comédie humaine,* and has an
awareness not only of how and in which texts characters reappear, but also
of how they evolve in and between different works. This reader's familiarity cannot be limited to the characters, however; we must remember Léo
Mazet's essential point that the circulation of characters is merely the
paradigm for other circulations within *La Comédie humaine*. The *lecteur
initié* should be aware of recurring themes and of the different idiosyncra-

sies of Balzac's work and worldview. The opposite of the *lecteur initié* is the naive reader, in this sense the reader of a given text, novel or *nouvelle,* as a unity in and of itself, rather than as a fragment of the great Balzacian whole. That said, I do not propose that there is necessarily a fixed body of knowledge that identifies this sort of reader. Individual readers of *La Comédie humaine* will make their own judgments about the importance or meaning of a given character, theme, or event. And any discussion of what happens between the texts is necessarily subjective, perhaps even contentious. I do not think that anyone would dispute the point that broader and deeper knowledge of *La Comédie humaine* enriches our understanding and appreciation of the individual texts that make up the whole; but a text so complex is bound to give rise to many different interpretations. Reading and individual interpretation are the variables in the equation that produce the sum of knowledge that I referred to earlier as a reader's personal Balzacian baggage. This collection of knowledge, assumptions, and beliefs form the prism through which we see the motion of Balzac's textual mobile.

Revealing Changes: Recasting the Role of Narratee

Virtually until his death, Balzac was at work changing and adding to his creation, shifting the parts of his mobile to change the way it looked and moved in his readers' imaginations. These changes, some of which significantly alter the sense of the texts in which they appear, do much to support the idea that Balzac was conscious of the effect of narratees in his framed stories, and that he deliberately sought to create this effect. One notable and much-discussed case that illustrates this theory is *Le Lys dans la vallée.* This novel takes the form of a long letter in which Félix de Vandenesse recounts the history of his first love to his current lover, Natalie de Manerville. Félix's story is a lyrical portrait of his ideal but chaste love for an older woman, Mme de Mortsauf, who loves and nurtures the younger man. He betrays her with the passionate, sensual, and cruel Lady Dudley. This betrayal is fatal for Mme de Mortsauf, whose memory haunts Félix throughout his life. This very long letter is followed by the very brief and trenchant response of Natalie, who, declaring she cannot compete with either "la Vierge de Clochegourde" or the "intrépide Amazone" (9:1226), ends her relationship with Félix. Far from being a mere "coup de théâtre," as Nicole Mozet maintained (*Balzac au pluriel*, 33), Natalie's letter is essential to the work as a whole. Natalie's caustic response changes our whole perception of Félix, throwing a harsh light on his narcissism and retroactively undermining any sympathy the reader might have had for him (Lastinger, "Narration et 'point de vue,' " 282). Natalie's response complicates the novel by destabilizing, at least momentarily, both the readers' sympthies and—perhaps more importantly—our assumptions about the author's sympathies, which are at first encouraged by the obvious and oft-noted parallels between Félix and Balzac.

Both Natalie's letter and the short epistolary introduction by Félix were added by Balzac after the initial composition of the novel (J.-H. Donnard, "Histoire du texte," éd. Pléiade, 1638). This addition not only further complicates the individual novel, but demonstrates how ambiguous *La Comédie humaine* can be when considered as a whole. Just as reading Natalie's letter undermines our faith in and sympathy for Félix, so does reading *Le Contrat de mariage* or *Une Fille d'Eve* complicate our view of Natalie. Nothing in *Le Lys dans la vallée* lets us know that Félix's correspondent is a heartless coquette, but in *Le Contrat de mariage,* we see Natalie's true colors. In that novel, the shrewd and ruthless Madame Evangelista, Natalie's mother, marries her daughter to Paul de Manerville, a rather dull-witted, second-class Parisian dandy who, having sowed his wild oats in the capital, returns home to Bordeaux to find a wife. Aided by an unscrupulous lawyer, the impoverished Evangelistas arrange a marriage contract that favors the bride in every way. In time, Natalie, "ce petit crocodile habillé en femme" [*that little crocodile disguised as a woman*] (3:619), becomes one of the queens of the Parisian *monde,* while her husband is mystified to find himself bankrupt. At the novel's end, Paul leaves France in an attempt to remake his fortune in the Orient, never to return. A last letter from his wife contains promises of eternal love and fidelity, and the news of her pregnancy; a last letter from his friend de Marsay opens Paul's eyes to the truth about his wife and his mother-in-law. Madame Evangelista, "qui s'entend en affaires comme un vrai procureur" [*who understands business as well as any lawyer*] (634), has stolen Paul's fortune and driven him into bankruptcy; as for Natalie, de Marsay tells his naïve friend that she has shown very little regret about her husband's abrupt departure and strongly suggests that the baby Natalie is carrying is not Paul's. The father is, in fact, the romantically melancholy Félix de Vandenesse.

Armed with this broader knowledge of Natalie's character, the *lecteur initié* might well question the validity of Natalie's outrage and the value of her condemnation of Félix. Natalie expresses compassion (of debatable sincerity) for "cette pauvre Mme de Mortsauf" (1226), but she also reveals a definite sympathy for Lady Dudley, "une femme extrêmement distinguée," whom Félix had "fatigué[e]" (1227) and "considérablement ennuyé[e]" [*an extremely distinguished woman whom Felix had bored considerably*] (1226). For the *lecteur initié*, Natalie seems closer in character to Arabella than to Henriette: both are adulteresses, and, more importantly, both are devious and cruel; both are in some sense foreigners— Natalie, though born in Bordeaux, is of Spanish descent; finally, Jean-Hervé Donnard has underlined an important similarity between the descriptions of these two characters (Introduction; éd. Pléiade, 892-93). While I would not go so far as Donnard in saying that Balzac "emploie des termes presque identiques" to describe the two women, two common details are quite revealing: Arabella and Natalie are both described as having "fauve" [*tawny, lion-colored*] hair, suggesting in both women a wild, predatory, and even ferocious nature; both are also said to have an "organisation de fer," [*an iron constitution*] implying not only *dureté*, hardness, but *froideur*, coldness, as well. Given the similarities in their respective portraits, we can reasonably infer a certain kinship between the two, which is further suggested by their friendship, described in *Une Fille d'Eve*. In that novel, Félix's two former lovers join forces with Mme d'Espard (who seems to be acting out of selfless malice) in a plot to disrupt the domestic contentment—we cannot really say happiness—of Félix and his very young and extremely naïve bride, Marie de Grandville.

If Natalie does indeed identify with Lady Dudley, then what Félix says of the "Amazone" in his letter would resonate strongly with his correspondent. Not only is Lady Dudley contrasted unflatteringly with Mme de Mortsauf in a moral sense, Félix also describes his purely physical relationship with Lady Dudley as ultimately unsatisfying:

> lady Arabelle [. . .] était la maîtresse du corps. Mme de Mortsauf était
> l'épouse de l'âme. L'amour que satisfaisait la maîtresse a des bornes

[. . .] L'infini est le domaine du cœur [. . .] je sentais souvent je ne sais
quel vide à Paris, près de lady Dudley. (1146)
Lady Arabella was the mistress of the body. Mme de Mortsauf was the
wife of the soul. The love that a mistress satisfies has limits. . . The infi-
nite is the realm of the heart. . . I often felt an indescribable emptiness
in Paris, next to Lady Dudley.

Natalie is implicitly placed in the same inferior position of mistress, beneath Mme de Mortsauf, the spiritual wife. This impression is supported
by a sentence in Natalie's letter that is almost certainly intended as a double entendre. The frequent references to Lady Dudley's passion for horse-
back riding are not merely a stereotype of the British aristocrat; they are
also meant to subtly suggest her sexual appetites. Having read Félix's
story, Natalie reminds her lover that "Vous avez oublié que nous montons
souvent à cheval. Je n'ai pas su réchauffer le soleil attiédi par la mort de
votre sainte Henriette, le frisson vous prendrait à côté de moi" [*You have*
forgotten that we often went riding. I was unable to give heat to the sun
that the death of your sainted Henriette had cooled, you would take cold at
my side] (1226). The implication is that Natalie understands that she has
been only a *maîtresse de corps,* like her fellow *écuyère.* Just as Lady
Dudely's presence gave Félix a vague impression of emptiness, Natalie
now knows that she leaves him cold—or rather she announces that she
will do so in the future.

Eventually, Natalie will become Félix's bitter enemy, as we see in
Une Fille d'Eve, where she acts in concert with Lady Dudley to destroy
the happiness of Félix's marriage. This friendship, very probably born of a
shared hatred, serves to point out once again the complexity of the construction of *La Comédie humaine.* The individual texts are not merely tied
one to the other, they are woven together in an incredibly complex pattern,
the smaller threads of which are not always immediately visible to the observer. Balzac's additions and replacements have further complicated this
pattern, creating new meanings in *La Comédie humaine,* both the whole
and the fragments.

As with any work of art that contains an extremely complex pattern, there are two ways to better understand *La Comédie humaine:* by
close examination of small parts and, paradoxically, by stepping back to
take in the whole. When we as *lecteurs initiés* step back to consider *Le Lys*

as a part of Balzac's larger world, another question about this long narration presents itself. Félix, in the brief letter that opens the novel, says that he is telling Natalie his story at her jealous insistence, seeking to explain the melancholy fits that he is subject to. This letter supposes, obviously, that Natalie knows nothing about Félix's history with Mme de Mortsauf. This is highly unlikely. Balzac's world, especially his *grand monde,* is a place where secrets are very hard to keep, and the affair between Félix and Henriette is no secret. Félix suspects Mme de Mortsauf's father, the duc de Lenoncourt, of having gossiped about it with Louis XVIII (1139); Lady Dudley decides to seduce Félix because she learns of this pure love: "Je suis, dit-elle, ennuyée de ces soupirs de tourterelle" [*"I am," she said, "bored by all these turtledoves' sighs"*] (1143). It seems illogical that no one, whether motivated by malice or simple boredom, would have informed Natalie of her lover's past history, just as the old duchesse de Lenoncourt tells her daughter, Mme de Mortsauf, of the affair between Félix and Lady Dudley (1149). Perhaps de Marsay, declared enemy of the Vandenesse family (*Le Contrat de mariage,* 3:647) for reasons no doubt as much personal as political, took it upon himself to inform Natalie. In doing so, he would have been avenging both himself and Natalie's husband, a good friend of de Marsay.

If we accept the possibility that Natalie knew the story of "La Vierge de Clochegourde" before reading Félix's letter, the next question that presents itself is: why would she have demanded that Félix tell her a story that she already knew? I think two answers are possible. The first, that she had grown bored with her lover and was seeking to provoke a *rupture.* The second, more interesting possibility is that by persuading Félix to reveal his secret to her, Natalie was attempting to force Félix to tacitly acknowledge that she had eclipsed Mme de Mortsauf. The surrender of the story, a sacrifice of Mme de Mortsauf to Natalie, would represent a total submission on Félix's part, and would mean that Mme de Manerville had succeeded where Lady Dudley had failed. In either case, it appears that, just like the *jeune personne* of *L'Auberge rouge,* Natalie got more than she bargained for by asking for a story. Not only has she not dislodged the ghost of Henriette from Félix's heart, she finds herself cast in the role of the *pis-aller,* a mere physical distraction for a man in love with a memory.

Obviously, these conclusions are based on some very subjective and very personal interpretations. I can present no textual evidence for them, other than the general atmosphere that I infer from the whole of the Balzacian text. What cannot be disputed, however, is that *Le Lys dans la vallée* is a text profoundly, even disproportionately, altered by the two very brief letters added to the beginning and the end of the original novel; this could only be denied by those who would dismiss the frame altogether, and many do just that. Another point difficult to dispute is that the choice of the narratee has a specific and marked effect on the interpretation of the *lecteur initié*. Natalie de Manerville was not chosen at random from a stable of characters or a list of names, and we cannot thoroughly or accurately discuss her role in *Le Lys dans la vallée* without considering her character as a part of *La Comédie humaine*.

A Change for the Better: From Foedora to Béatrix in *Sarrasine*

Another illustration of the effect of a narratee resulting from changes made in that role after the initial composition of a text is to be found in *Sarrasine*. The role of narratee was filled by two characters before Balzac finally settled on Mme de Rochefide. The first, the "comtesse de F. . ." became Foedora, the "femme sans cœur" from *La Peau de chagrin* in 1835 (Pugh, 96); in 1843, Foedora was replaced by Mme de Rochefide (341). The reason for the first change is obvious: Balzac had invented his system of recurring characters, and Foedora at first glance seems well suited to the role of the flirtatious but ultimately reserved *mondaine* who listens to the strange tale of Sarrasine and La Zambinella. Anthony Pugh has offered a very plausible reason for the removal of Foedora from *Sarrasine*, as she was removed from other works, and ultimately, from the system of recurring characters altogether. In *La Peau de chagrin*, Foedora has an intangible quality, she is, as Emile Talbot put it so well, "la fée d'or" [*the golden fairy*] ("Pleasure/Time or Egoism/Love: Rereading *La Peau de chagrin*," 78). This quality is complemented in the main part of the novel by Foedora's calculated virtue—she makes herself untouchable—and is made (too) explicit in the epilogue by an unseen narrator's final comment on Foedora: "elle est partout, c'est, si vous voulez, la Société" [*She's everywhere, she is, if you like, Society*] (10:294). By limiting this character to a unique appearance in *La Peau de chagrin,* Balzac insists upon her elusive quality and strengthens the character as an element in that novel. Less attention has been given to other reasons why Foedora—as a character rather than as an "allegorical figure" (Pugh, *Balzac's Recurring Characters,* 341)—is ill-suited to play the role of the narratee in *Sarrasine.*

In *La Peau de chagrin,* Foedora is marked above all by two character traits: intelligence and self-control. It would be completely out of character for Foedora to perform the actions that the young woman of *Sarrasine* does, and these actions are essential to the development of the plot: that is, touching the old man as if he were an inanimate object, fleeing to the boudoir, becoming visibly fascinated by the portrait, etc. Foedora's intelligence and cool reserve would make the narratee's reaction to the object story illogical for Foedora; she might well be repulsed by the story, but it is doubtful that she would show her reaction with as much emotion as the narratee of *Sarrasine* does. This leads to a final reason, the most important one, for Foedora's inappropriateness as the narratee for the object story in *Sarrasine.* An essential element in the *nouvelle* is that the narratee breaks the implied sex-for-story contract with the narrator. If it is Foedora who does this, we cannot tell if she does so because of the story, or because she has—to borrow Barthes's rather harsh terminology—psychologically castrated herself. Foedora's most remarkable trait in *La Peau de chagrin* is her lack of any acknowledged lover (*PC,* 10:146), an unheard-of restraint for a rich and beautiful young widow in Balzac's *monde.* For reasons that are never fully explained, Foedora rejects the many suitors who present themselves. She has attendants, but no lovers. If Foedora had entered into the implied contract with the narrator, the agreement would have been null and void from the start, because made in bad faith by Foedora. In order for the story of the castrato and the sculptor to have its full force, we must know for certain that the contract is broken because of the story, not because of duplicity on the part of the narratee.

There were as many reasons for Balzac to remove Foedora from *Sarrasine* as there were reasons to select Béatrix de Rochefide to fill the role. The two women are about the same age, born around 1808, but they show sharply different degrees of maturity. Foedora at twenty-two is all cool self-possession in dealing with men; in *Sarrasine,* Mme de Rochefide is, as Barthes put it, a "femme-enfant" (*S/Z,* 57), a phrase that could never be used to describe Foedora. This immaturity is not inconsistent with the portrait of Mme de Rochefide given by Félicité des Touches in *Béatrix*. She was a somewhat naïve provincial girl when she married in 1828. Although Félicité acknowledges that Béatrix's intelligence was remarkable even then, the brilliant author also points out that her friend is known for a certain "exaltation" (*Béatrix,* 6:712), and Béatrix is said to have experienced an "étourdissement" during her first years in the Parisian social world (716). It is far more likely that this character, at twenty-two, should commit the *faux pas* that will lead to the discovery of the painting in *Sarrasine*. Furthermore, Béatrix has far less talent for disguising her emotions than Foedora, as is evidenced by her bursts of unspeakable anger in *Béatrix*. Another point in character: Béatrix's strong attraction to the beautiful young man in the portrait. This character has a weakness for handsome young men: Conti, Calyste du Guénic, La Palférine. Finally, it is completely in character that Béatrix should break the contract with the narrator. According to Félicité des Touches, Béatrix is one of those unfortunate *mal-mariées* of *La Comédie humaine,* married off at a young age to a man with whom she is sexually incompatible. Her loutish husband, assuming their incompatibility to be due to his wife's sexual frigidity, abandons her for the pleasures of Parisian life (*Béatrix,* 2:713). Béatrix at twenty-two is not only socially but sexually naïve, far more vulnerable to "contamination" from the story (to borrow again from Barthes) than Foedora. It is completely logical that the character described in *Béatrix* should have the reactions attributed to the narratee in *Sarrasine*.

Another trait of Béatrix that makes her a well-chosen character for the role of narratee in *Sarrasine* is a certain pretentiousness. Félicité des Touches, a highly credible source, informs us that Béatrix is frequently motivated by jealousy of Félicité, establishing a superficial literary salon in imitation of that of the *femme-artiste*. In *Sarrasine,* this literary and social pretension is not yet visible, but we do see a certain moral pretention in Mme de Rochefide's final words to the narrator: "Vous m'avez dégoûtée de la vie et des passions pour longtemps [. . .] Demain je me ferais dévote si je ne savais pouvoir rester comme un roc inaccessible au milieu des orages de la vie" [*You have have ruined life and passion for me for many years. . . Tomorrow I would become a puritain if I were not sure I could remain like an inaccessible rock amidst the storms of life*] (1075). And a bit further on: "Oui, les âmes pures ont une patrie dans le ciel! Personne ne m'aura connue! J'en suis fière" [*Yes, pure souls have a place in heaven! No one will ever know me! I am proud of it!*] (1076). For the *lecteur initié*, these words are rich with irony. Mme de Rochefide's life will not reflect her disgust for passions, and she will become the eye of the storm rather than a rock in *Béatrix*. I think what we see in these words is a reflection of the character's sexual naïveté that Félicité des Touches alludes to in *Béatrix*. When she listens to the story of the Italian soprano in *Sarrasine*, Mme de Rochefide had not yet learned about passion from her first extramarital lover, the Italian tenor Gennaro Conti.[4]

A final aspect of Béatrix's personality that makes her so well suited to the character described in *Sarrasine* is her taste for literature and the arts. As a girl, Béatrix had been considered an *originale* among the provincial Norman nobility because of her strange ideas, "un sentiment pour le beau [et] un certain entraînement pour les œuvres d'art" [*a feeling for beauty and a certain taste for works of art*] (*B*, 2:712). It is a safe bet that her tastes run along the same lines as those of the *jeune personne* in *L'Auberge rouge:* Scott and Hoffman; the romantic and the fantastic. These twin strands are strongly present in the atmosphere of the Lantys' ball, from the curious old man who has inspired so many strange rumors to the portrait of Endymion in the boudoir. These are the two elements that pique Mme de Rochefide's curiosity, that draw her into making her pact with the narrator. The narrator's story, the one that he hopes will win him Mme de Rochefide's affections, weaves these twin strands into one, bringing together the grotesque old man at the ball with the beautiful young man in the portrait. Mme de Rochefide, having been irresistibly drawn to both the *beau* and the *laid,* learns that they are one. Furthermore, she learns that she was doubly attracted to a castrato, a creature (created thing) that repulses her. The inexperienced young bride reacts in a way that is perfectly logical for her, but that would not have been so consistent had the narratee of this strange tale been the cool widow Foedora.

The *lecteur initié* definitely has a greater appreciation of the narratee's role in *Sarrasine* than the naïve reader, but that is not to say that this role is without interest to the reader of *Sarrasine* as a totality rather than a fragment. The narratee of this *nouvelle* is important and interesting

---

[4] According to Félicité des Touches, Conti's voice has an effect on women similar to the one that La Zambinella's has on Sarrasine (*Béatrix*, 717)

in her (perhaps I should say "its") own right. The role is essential to the
links between story and frame, and very interesting even without reference
to the system of recurring characters. For example, it is not really necessary that the narratee be a recurring character to appreciate the importance
of the character's literary tastes in her role as narratee. As the texts of *Sarrasine* and *L'Auberge rouge* indicate to us, the *amis du fantastique* were a
rather large group in Paris in 1830, and the *bas-bleu* [bluestocking] was a
contemporary stereotype. There is also, however, a direct and under-
discussed link between frame and story that is based on the narratee.
Barthes, following his theme of castration and its power to contaminate
others, sees a link between frame and story in the narrator's resemblance
to Sarrasine (*S/Z*, 94). Both fall in love with a woman who ultimately rejects their advances, for very different reasons. The initial castration of La
Zambinella effectively renders both men impotent as well. This view implicitly places Mme de Rochefide in the role of La Zambinella, both as an
object of desire and, because of her refusal of the narrator's advances, as a
castrating woman as well. At least as important as this is the resemblance
between Béatrix and Sarrasine.

Both are strongly attracted to Zambinella, a person who is neither
male nor female, who cannot satisfy either of them sexually. The similarity between the two characters and their desire for the castrato is underlined by the similarity between the scenes that describe the initial
attraction in both cases: Sarrasine is at the opera in Rome when he hears
the unnaturally beautiful voice of La Zambinella; it is the voice that causes
him to look at the stage, and then to fall in love with the singer. Many
years later, in Paris, it is while Mariannina is singing that Béatrix finds
herself irresistibly drawn by the grotesque figure of Zambinella grown old.
After his initial attraction to the singer, Sarrasine takes a private box (*loge*)
at the opera, where night after night he lies on a sofa waiting for the voice
to enthrall him. After Béatrix touches the old man, she runs to the boudoir,
"un petit cabinet demi circulaire" [*A small semicircular room*] (1053), not
unlike a *loge* or even a theater in miniature, where she throws herself on
the sofa ("un divan") in despair. It is while lying on the sofa that she notices the portrait of Zambinella, which—at the focal point of the room like
a stage in a theater—fascinates her, even seduces her. In both cases, beautiful works of art stir sexual desire in admirers who do not really under-

stand what they are seeing. When they learn the truth, both are horrified—at least as much by their own desire as by the object of their desire.

The replacement of Foedora with Béatrix de Rochefide further supports the idea that Balzac was cognizant of the potential effect of the narratees in his frames and deliberately sought to exploit these possibilities. Studying Mme de Rochefide in this role reveals the often subtle and understated complexity of *La Comédie humaine*. She is far more than a passive link between the fragment and the whole, and she is much more than a name. We must learn to be very skeptical of the notion, too frequently accepted, that Balzac's frame-characters were chosen almost at random to fill in certain blanks. If Béatrix is not precisely irreplaceable in the text, it would certainly be a much different text if another character had been chosen for this work. Balzac could not have written the same ending to this story if the narratee had been Diane de Cadignan or Natalie de Manerville, or Félicité des Touches, all characters whose personalities would make them ill-suited, for different reasons, to act as the narratee of *Sarrasine*. One can imagine that if Balzac had left Foedora in this role, critics would have been quick to point out the inconsistency and to accuse Balzac of sloppy work; yet the skill with which he chose Mme de Rochefide for this role has received relatively little attention. It is a curious commentary about the relationship between Balzac and his readers, even those of us who admire him greatly, that we are sometimes quicker to point out his putative weaknesses than his less obvious strengths.

Hearing Their Own Stories: Félicité, Onorina, and *Honorine*

With *Sarrasine*, we can see how a working knowledge of *La Comédie humaine* provides the *lecteur initié* with a richer experience of reading. The naive reader is by no means cheated, however, as the *nouvelle* stands alone quite well, even if one does not go as far as Barthes, who found it to be the most fascinating text of *La Comédie humaine*. *Sarrasine* must be able to stand alone, as the original text predates the system of recurring characters and the concept of Balzac's work as a whole composed of fragments. Mme de Rochefide was added to an existing text, enriching and complexifying it, but not really completing it. The same can be said of another late addition to a Balzacian text, the addition of Félicité des

Touches to *Honorine.* This long *nouvelle* was originally an unframed story
with a happy ending. This version, written in three days at the end of December, 1842, begins with the same premise as the object story in the version we know today: A young man, Maurice de l'Hostal, goes to work for
a somber magistrate known only as "le comte Octave." The two men form
a strong, almost father-son bond, and Maurice learns the secret cause of
his patron's melancholy: the count is married to a young woman he has
known all his life, Honorine. Their marriage turned out to be an unhappy
one—Balzac subtly intimates to the readers that the cause of the bride's
discontent is sexual incompatibility—and Honorine ran away with a lover,
who abandoned her shortly after she became pregnant. Rather than return
to the perfectly respectable and forgiving Octave, Honorine attempts to
live on her own, all the while being secretly supported by her estranged
husband. In a last effort to win back his wife, the count uses his young
secretary as a go-between, as an emissary to his wife. Maurice eventually
gains the countess's trust, she is persuaded to return to her husband, and
the two live happily ever after.

The frame as we know it was added in late January, 1843, with the
considerable revision of the end of the tale coming just a few days later
(Pierre Citron, Introduction, éd. Pléiade, 2:507-8). In the revised version
of the *nouvelle,* which is also the final version, Maurice falls in love with
his patron's wife and must leave France in an attempt to forget his love
and preserve his friendship with Octave. Honorine still returns to her husband, but is desperately unhappy and eventually dies of a broken heart.

I have already touched on the role played by Félicité des Touches
in the interpretation of the object story: Maurice's story wins the celebrated author's sympathy for Honorine, and her condemnation of Octave's
conduct guides the readers' reaction to the story, leaving—at first
glance—little doubt as to what conclusions we should draw from it. Félicité des Touches is well known to the *lecteur initié;* she is one of the
most remarkable characters of *La Comédie humaine,* but a broad familiarity with the larger text is not essential to understand this aspect of the
character's role in *Honorine.* For the naive reader, the reader of *Honorine*
as an independent text, her credibility is established in the opening part of
the frame. It is clear in this portion of the text that Félicité's renown has
spread beyond the intellectual and artistic community of Paris, even beyond the borders of France. Mlle des Touches's reluctant presence at the

consul's dinner is an honor not only for the French diplomats in Genoa, but also for the Italians who have played host to Félicité's traveling companion:

> Léon de Lora dit à Camille que sa présence était la seule manière qu'il eût de remercier l'ambassadeur et sa femme, les deux marquis génois, le consul et la consulesse. (527)
>
> *Léon de Lora told Camille that her presence was the only way that he could thank the ambassador and his wife, the two Genovese marquis, the counsel and his wife.*

The bona fides given at the beginning of the frame, and the fact that Félicité's reaction is the only one given in the closing portion, establish this character's authority, inducing the reader, naive or experienced, to trust her judgment. This credibility is reinforced by the display of a certain *science divinatoire* on the part of this narratee. Félicité, an author and therefore an observer, senses some vague trouble beneath the apparent domestic tranquility of the consul and his wife: "Mlle des Touches trouvait au consul un air un peu trop distrait chez un homme parfaitement heureux [. . .] Camille se disait tour à tour: « Qu'y a-t-il? —Il n'y a rien! »" [*Mlle des Touches found the Consul a bit too distracted for a perfectly happy man. She said to herself repeatedly: "What is it? It's nothing"*] (530). In the closing part of the frame, it is the perspicacious *femme-artiste* who explicitly confirms for the reader what is only hinted at in Maurice de l'Hostal's narration, that Honorine was in love with the young messenger sent by her estranged husband, and that Maurice was completely unaware that his feelings were reciprocated. This *seconde vue* that Mlle des Touches displays vis-à-vis Maurice also underlines the importance of Balzac's description of the diplomat as Byronian. There is an affinity and a sympathy between the great writer and the sensitive diplomat who is poetic, if not actually a poet.

As a narratee, Félicité des Touches is essential to our full understanding of the *nouvelle*, but she is not the only important narratee in *Honorine*. There is also Onorina, the beautiful Italian wife of the French consul. Onorina is a hidden narratee, not meant to hear the story her husband tells. Before he begins his tale, he sends his wife away. It is only at the end of the *nouvelle* that Camille Maupin realizes that Onorina has

heard the whole story of her husband and Honorine: "Oh! fit-elle en voyant venir la consulesse, sa femme l'a écouté, le malheureux!. . ." ["*Oh!*"
she exclaimed on seeing the consul's wife coming, "his wife overheard,
the unhappy man!"] (596) It is curious that Félicité sees this as more of a
problem for the husband than for the wife—"le malheureux!" By un-
knowingly revealing his story to his wife, Maurice has undermined the
stability and the happiness of the marriage that he had worked to make
succeed. As for his wife, it is made clear to the reader that Onorina knew
that Maurice's melancholy hid a romantic secret:

> les femmes ne se plaignent jamais d'être victimes d'une préférence,
> elles s'immolent très bien à la cause commune. Onorina Pedrotti, qui
> peut-être aurait haï le consul si elle eût été dédaignée absolument, n'en
> aimait pas moins, et peut–être plus, *suo sposo,* en le sachant amoureux.
> (529)
>
> *Women never mind being the victims of a preference, they sacrifice*
> *themselves to the common cause. Onorina Pedrotti, who would perhaps*
> *have hated her husband had she been absolutely disdained, loved him*
> *no less, and perhaps more, knowing that he was in love.*

But it is only in hearing her husband's story that Onorina can understand
the true nature and the force of her husband's love for another woman.
This was not some adolescent infatuation, but a profound and enduring
emotion. Perhaps Onorina, like Félicité, recognized that this love was mutual, and now wonders whether things would have been different had her
husband known his feelings were reciprocated.

Onorina also learns through this story that her husband had turned
down a financially and socially advantageous marriage to a beautiful
young woman (the best of the Balzacian world) because of his love for
Honorine. As Maurice himself puts it in his story:

> Entre les plaines de la Champagne et les Alpes neigeuses, orageuses,
> mais sublimes, quel est le jeune homme qui peut choisir la crayeuse et
> paisible étendue? Non, de telles comparaisons sont fatales et mauvaises
> sur le seuil de la Mairie [. . .] le mariage exclut la passion, [. . .] la Fa-
> mille ne saurait avoir les orages de l'amour pour base. (584)

Between the plains of Champagne and the Alps, snowy, stormy, but
sublime, what young man could have chosen the chalky and peaceful
stretches? No, such comparisons are fatal and unhappy on the steps of
the Church. . . marriage excludes passion. . . the Family cannot have
as its foundation the storms of love.

Onorina cannot fail to recognize that the marriage that her husband had refused is directly parallel to their own, to which Maurice only consented after Honorine had given birth to Octave's son, thus consummating their re-union. Onorina would also surely have understood that she is implicitly compared to the peaceful and chalky stretches of Champagne, against the passionate and sublime Honorine. It is only now that Onorina learns exactly how her husband views their marriage—as a passionless union, founded as a family, not as a couple. A final insult to this *Italienne,* who is described as being beautiful and maternal—in short, a good woman—is to be found in the explanation given for the all-consuming passion that Honorine inspires. It is the comte Octave who decribes Honorine's attractions, explaining to his young protégé that the "passion physique" he feels for his estranged wife "n'est rien en comparaison de l'adoration qui m'inspirent l'âme, l'esprit, les manières, le cœur, tout ce qui dans la femme n'est pas la femme" [*is nothing in comparison to the adoration inspired by the soul, the spirit, the manners, the heart, everything in a woman that is not the woman*] (559). Onorina cannot ignore the implication that the domestic tranquility she brings to her husband's life cannot compare to the intellectual and spiritual bond he had formed with the woman whose ghost haunts their marriage. The similarity between the names of the beloved and the wife—an obvious and primary link between frame and story—is meant to suggest not a similarity between the two women, but rather to ironically underline the fact that the legitimate spouse is merely a pale shadow of the soul mate.

The similarity of names is not the only link between frame and story in this text; there is another, far more subtle than the first. If Félicité des Touches serves as guide to the reader of *Honorine,* and if her presence serves as a link between this fragment and the whole *Comédie humaine* for the *lecteur initié,* the character of Félicité also serves as the link between frame and story, in a way that is probably only detectable to the *lecteur initié.* Honorine de Bauvan is a woman in rebellion against society. Born into the highest stratum of society, almost unconsciously forced into a marriage that should have been perfect for her, Honorine finds that she cannot live according to the rules of the society that surrounds her, and so she attempts to make her own life outside of that society, in infraction of those rules. The same thing can be said of Félicité des Touches. There are some hints of Félicité's antisocial lifestyle in the frame of *Honorine*: this unmarried woman who writes books for a living is traveling in Italy in the company of two men, has been to Venice to conduct some business "affaire" (527), etc. All highly suspect behavior, but her unconventional nature is overshadowed by her artistic reputation and the respect that her work has earned her, giving her the aura of intelligence and authority that serves Balzac's purposes in this appearance. It is in *Béatrix* that the most complete portrait of Mlle des Touches is given, and it is there that her countercultural lifestyle can best be understood and appreciated:

> En 1816, elle eut vingt-cinq ans. Elle ignorait le mariage, elle ne le concevait que par la pensée, le jugeait dans ses causes au lieu de le voir dans ses effets, et n'en apercevait que les inconvénients. Son esprit se refusait à l'abdication par laquelle la femme mariée commence la vie; elle sentait le prix de l'indépendance et n'éprouvait que du dégoût pour les soins de la maternité [. . .] Placée entre le mariage et la passion, elle voulut rester libre. (592-93)
>
> *In 1816, she was 25. She knew nothing of marriage, she conceived it only in thought, judged it in its causes rather that seeing its effects, and saw only its disadvantages. Her spirit refused the abdication by which the married woman begins her life; she sensed the value of independence and felt only disgust for the cares of motherhood. Forced to choose between marriage and passion, she decided to remain free.*

Rejecting both marriage and motherhood, Félicité lives and succeeds in the man's world that is Balzac's literary and journalistic milieu. Having inherited and successfully managed a great fortune, Félicité has the money necessary to sustain her unorthodox choice. She also maintains her connections in the *monde*—cousin of the Grandlieu family, Félicité is not only *reçue* but apparently well respected by Mme de Grandlieu, the most reactionary and devout duchess of Balzac's aristocracy. But in her ancestral province of Brittany, this exotic and masculine woman is viewed with suspicion, even hostility, by her *hobereaux* neighbors.

Honorine arrives at similar conclusions about marriage, but only after the fact; having experienced married life, the countess judges the effect rather than the cause. She explains her views on this subject to Maurice, in terms that clearly express a (proto-)feminist point of view. Speaking of the pride she receives from selling her artificial flowers (which her husband secretly buys at prices far beyond their real value), she says: "Gagner sa vie en s'amusant, être libre, quand les hommes, armés de leurs lois, ont voulu nous faire esclaves!" [*To earn one's living while amusing oneself, to be free, when men, armed with their laws, have sought to make us their slaves*] (572) For both women, the state of matrimony is seen in terms of slavery and abdication, directly opposed to liberty and independence. Balzac being Balzac, money is sharply present in both women's conception of liberty. Félicité, unmarried, has preserved the right to manage her own money, and her unorthodox, masculine education has helped her to do so quite successfully. As for Honorine, her aristocratic upbringing and traditional, feminine education have deprived her of any sense of the true value of things, and this ignorance allows her husband to build a gilded cage around her. She has money of her own, but as a married woman, her fortune is "en puissance de mari" [*under her husband's power*], to borrow a very appropriate phrase from *Gobseck* (2:992). While Félicité has been able to live a life of independence, Honorine perhaps because her independence has been harder won and more precarious, is more militant in her expression of it. In a sentence that is chillingly prescient for the rereader of *Honorine*, she declares that "Lucrèce a écrit avec son poignard et son sang le premier mot de la charte des femmes: *Liberté!*" [*Lucrecia wrote with her dagger and her blood the first word in the charter of women: Liberty!*] (571). The reference to the classical heroine suggests that death is the only end possible for women who refuse to submit.

The connection between these two rebellious women is complemented by another affinity between them, one that is perhaps related to their status as social misfits. If Félicité is linked to Maurice by a certain artistic temperament, Balzac also implies the same sort of kinship between Félicité and Honorine. It may seem a bit bizarre for us to think of Honorine's business of manufacturing artificial flowers as an art, but the *fleuriste* sees herself as an artist, and Maurice, as narrator, supports her conclusion: "La comtesse avait, à la longue, poétisé, pour ainsi dire, ce qui est l'antipode de la poésie, une fabrique"[5] [*The countess had, over time, poeticized, so to speak, that which is the antithesis of poetry, a workshop.*] (567); and a bit further on:

> Elle déployait le génie des peintres dans ses audacieuses entreprises, elle copiait des feuilles flétries, des feuilles jaunes; elle luttait avec les fleurs des champs, de toutes les plus naïves, les plus compliquées dans leurs simplicité. "Cet art, me disait-elle, est dans l'enfance . . ." (568)
> *She displayed the genius of an artist in her audacious entreprises, she copied faded flowers, yellow leaves; she rivaled the flowers of the fields, the most naïve of all, the most complicated in their simplicity. "This art", she told me, "is in its infancy. . ."*

This art of flowermaking suggests another connection between Félicité and Honorine, probably coincidental but nonetheless interesting. In *Balzac au pluriel,* Nicole Mozet alludes to a passage from George Sand's correspondence in which the author specifically mentions flowermaking as one of the few options—literature being another—open to a woman who wishes to be self-sufficient: "Pour elle [. . .] écrire ou fabriquer des fleurs artificielles, comme l'héroïne d'*André* ou l'héroïne balzacienne qui s'appelle Honorine, c'est tout un" [*For her. . . to write or to make artificial flowers, like the heroine of* André *or the Balzacian heroine called* Honorine, *it's all the same*] (171). George Sand thus becomes another liaison between Honorine and Félicité des Touches, whose resemblance to the real author—which was neither accidental nor unacknowledged by Balzac—is universally recognized and has been abundantly analyzed; all three women are artists, and all three are unwilling and unable to conform to the social norms imposed on women by society.

While listening to the story of Honorine, Félicité des Touches is hearing her own story, the story of woman in revolt. Consciously or unconsciously, she develops a strong sympathy for this fellow rebel, which explains both her complete change of opinion on the guilt of adulterous women, and—more specifically—the harshness of her judgment of Octave

---

[5] Maurice's hesitation in this sentence makes the reader wonder if Balzac himself was not somewhat hesitant to describe this craft as an art.

pronounced at the end of Maurice's narration. There are more similarities between Félicité and Honorine than even Félicité is aware of. Not only are they alike in their rebellion, they are also alike in the ultimate failure of their rebellion. Honorine, having had a passionate but ultimately disappointing love affair, attempts to continue to live independently by creating a cloistered life for herself. When she learns that even this solitary liberty is illusory—she has been under her husband's protection since the departure of her lover—she surrenders. Her return to her husband lasts only long enough for her to bear a son, thus honoring her end of the social pact she now understands is unbreakable. Having lived up to her name, she dies, a death that is for all practical purposes a suicide in the name of freedom, like Lucretia's. Félicité des Touches, having lived a long and successful period of independence, will return to Brittany after her trip to Italy. There, she will fall in love with Calyste du Guénic, who, at 21, is 24 years younger than Félicité. This love is impossible, not only because of the vast age difference, but because the astute Félicité realizes that Calyste's feelings for her—a combination of affection and admiration—have more to do with the desire to love than with love itself: "Ce sentiment, qui est plus le besoin d'aimer que l'amour, n'avait pas échappé sans doute à la terrible analyse de Camille Maupin" [*This sentiment, which is more the need to love than love itself, had not escaped the terrible analysis of Camille Maupin*] (*Béatrix*, 2:706). Ultimately, both women choose honor over passion, Honorine returning to her husband and Félicité choosing a strangely and equivocally maternal role vis-à-vis Calyste, facilitating both his adulterous affair with Béatrix de Rochefide and his socially acceptable and financially advantageous marriage to the beautiful young Sabine de Grandlieu.

For the *lecteur initié*, this failed revolt is a part of the privileged knowledge that the Narrator has shared with us. By reading *Béatrix* before (re)reading *Honorine*, we are able to recognize another similarity between two characters whose similarities are only barely noticeable in *Honorine* taken as a whole. The broad perspective of the *lecteur initié* allows us to see another link between them, the theme of the convent. Honorine, before she discovers the truth about her false independence, assures Maurice that she is as immune to the *monde* and its temptations as an old nun: "Moi [. . .] je ne suis pas une femme, je suis une religieuse arrivée à soixante-douze ans [. . .] Je suis religieuse, et vous me parlez d'un monde où je ne puis plus mettre les pieds" [*I. . . I am not a woman, I am nun who has reached the age of 72. I am a nun, and you speak to me of a world where I can no longer set foot*] (571). When Honorine discovers that her husband still watches over her, she proposes a convent as a last possible refuge, but Maurice assures her that this is not possible. The convent is not an option for her, because she is married; her husband, the magistrate, armed with the law, will not allow her to seek refuge in a cloister. Legally, she is under his power, like a slave. Félicité, unmarried, can and does choose the convent when the world finally crushes her revolt. Abandoning her fortune to her two protégés, Calyste and Sabine, she renounces her literary work and takes the veil. This surrender is as much a figurative suicide as is Honorine's return to Octave. Furthermore, the refutation of her literary work means that Camille Maupin commits suicide as well as Félicité des Touches. This remarkable woman not only removes herself from society, but attempts to remove as well all traces of the intellectual contribution she had made in the world of arts and letters where she flourished.

A careful study of the evolution of *Honorine* suggests that Balzac was conscious of the similarities between Félicité and Honorine, and that he sought to exploit them quite purposefully in the text. This *nouvelle* began, as we have seen, as an unframed tale with a happy ending. The frame was the second major step in the composition. When Balzac added Félicité des Touches, Léon de Lora, and Claude Vignon to *Honorine*, he took care to change the time-setting of the nouvelle from 1839 to 1836. This was completely logical, as we know from *Béatrix* that Félicité entered a convent in 1838, but this is just the sort of detail that Balzac was prone to overlook in his rewritings; the fact that he paid close attention to the dates in this case suggests that the author had the novel *Béatrix* on his mind when he wrote *Honorine*. The first part of *Béatrix*, which ends with Félicité's entry into the convent, was written in 1842, so we know that Balzac had decided on Félicité's fate when he placed her in the frame of *Honorine*. However, it was not until after Félicité was added to the frame that Balzac changed the ending of the story of Honorine and Octave. This is evidenced by a suppressed passage from the opening part of the frame, in which Balzac mocks the motif of the framed narrative: "vieille machine fourbie dont abusent les éditeurs" [*a clumsy old gimmick overused by editors*] (2:1415-16, var g). This detail suggests that the addition of Félicité des Touches to the frame preceded the decision to change the ending, as this lighthearted tone is wholly inconsistent with the tragic fate of the characters in the framed story. We can only speculate as to Balzac's reasons for this change in the ending of Honorine's story, but the evolution of the text and the order in which changes were made lead me to conclude that at some point, either before or after the addition of Félicité des Touches to *Honorine,* Balzac saw the similarities between his two characters and decided to give them a similar ending.

A final comment remains to be made on the presence of Mlle des Touches in *Honorine:* Even without the similarities between the two characters spelled out in the preceding pages, Félicité serves as a link of the most obvious and superficial kind between *Honorine* and *Béatrix.* This obvious connection lies over the more subtle thematic connections; not only the theme of the rebellious woman, but also the related yet distinct theme of the renegade wife. At first glance, Félicité des Touches and Béatrix de Rochefide would seem to be two characters with nothing in common, but considering *Béatrix* in light of *Honorine* highlights the fact that Béatrix is herself a woman in revolt. The virtuous Honorine has as much in common with the immoral Béatrix as she does with the admirable Félicité. Both are aristocrats married to men with whom they are sexually incompatible; both flee with a lover who later abandons them; both eventually return to their husband. The similarities end there, of course: Honorine rejects a second lover, Béatrix seduces Calyste out of spite; Honorine returns to her husband in spite of her love for Maurice, while Béatrix returns to her husband because of her desire for La Palférine—her third *amant en titre.* Balzac wrote in the preface to the first edition of *Béatrix:*

> Sans Béatrix, l'auteur aurait oublié de peindre les sentiments qui retiennent encore les femmes, après une chute. Quand certaines femmes du haut rang ont sacrifié leur position à quelque violente passion, quand elles ont méconnu les lois, ne trouvent-elles pas dans l'orgueil de la race, dans la valeur qu'elles se donnent et dans leur supériorité même, des barrières presque aussi difficiles à passer que celles déjà franchies, et qui sont à la fois sociales et naturelles? N'était-ce pas aussi l'un des plus beaux accidents de la passion, que cet ennoblissement dû à l'amour vrai et qui peut relever une femme tombée? (635)

Without Beatrix, the author would have neglected to paint the senti-
ments that still hold women after a fall. When certain women of high
rank have sacrificed their position to some violent passion, when they
have scorned laws, don't they find, in the pride of their race, in the
value that they give themselves and in their very superiority, barriers
as difficult to pass as those that they have already crossed, and which
are at once social and natural? Isn't that also one of the most beautiful
accidents of passion, that ennoblement due to true love which can raise
up anew a fallen woman?

Honorine, a character created three years after this preface was written, is
an example of the fallen woman who raises herself up again, by respecting
that second set of barriers. Béatrix, who is quite different in the novel from
the romantic heroine described here, is a woman who falls again and
again.

In his study of Balzac's recurring characters, Anthony Pugh suggested that the addition of Félicité des Touches to *Honorine* was merely
the result of the contemporaneous composition of the two texts (308-9).
This is only a small part of the explanation, but the multiple links between
Honorine and *Béatrix,* and between the three principal female characters
involved, suggests that there were much more profound and much more
complicated reasons for this addition. Studying them together suggests
that the intertextuality between these two works is much stronger than
merely a shared character. When viewed as intertexts, *Béatrix* and *Hon-*
orine shed a great deal of light not only on Balzac's views on marriage
and adultery, but also the larger question of the social role of women, all
important themes in *La Comédie humaine.* Finally, we should note that
none of these connections is explicitly mentioned either by the Narrator, or
by the novelist who allegedly tells us everything. If we as readers become
complacent, and pay too much attention to Balzac's reputation and not
enough to his text(s), it becomes easy to overlook what the Narrator does
not explicitly point out for us.

People Listening and Not Hearing: *Gobseck* in the Faubourg Saint-Germain

In Honorine, a narratee's explicit commentary helps guide the readers' reaction to an object story. In *Gobseck,* it is the lack of response on the part of the diegetic narratees that stands out, leading the reader to ask questions about what the frame contributes to the *nouvelle* as a whole. Like *Sarrasine, Gobseck* is a case in which the original version of a text, in this case *Les Dangers de l'inconduite* (1831), predates the system of recurring characters. In *Les Dangers,* a lawyer tells an aristocratic family the tale of a noblewoman who is led astray, eventually falling victim to a ruthless moneylender as well as to her unprincipled lover. The principal narratee of *Les Dangers* is the daughter of the family, for whom the lawyer's story is meant to be a lesson in good conduct, as the title indicates (Citron, intro, 2:945-46). As *Les Dangers de l'inconduite* evolved into *Gobseck,* as the family became the Grandlieus, as the lawyer became Derville, the moneylender Gobseck, etc., the import of the object story became far more complex, and the focus of Derville's narration changed. Camille de Grandlieu, the young girl whose marital project gives Derville a reason to tell his story, has lost much of her importance as a narratee; she is even dismissed from the Grandlieu *salon* halfway through the story. The primary motivation for storytelling is no longer to advise the young girl, but to arrange her marriage; Derville is acting more as the agent of the Restaud family and Gobseck than as an adviser to Camille. Yet this act of narration does retain an underlying didactic purpose. In the first chapter, I discussed the political aspect of Gobseck's metadiegetic narration, seen in the old man's hatreds and class resentments. These resentments, joined with the occult powers that he gains through the manipulation of money, make him an extremely formidable character. By telling this story, Derville is revealing to the Grandlieus—and Balzac to the reader—the power of money in the new society of the nineteenth century, demonstrating how laws and even great names are subject to those who understand the power of gold in the new era. Even with Gobseck dead, his victims remain vulnerable, and his *compères,* the dozen or so "rois silencieux et inconnus" [*silent and unknown kings*] of the café Thémis (976), remain active. With this story Balzac seems to be, as Allan Pasco said, "sounding the alarm" among the ruling classes that the old order is gone, that new rules have been established. The greatest danger comes not from the power of gold and the little men who manipulate it, but from the refusal or inability of the great aristocrats to understand the new rules and the very real "danger that threatens them" (Pasco, *Novel Configurations,* 65). This lack of understanding is personified in *Gobseck* by the vicomtesse de Grandlieu and her brother, the comte de Born.

Mme de Grandlieu, living again in her Parisian *hôtel,* her fortune and her social position restored to her, shows herself to be of the same mind-set as so many of Balzac's old-line aristocrats. She thinks that the Restoration has completely erased the Revolution. She continues to think in terms of titles and noble clans, defending her family name against a *mésalliance.* Her *snobisme* is clear not only in her objections to her daughter's marrying the grandson of a *vermicellier,* but also, and even more interestingly, in her condescending attitude toward Derville. When Derville informs the vicomtesse and her brother that he in fact married Fanny Malvaut—the beautiful and virtuous working girl that Gobseck told him about—Mme de Grandlieu says, with an amused wonder that borders on the contemptuous: "Le pauvre garçon [. . .] avouerait cela devant vingt personnes avec sa franchise ordinaire" [*The poor boy would admit that in front of twenty people with his usual frankness*] (978). The *pauvre garçon* is the man to whom she owes the restitution of her fortune. This anachronistic elitism might seem nothing more than a rather banal character trait of a *grande dame,* but this arrogance and shortsightedness are the blinders that prevent Mme de Grandlieu and the rest of her class from seeing either the strength of the new moneymen or the weakness of their own position in the new society.

Mme de Grandlieu fails to understand how the story of Derville's former neighbor can possibly affect her existence: "Mais je ne vois rien là-dedans qui puisse nous concerner" [*But I can see nothing in any of this which could possibly concern us*] (978). When she makes this objection, Derville has already told some remarkable aspects of Gobseck's story. Most notably, she has heard the old miser expound on his philosophy of gold ("l'or est le spiritualisme de vos sociétés actuelles" [*Gold is the spirituality of your modern-day societies*] 976); she has also witnessed a demonstration of the power Gobseck derives from gold, as he makes an elegant countess tremble. Most strikingly, she has heard of the mysterious men who sit under the sign of justice at the café Thémis,[6] and who are, according to Gobseck, "les arbitres de *vos* destinées" [*the arbiters of* your *destinies*] (976, emphasis mine). These last two points hit especially close to home. Even if she has not yet recognized Mme de Restaud in the anonymous countess of the rue du Helder, Mme de Grandlieu should acknowledge that Gobseck's reach extends quite high in the social world. Furthermore, Gobseck's jurisdiction among the judges of the café Thémis—"Moi, j'ai l'œil sur les fils de familles [. . .et] les gens du monde" [*I keep an eye on the sons of noble families and the society people*] (977)—is essentially Mme de Grandlieu's world. Her lack of comprehension stems from an inability or an unwillingness to recognize that someone of her stature could be threatened by a miser living in a run-down building in a bad neighborhood. Safe in her *hôtel*, protected by her name and her fortune, she does not understand how far Gobseck's tentacles extend into the faubourg Saint-Germain.

This refusal to acknowledge the world socially beneath her is Mme de Grandlieu's flaw as a listener, and it is the fatal flaw of her class. The shortsighted arrogance of the upper class is further underlined by the presence of the comte de Born in the *nouvelle*. His presence in the text might seem virtually superfluous; at one point, as he nods off in the middle of Derville's narration, it seems that he is meant only to provide comic relief. Perhaps he is meant also to suggest a nominal male authority at this familial gathering where the all-important question of a marriage for the fatherless Camille will be decided, although it is clear that his sister is the real authority in this matter. The dozing count does perform a brief but important role as a narratee, when his interest is piqued by the mention of a familiar name in Derville's story, Maxime de Trailles: "le comte Maxime de Trailles est un être singulier [. . .] anneau brillant qui pourrait unir le bagne et la haute société" [*Count Maxime de Trailles is a singular person. . . a brilliant ring who can link the prisons and the highest society*] (983). The comte de Born can recognize de Trailles, who is part of the masculine world of clubs and theaters and actresses' apartments that his sister—at least officially—would be unfamiliar with. As a recognizable link between Gobseck and the aristocracy, de Trailles serves to bring the

---

[6] In Greek mythology, Themis is the muse of Justice. The name of the café, which did not exist, was added to the *Furne corrigé* (Pléiade, 1566-67, var *a* and nb 1).

story home for the two aristocrats listening. The old moneylender's close-
ness to the *monde* should become even more obvious when Derville
recounts the scene in which Maxime and Gobseck face off, and the
symbiotic nature of the relationship between the dandy and the usurer is
revealed:

> Vous faites une éponge de moi, mordieu! et vous m'encouragez à me
> gonfler au milieu du monde, pour me presser dans les moments de crise
> [. . .] Sans les dissipateurs, que deviendrez-vous? nous sommes à nous
> deux l'âme et le corps. (986)
> *You make a sponge out of me, by God! You encourage me to fill myself*
> *up in society, just so you can wring me out in moments of crisis. With-*
> *out the dissipators, what would become of you? The two of us are body*
> *and soul.*

Derville mentions another name, probably by inadvertance, that shows
that Maxime is not the only link between the lowest and highest levels of
society:

> le jeune homme revient en donnant la main à une jeune femme en qui
> je reconnus cette comtesse dont le lever m'avait autrefois été dépeint
> par Gobseck, l'une des deux filles du bonhomme Goriot. (987)
> *The young man came back holding the hand of a young woman in*
> *whom I recognized that countess whose morning had once been de-*
> *scribed for me by Gobseck, one of the two daughters of old man Goriot.*

This reference to Mme de Restaud, already named as a "demoiselle Goriot" by the vicomtesse (962), further demonstrates how close Gobseck is
to the Grandlieus. It should now be evident that Gobseck's story directly
affects not just Mme de Grandlieu's caste, but potentially her family as
well. If de Trailles is a brilliant ring that could link "la bagne à la haute
société," Gobseck is the ring of gold that actually does so. The all-
consuming need for cash in the aristocratic circle of de Trailles and
Anastasie de Restaud has given Gobseck great power in Paris, even in the
noble faubourg. Mme de Grandlieu may not have fallen so far as to have
to sign her name to papers in Gobseck's spare cell, but she is as keenly

aware of the importance of money as is Maxime de Trailles, ready as she is to consent to a problematic marriage if the price is right.

Even after it is made plain to Mme de Grandlieu that Gobseck's reach has extended literally to the heart of her family, she remains blinded. Although we can assume a definite intelligence on the part of this character—she is described as "l'une des femmes les plus remarquables du faubourg Saint-Germain" (962)—she is utterly insensitive to what the reader finds most important in Derville's story: the awesome power of the philosophical miser, as well as that of the miser's philosophy. The whole story told, she rather brusquely returns to matters that fall within her very narrow scope of interest and comprehension, namely whether or not Ernest de Restaud has enough money to compensate for his mother's low birth:

> —. . .nous y penserons, répondit Mme de Grandlieu, M. Ernest doit être bien riche pour faire accepter sa mère par une famille comme la nôtre [. . .]
> —Mais, dit le comte de Born, Restaud *porte de gueules à la traverse* [etc.]. . . et c'est un très vieux blason.
> —C'est vrai, dit la vicomtessse, d'ailleurs Camille pourra ne pas voir sa belle-mère qui a fait mentir la devise RES TUTA!
> —Mme de Beauséant recevait Mme de Restaud, dit le vieil oncle.
> —Oh! dans ses raouts », répliqua la vicomtesse. (1013)

> *"We will think about it," replied Mme de Grandlieu, Monsieur Ernest will have to be quite rich for his mother to be accepted by a family like ours. . . ."*
> *"But," said the Count de Born, "Restaud bears the* porte de gueules à la traverse. . . *a very old coat of arms."*
> *"That's true," said the vicomtesse, "and in any case Camille could always refuse to receive her mother-in-law, who betrayed the family motto of* Res Tuta!"
> *"Mme de Beauséant received Mme de Restaud," said the old uncle.*
> *"Oh, at her open-houses," replied the vicomtesse.*

This brief dialogue, which has nothing to do with Gobseck, closes the *nouvelle*. At a first reading, this ending is anticlimactic, especially after the haunting scene of Gobseck's death, and the last reference to *Le Père*

Goriot may seem a bit gratuitous. But this passage actually makes an important point about the Grandlieu and Gobseck. Both Mme de Grandlieu and her brother are immune to the force of the story that Derville has just told. They are blind to the importance of anything outside of their mindset, questions that have long since outlived their importance, such as heraldry and arcane questions of etiquette, who is received by whom and under what circumstances. Mme de Grandlieu briefly, perhaps even unconsciously, articulates the importance of money—it is as important as her name—but her psychology and her self-image will not allow her to acknowledge that importance, or the man who incarnates the power of money.

The aristocrats' inability to appreciate Gobseck's story is an important part of the *nouvelle*. Thematically, it serves to link this fragment to the larger text in a way that is at least as important as the system of recurring characters. A first theme concerns *La Comédie humaine* as a historical reproduction, as a portrait of a specific time and place. In this regard, it is significant that this *nouvelle* is set in "l'hiver de 1829 à 1830" (961). This time-setting vividly underlines the fact that Mme de Grandlieu is fighting a rearguard action. A new revolution is about to take place, and the vicomtesse and her kind will lose still more of their social and political power. As the new society continues to evolve, further away from the one the vicomtesse thinks she still lives in, her daughter and daughter-in-law will share the social scene with such figures as Mme de Portenduère (*née* Ursule Mirouët) and the comtesse de Rastignac (the daughter of another *demoiselle Goriot*). In time, the vicomtesse's cousin, the duchesse de Grandlieu, will agree to become the social patroness of Maxime de Trailles's wife, still another *roturière* (*Béatrix*, 8:910-11). This theme parallels the point made by Pasco, that *Gobseck* is meant in part to serve as a warning, not just to the aristocracy, but to all people, that the insatiable need for money has weakened the very foundations of society, represented by the Grandlieu family: "One can sense Balzac's horror when Mme de Grandlieu fails to perceive how the story of Gobseck affects her family" (*Novels Configurations*, 65). Whether this horror is expressed as a warning of events to come or a regret for things already passed is debatable, but the fact of Balzac's frustration is hard to dispute.

The second thematic link between *Gobseck* and *La Comédie humaine,* discussed by Jean-Luc Seylaz in his "Réflexions sur *Gobseck,*" is more subtle; it has to do with the key Balzacian themes of power and secrecy. Secret power and the power of secrets are important and frequently seen elements of *La Comédie humaine.* The famous secret associations in Balzac's fictional world, the *Treize* and Vautrin's *Société des dix mille* are only the most obvious manifestations of Balzac's fascination with secrecy. On the other side of the Law—if not necessarily of Justice—is the secret police, represented by Malin de Gondreville, Peyrade, and Corentin, with the specter of Fouché floating obliquely behind them. The half-hidden actions of these shadowy characters animate the plots of *Les Chouans* and *Une Ténébreuse affaire.* The two sides clash, and ultimately fuse, in *Splendeurs et misères des courtisanes.* It is when Vautrin reaches the apex of his power, when the master criminal becomes chief of the secret police, that he slips away from the reader's view. We know that his career continues, but we never learn exactly what he does. It's a secret.

The Balzacian text is riddled with secrets. Reading a work of fiction often involves the discovery of a secret, the resolution of an enigma, but in Balzac's world, secrets are often the basis for an entire text. The whole of *Le Curé de village,* for example, is built on Véronique Graslin's secret passion. The princesse de Cadignan has lots of secrets, and in the end no one, not even the reader, is privy to all of them. Plots are often composed of multiple secrets running along a single plot line. *La Cousine Bette* probably offers the paradigmatic example of a text swarming with secrets: Baron Hulot's hidden debauchery causes his family's secret poverty, which leads Adeline to offer herself to Crevel; Hortense's discovery of Bette's secret 'lover' leads to the girl's own secret liaison with Wenceslas, which, when discovered, fuels Bette's secret hatred for her cousin's family, leading to Bette's secret alliance with Valérie Marneffe. In particular, an act of storytelling almost always involves the revelation of secret, and this is certainly the case in *Gobseck,* where Derville lifts the veil on the secret of the old miser.

Seylaz theorized that in Balzac's world, to have one's secret discovered is often to lose power. Vautrin's (temporary) defeat illustrates this point; he is arrested because his secrets have been discovered by Mlle Michonneau. Nucingen, who conducts many of his financial operations in secret, falls prey to Vautrin after the secret of his fortune is deduced by his fellow speculators. Gobseck is one of the few characters in *La Comédie*

humaine whose veil of secrecy is never penetrated.[7] If Derville knows the
old man's secrets, it is only because Gobseck chose to reveal them to him;
and on the one occasion when Derville chooses to share this secret knowledge, its importance is not grasped by the audience, and the secret remains
intact, as if the story had never been told within Balzac's fictional world.
The story has passed from Gobseck to Derville, and from Derville to the
Narratee and the reader, bypassing the Grandlieus completely. Thus even
after his death, Gobseck's secrets remain safe, and his power remains intact. Not even Vautrin, who speaks almost derisively of "le papa Gobseck," seems to grasp the raw power that is hidden beneath the plain
exterior, beneath the image that this old man has carefully cultivated. The
force of Gobseck, the transcendant power that other people's greed has
given him, is one of those things the reader knows about Balzac's world,
but that the inhabitants of that world are unaware of. Sharing secrets like
these with the author is one of the pleasures of Balzac's text. We observe
this world from the same, almost god-like point of view of the author.

For the reader, this hidden power and the danger that Gobseck represents illuminate the character, infusing him with a force and an energy
that is not immediately evident in his other appearances in other texts.
This case offers an excellent demonstration of the power of the system of
recurring characters. Once we have read this *nouvelle,* the character is
changed for all further readings of *La Comédie humaine.* For the *lecteur
initié,* Gobseck becomes not the name of a mere usurer—again, a very
common type both in Balzac and in European literature in general—but a
symbol that represents the awesome power of gold, a power created by the
force of human greed and ambition. Having read *Gobseck,* we understand
that those who do business with him are not merely borrowing money, as
the cruelly lucid Gobseck himself says: "le premier pas fait de ma porte à
mon bureau dénonce un désespoir" [*The first step from my door to my
desk announces despair*] (971). Those who enter the miser's room have
abandoned all hope. It is worth repeating that Gobseck is different from
the other misers of *La Comédie humaine.* He represents neither the force
of capitalism (like Nucingen), nor the vulgar obsession with a base metal

---

[7] Lizbeth Fischer is the exception to the rule. No one ever discovers the full extent of
Bette's machinations, but her plans are frustrated by arbitrary twists of fate (the hidden
hand of her creator).

(like Grandet), nor even this obsession taken to the level of the supernatural (like Facino Cane). Gobseck looms larger than his *confrères* because he is the incarnation of a moral force in Balzac's world, for his strength is the creation of human frailty.

Listening and Watching: *Je* and Taillefer in *L'Auberge rouge*

The narrating *je* of *L'Auberge rouge* plays as important a role as narratee as he does as narrator. In fact, the two roles are tightly intertwined. The narrator serves as the reader's eyes even as he relates the tale of the murder in Germany; even before the narration begins, the attention of this *chercheur de tableaux* is drawn to an enigmatic sadness in Taillefer's face. This initial connection between the two is essential to the development of the *nouvelle*. As Monsieur Hermann tells his story, Balzac uses the narrator to suggest Taillefer's guilt through the comments the narrator makes on Taillefer's actions as a listener. The banker's discomfort is obvious and increases as the story continues: he visibly reacts to the mention of Prosper Magnan's name, he develops a powerful thirst, begins to perspire noticeably, etc. Balzac also uses the narrator's female dinner companion to advance our suspicions about Taillefer. When Hermann remembers that Prosper's traveling companion's first name was Frédéric, this anonymous woman playfully kicks the narrator under the table and whispers: "Hein. . . S'il se nommait Frédéric" [*Ah, ah... and what if his name was Frederic*] (11:110). But this woman is merely playing a mildly malicious game; she knows Taillefer and seems to find him quite likable and sympathetic:

> C'est un ancien fournisseur des armées impériales, un bon homme assez original. Il s'est remarié par spéculation, et rend néanmoins sa femme extrêmement heureuse. Il a une jolie fille que, pendant fort longtemps, il n'a pas voulu reconnaître; mais la mort de son fils, tué malheureusement en duel, l'a contraint à la prendre avec lui, car il ne pouvait plus avoir d'enfants. [. . .] La perte de son fils unique a plongé ce cher homme dans un chagrin qui reparaît quelquefois. (91-92)
> *He's a former supplier for the imperial armies, a fairly odd fellow. He remarried in speculation, and nevertheless makes his wife extremely*

> *happy. He has a pretty daughter, whom, for quite a long time, he re-*
> *fused to recognize as his own; but the death of his son, sadly killed in a*
> *duel, forced him to take her in, because he cannot have anymore chil-*
> *dren. The loss of his only son plunged the dear man into a sorrow that*
> *comes back to him from time to time.*

And so the banker's melancholy is explained innocently enough. Ironically, it is this very justification that would convince the *lecteur initié*
of Taillefer's guilt, as soon as that name is attached to the "ancien four-
nisseur."

　　The reader of *Le Père Goriot* will recognize in Taillefer the cruel
and unjust father of Victorine and the eventual victim of Vautrin. The
anonymous dinner guest of *L'Auberge rouge* relates part of the story of
Taillefer and his daughter, but apparently she does not know it all. Her
version of the story mentions nothing about the reasons that lead Taillefer
to deny Victorine's paternity. Her description of him—as a "cher homme"
who is "contraint de la prendre"—implies that there is some justification
in his refusal. In *Le Père Goriot,* however, the Narrator tells us expressly
that Taillefer has rejected his daughter "enfin de pouvoir...transmettre [sa
fortune] en entier à son fils" [*In order to be able to leave his entire fortune
to his son*] (2:59); and Victorine's guardian, Mme Couture (an admittedly
biased witness) tells us that Victorine and her father resemble each other
"comme deux gouttes d'eau" (90). Finally, Vautrin, who naturally knows
the whole story of the crime committed in Germany, tells Rastignac that
Taillefer is guilty of "injustices" toward Victorine (144). But the reader of
L'Auberge rouge who has not read *Le Père Goriot* knows nothing of this;
this naive reader can only go by what the narrator sees and what his dinner
companion tells him (and us). For the naive reader, Taillefer's guilt is a
remote and perhaps somewhat surprising possibility.

　　When the story is finished, the narrator has become firmly convinced that Taillefer is guilty, but his companion recoils from the idea. She
even reproaches the narrator for his suspicions:

> Vous agissez en jeune homme, et bien légèrement, me dit ma voisine.
> Regardez Taillefer! tenez!. . . Un assassin, que le récit de cette aventure

aurait dû mettre en supplice, pourrait-il montrer autant de calme? N'a-
t-il pas un air vraiment patriarcal?[8]
"You're acting like a young man, and quite lightly," said my neighbor.
"Look at Taillefer! Come now!. . . an assassin, whom the telling of this
tale would surely have tortured, could he show as much calm? Doesn't
he seem like a real patriarch?"

The narrator persists and suggests that his friend ask Taillefer if he has
ever traveled in Germany; Taillefer responds that he has not, and another
guest challenges him:

—Que dis-tu donc là Taillefer? . . . n'étais-tu pas dans les vivres, à
la campagne de Wagram?
—Ah, oui! répondit M. Taillefer, cette fois-là, j'y suis allé. (113)
"What are you saying there, Taillefer? Weren't you in supplies
during the Wagram campaign?
"Oh yes," M. Taillefer responded, "at that time, I went there."

This lie is a strong indication for the reader—naive or experienced—that
Taillefer is guilty. Nevertheless, the narrator's friend persists in believing
in his innocence ("Vous vous trompez, c'est un bon homme" [*You're*
wrong, he's a fine man]) and in trying to pull the narrator back from his
quest for the unpleasant and socially inconvenient truth. Eventually, her
own words become evidence of Taillefer's guilt, as his discomfort becomes actual physical agony, *une supplice.*
    Balzac gives no indication as to whether this lady changes her
mind about Taillefer, for the story quickly progresses to its second phase.
We now see that Monsieur Hermann's narration, fatal for Taillefer, has
become a vital matter for the narrator. After he has become convinced of
Taillefer's guilt and for all practical purposes hounded the man to his
death, the narrator sees a girl who has very recently caused him a *coup de*
foudre. This girl is, of course, Victorine. Torn between his love and his
personal ethical code, the narrator tells his story to a group of friends, "un
sanhédrin de consciences pures. . .ceux de mes amis auxquels j'accorde le
plus de probité, de délicatesse et d'honneur," [*a sanhedrin of pure con-*

[8] For the reader of *Le Père Goriot*, the use of this adjective is an additional irony.

sciences. . . those of my friends in whom I saw the most probity, delicacy, and honor] including a priest, a judge, "un puritain," and a duke "dont la fortune consistait en biens confisqués à des protestants réfractaires lors de la révocation de l'édit de Nantes" [*a duke whose fortune consisted of goods confiscated from refractory Protestants at the revocation of the Edict of Nantes*].[9] This council, which represents "toutes les opinions sociales, toutes les vertus pratiques" (118-19), does nothing to help the narrator resolve his dilemma. Indeed, for the most part, they do not seem even to understand why there is a dilemma; his older friends criticize his excess of scruples, and his younger friends hope to profit from it by finding out the name of this beautiful heiress. In the end it is the Puritan who formulates what seems to be the general opinion of this Parisian Sanhedrin, and of society in general: "Imbécile, pourquoi lui as-tu demandé s'il était de Beauvais!" [*Imbecile, why did you ask him if he was from Beauvais!*] (122).

The ending of *L'Auberge rouge* has been criticized for this shift in tone, from the heavy atmosphere that surrounds Hermann's act of narration and the narrator's harassment of Taillefer, to the comedic, almost theatrical tone of the "sanhédrin" scene. There is nonetheless a connection between the two parts of the *nouvelle*. The bemused indifference of the narrator's friends matches the determined goodwill of his dinner companion. Just as she insists on believing in Taillefer's innocence in spite of all evidence, so do the narrator's virtuous counselors advise him to take the easy way out, as they variously see it. The truth is ugly and inconvenient, and abstract notions of right and wrong will do no one any real good—Taillefer is dead and Prosper Magnan has left no heirs. The refusal of all these people to confront the truth is not completely dissimilar—although more willful—to the vicomtesse de Grandlieu's inability to recognize Gobseck's power; both stories present the theme of a society unwilling to recognize unpleasant truths. In *L'Auberge rouge,* the narrator is the only man in Paris offended by the crime that lies behind the Taillefer fortune. This is true not only of the nouvelle, but of *La Comédie humaine* in general; Vautrin knows all about the murder, but he of course is a special case, he sees Taillefer as something of a spiritual brother: "C'est un de

---

[9] This, of course, is a highly ironic reference for Balzac, whose views on this source of wealth are to be found in *L'Interdiction* and *Madame Firmiani.*

mes gaillards qui ont de l'indépendance dans les opinions" [*He's one of my boys who have a bit of independence in their thinking*] (*PG*, 3:143). In *La Peau de chagrin,* Emile also knows the truth about Taillefer's wealth (*PC*, 10:96), but has no compunctions about exploiting that wealth for his own purposes. Even the narrator is not presented as being above reproach, for at the end of the *nouvelle,* it is unclear to the reader what, if any, decision he has made or indeed what decision he should make.

When we say that the act of narration is rarely innocent in *La Comédie humaine,* we must bear in mind that this act includes not only the storytellers, but the story's audience as well. Narrators and narratees very often play equally important roles in the interpretation of Balzac's framed narratives. As we have seen, Balzac's listeners are chosen with great care. A character listening to an object story is very often touched by the meaning or meanings it contains, and then serves as either a conduit out to the larger text, or as a reflector back into the object story. Sometimes a narratee can perform both functions, like Félicité des Touches in *Honorine.* In either case, these characters comment and complicate, destabilize and confuse both text and reader, creating an ambiguity that enriches the text and challenges the reader. The questions raised by the relationship between story, narrator, and narratee become more complicated when the roles for a given story are not so clearly delineated. In the next chapter, I will examine some of these cases where the act of storytelling is shared by different characters, when no single character acts as a sole narrator or narratee, and some characters play both roles in the same text. In these texts, the use of multiple characters, each one bringing his or her own history and textual connections to the story/frame construction, adds remarkable resonance to the stories told.

Chapter III

Sharing Tasks and Blurring Lines

IN THE FIRST TWO CHAPTERS, WE SAW how Balzac used the figures in his frames to influence our interpretation of stories told, and to bind his many works into a greater textual whole. In some works, these characters, whether narrarors or narratees, affect our perception of an object story directly, through explicit commentaries or reactions; in other cases the effect is much more subtle, the result of some details unmentioned by either the Narrator or other characters, but apparent to us because of what we know about a character or situation from other texts. These characters can change our perceptions of other characters, of the object stories they tell or hear, of individual texts and of *La Comédie humaine* as a whole. In most cases, the structure of Balzac's framed stories is fairly straightforward, and can be represented by the following schema:

$$Balzac—\{Narrator—[narrator—(object\ story)—narratee(s)]—Narratee\}—reader$$

| A | B | C | D | C | B | A |

This model is in itself overly simplified, of course; there are several variations, most notably in the *je*-narrated stories, where the Narrator and Narratee are not explicitly present and where the narratee is ambiguous. While this basic structure is in general adhered to, we do sometimes find very complicated structures that raise new questions in the reader's mind, further complicating our task as readers, as well as the structure and the movement of Balzac's textual mobile.

The texts already discussed present us with some idea of these more complicated structures and the questions they create. In *Gobseck,* for instance, Derville's diegetic narration contains the miser's metadiegetic, autobiographical narration. This technique adds several important nuances to the text. Most significantly, the reader is allowed to "hear" Gobseck in his own words, sharing with Derville the experience of learning about the old man's philosophy and subterranean power. To this is added the spectacle of the Grandlieus' incapacity to comprehend these same words, passed to them through the neutral conduit of Derville. Further examples are to be found in *Facino Cane* and *L'Auberge rouge,* where the *je* serve both as diegetic narrators and metadiegetic narratees. This strategy draws the reader into the heart of the story, along with the narrating *je,* as Balzac manipulates us through these anonymous, amorphous first-person characters, guiding our reaction to the object stories that they relay to us. In *Facino Cane,* the story of the blind Venetian gains at least a temporary credibility as we, along with the narrator, are infected with the old man's gold fever. In *L'Auberge rouge,* the detective story aspect in the first part of the *nouvelle* depends on the reader's willingness to be persuaded of the efficacy of the narrator's talents of observation, just as the moral effect of the second half of the story depends on our willingness to share his sense of outrage.

Three *nouvelles* from *La Comédie humaine* contain object stories set in narrative structures that go well beyond the simple one diagrammed above. Each of them presents us with two basic questions: 1) why Balzac chose to depart from the classic model in these cases; 2) what is the effect of this deviation from the norm. In *La Maison Nucingen, Autre étude de femme,* and *Un Prince de la bohème,* we have three opportunities to explore some more complicated narrative structures and to address those questions they raise.

Into the Abyss: Reading the *mises-en-abyme* in *La Maison Nucingen*

In 1836, in an elegant but unspecified Parisian restaurant, a man and a woman are sharing an intimate dinner in a private dining room. In the adjacent room, on the other side of a thin wall, a party of four men are having a rather more boisterous evening, and the subject of their conversation captures the attention of the couple next door. The story the four men share is so fascinating—and so well told—that it is "sténographiée" in the memory of the eavesdropping man (6:331), and it is his version of this story that we read in *La Maison Nucingen*. The subject of that conversation—or at least its point of departure—is the origin of Rastignac's fortune, and that story is inextricably tied to the story of the baron de Nucingen, the banker who is the symbol of unprincipled capitalism in *La Comédie humaine*, and who is also the husband of Rastignac's lover. As Bixiou tells the story, Nucingen's colossal fortune is the sum of several more modest fortunes invested with Nucingen's bank. Through a complicated series of market manipulations and one fraudulent bankruptcy, Nucingen essentially swindled a great many people, committing the great crime that lies behind not only his own great fortune, but Rastignac's as well. As narrator, Bixiou benefits from the active participation of his narratees: the journalist Emile Blondet, the publisher Finot, and the stock speculator Couture. Thus we have an already complicated structure for this story—the eavesdropping man becomes a narrating *je*, and he narrates the story of another act of narration, the one performed by Bixiou—which is made more complicated by Bixiou's unorthodox style of narration. Before addressing the possible reasons for and interpretations of this double frame, there are some basic remarks to be made on the characters in the frames, and why they are well chosen for this storytelling situation.

We know very little about the narrating *je* who presents Bixiou's act of narration to us. He is a Parisian, has some familiarity with the better restaurants, and is in a social and financial situation that allows him to share a private and probably expensive dinner with a female companion, who, unfortunately, he has the discretion not to name. Most importantly, he recognizes the four men in the next room without even seeing them— he knows them well enough to recognize their voices. All of these men are recurring characters: Bixiou and Blondet are well known to the *lecteur initié*, as both are frequent if usually secondary actors in many different works; Finot is less prominent, but is an important player in those works that deal with the world of publishing and journalism; Couture is the least prominent of the four, but the narrator obligingly provides us with all the information we need about him. In this, the narrating *je* of the text greatly resembles the Narrator. In fact, a close parallel can be drawn between the narrator of *La Maison Nucingen* and the way that the Narrator functions in

Honorine: in both cases, a specific setting and date are given, and the characters present in the frame, gathered together for a meal, are described in much the same way. This is especially true as regards Camille Maupin, who is chiefly described by her reputation, as a brilliant, well-known, and well-respected author; Bixiou, Blondet, et al. are also described more by their reputations ("quatre . . . hardis cormorans," 330) than by Balzac's famously detailed physical descriptions.

Of course, the narrating *je* of *La Maison Nucingen* cannot be the Narrator. Like the other anonymous first-person narrators, the *je* in this story is as much a corporeal character as is Bixiou or Blondet; he is with another person, eats a meal, makes a noise as he leaves the restaurant, etc. This distinction leads us to a first discernable effect of the narrative structure of *La Maison Nucingen:* by using a narrator to set the scene for Bixiou's narration and to describe to the reader the reputations of the recurring characters present, Balzac succeeds in making those reputations seem more vital to us. We see firsthand, as it were, that these men are well known in the world they live in, and that they are all remarkable, if not necessarily admirable. The narrator's anonymity serves to expand, even to blur, the borders of Balzac's fiction. If this *nouvelle* were narrated by Bianchon, his presence would draw the reader back to what is really a rather limited group—the recognizable characters of Balzac's Parisian society—, limiting at the same time the reputations of these four men to a fixed social circle. By allowing the narrator to remain anonymous, Balzac creates the illusion that the fame of his created characters extends beyond the world familiar to the *lecteur initié,* perhaps even beyond the Narrator's field of vision. Also important is the narrator's use of the present tense when describing the four men, which gives their lives and reputations a sense "of immediacy that is lacking in the Narrator's usual past-tense expository passages. Combining the recurring characters with the anonymous narrator draws the reader that much closer to Balzac's fictional world; we are even given the illusion that we are a part of it, since the lack of an explicit narratee who corresponds directly to the narrating *je* casts the reader in that role. Thus the whole *nouvelle* seems to be a direct address to the reader. We are, for all practical purposes, in the same position as the narrator's anonymous dinner companion, right next to Bixiou as he spins his tale.

In the room next door, Bixiou's act of narration is quite unlike the others we have seen. Balzac's narrators, again, are generally quite straightfoward storytellers, they tend to go from the beginning, to the middle, to the end of their story. Bixiou's narration is a piece of performance art, full of digressions, asides, jokes; he insults his own "characters" and his narratees, who return the favor handsomely. Balzac's narratees have a habit of interrupting, but none do so as aggressively and disrespectfully as those who are listening to Bixiou. The narrator's introductory description prepares us for a lively and acerbic story with its presentation of Bixiou:

> le plus malicieux des quatre, son nom suffira : Bixiou! Hélas! ce n'est
> plus le Bixiou de 1825, mais celui de 1836, le misanthrope bouffon à
> qui l'on connaît le plus de verve et de mordant, un diable enragé
> d'avoir dépensé tant d'esprit en pure perte, furieux de ne pas avoir
> ramassé son épave dans la dernière révolution, donnant son coup de
> pied à chacun en vrai Pierrot des Funambules, sachant son époque et les
> aventures scandaleuses sur le bout de son doigt, les ornant de ses in-
> ventions drolatiques, sautant sur toutes les épaules commme un clown,
> et tâchant d'y laisser une marque à la façon du bourreau. (531)
>
> *the most malicious of the four, his name will suffice: Bixiou! Alas! It's*
> *no longer the Bixiou of 1825, but the Bixiou of 1836, the misanthropic*
> *buffoon who was known for having the most verve and mordant wit, a*
> *devil enraged for having spent so much wit at a pure loss, furious for*
> *not having made his pile during the last revolution, giving a kick to*
> *everyone like a real Pierrot of the Funambules theatre, knowing his*
> *times and all the scandalous adventures like the back of his hand,*
> *embellishing them with his own comic inventions, leaping on every-*
> *one's shoulders like a clown, and hoping to leave his mark like the*
> *executioner.*

This admirable portrait is not without its own *verve* and *mordant*—even the punctuation is revealing ("Bixiou! Hélas!")—and it tells us all we need to know about Bixiou: he has the privileged knowledge ("les aventures scandaleuses") and the talent that make his stories interesting to his listeners, and to us. In these respects, Bixiou is not very much different, as a narrator, from Bianchon, another talented storyteller, but there are essential differences between the two characters. The narrator's description of

Bixiou implies a great deal of comic energy, and several of the terms used suggest performance; both of these aspects are clearly demonstrated in the narration, and are in direct contrast to the professional gravity that is the cornerstone of Bianchon's reputation as a *raconteur*. Bixiou is also bitter and resentful, even cruel, a misanthrope where Bianchon is a healer. Bixiou's malice is clearly discernable in his story, making him more interesting both as a narrator and as a character.

The other characters in this framed frame are equally interesting, and their presence is equally important. First among the narratees is Blondet: " homme de beaucoup d'esprit, mais décousu, brillant, capable, paresseux, . . . Fin comme une soubrette de comédie" [*a man of great wit, but undisciplined, brilliant, capable, lazy, sharp as a* soubrette de comédie] (330). Blondet has some important knowledge that is essential to the main story, it is he who tells the others about Nucingen's earliest false bankruptcies (338), which served as the preludes to the final grand swindle that established Nucingen as the richest of Balzac's bankers, and established Rastignac at the same time. This journalist belongs to the same race of Bohemian quasi-artists as Bixiou, and his lazy wit makes him a perfect foil for the febrile narrator, as he returns Bixiou's barbs throughout the narration. Blondet thus serves as a balance, even as ballast, for Bixiou. We get the distinct impression that without Blondet's critical admonitions ("allons un peu plus vite! dit Blondet, tu marivaudes" [*"A bit quicker!" said Blondet, "you're doing Marivaux"*] 351; "mon cher, tu ne racontes pas, tu blagues" [*"My dear boy, you're not telling stories, you're telling jokes"*] 363), Bixiou's verbal play with Finot and Couture might lead him irretrievably farther away from the main line of his narration, and the final secret would never be revealed.

Also present is Finot: "Peu parleur, froid, gourmé, sans esprit" [*Taciturn, cold, stiff, without wit*] (330), Finot is a something of a buffoon; his attempts to join in the repartee among his three companions fall somewhat flat, and a good part of Bixiou's pleasure as a storyteller comes from the confusion his narrating style inspires in the *parvenu* editor. But if Finot lacks wit, this does not mean he is a complete fool; as his name implies, Finot possesses an indisputable if limited native intelligence. He is, after all, the only one of the four who is rich ("parvenu," 330), and he got rich by exploiting the work of the very *spirituels* Blondet, Bixiou, and the rest of their quick-witted brethren. This ironic situation is reflected in the text, albeit in a different context, by an exchange between the two *mystificateurs:*

> —Blondet, Blondet, pourquoi donc sommes-nous si pauvres? s'écria Bixiou.
> —Et pourquoi Finot est-il si riche? reprit Blondet. (362)
> *"Blondet, Blondet, then why are we so poor?" cried Bixiou.*
> *"And why is Finot so rich?" rejoined Blondet.*

Finot is in many ways the descendant of the *paysan rusé* of earlier French literature. His business sense is acute, but we sense that he will never have enough money to compensate for his essential vulgarity. "Je ne le formerai jamais!" [*I'll never educate him*], laments Bixiou at one point (346).

The relationship between Bixiou and Finot is the primary narrator-narratee relationship in *La Maison Nucingen,* as the publisher agrees to forgive a debt of 500 francs in return for the caricaturist's story. Blondet and Couture, who both have information that supplements Bixiou's narration, but do not seem to know the whole story, serve in some sense as auxiliaries both to the narrator and to the narratee. An interesting phrase in Bixiou's negotiation with Finot hints at another level in their relationship. Announcing that his story is worth 500 francs, the storyteller calls on Blondet and Couture as witnesses: "Vous êtes témoins, dit Bixiou, que je n'appartiens pas à cet impertinent [. . .] mon bon Finot, je dirai l'histoire sans personnalités, et nous serons quittes" [*"You're all witness," said Bixiou, "that I don't belong to this impertinent. . . my dear Finot, I'll tell the story without personal attacks, and we'll be even"*] (337). This insolent declaration of independence is in fact a recognition of a dependent relationship that Bixiou clearly resents, and that he attempts to avenge by repeatedly mocking the slow-witted editor as he tells the story. This is most evident during the long digression on "l'improper," which Finot never really understands. But Bixiou's efforts to reclaim his dignity through mockery are of course futile. This is Balzac's world, and Art remains in the service of Commerce.

Finally, there is Couture, the only one of the company who is not part of the journalistic milieu. The narrator recognizes this anomaly, after introducing Couture as someone who "se maintient par la Spéculation. Il ente affaire sur affaire, le succès de l'une couvre l'insuccès de l'autre," [*lives by Speculation. He piles deal on deal, the success of one covering the failure of the other*] the narrator acknowledges that, "[é]videmment, il n'est pas à sa place" [*evidently, he's not in his place*] (330-31). Couture would probably be a good listener in any case. Like Finot, his name suggests possible interpretations of the character, indicating sharpness (*couteau*, knife) and also—from *couture*, sewing—an ability to piece fragments together into wholes, be it the seemingly disparate parts of a story or the successful and failed speculations that he strings together to earn a living. It is this last trait that makes Couture a well-chosen narratee for this fractured story of high finance. Professionally speaking, he is a moneyman; his presence responds to the financial theme of Bixiou's story, for the dénouement of the story takes place largely on the Parisian *Bourse*. This professional identity that at first makes him seem out of place is in fact what makes Couture effective as a link between the three men of letters—or at least of the industry of the printed word—and the world of Finance where Nucingen moves. Couture's perceptiveness is evident as the story unfolds, and is recognized by his narrator. He guesses at the central point of the story before Bixiou even begins:

> —Il va nous démontrer, dit en souriant Couture, que Nucingen a
> fait la fortune de Rastignac.
> —Tu n'en es pas si loin que tu le penses, reprit Bixiou. (337-38)
> *"He's going to show us," said Couture with a smile, "that Nucingen made Rastignac's fortune."*
> *"You're not as far off as you might think," replied Bixiou.*

Couture's observations are often marked by the vocabulary of the financial world. A bit further on, while trying to encourage Bixiou to tell his story, he swears by the blessed name of the Stockholder, anticipating the subject before hearing it, displaying again the sort of prescience that Balzac often gives to his characters:

> —Hé, par le saint nom de l'Actionnaire, dit Couture, raconte-nous
> ton histoire?
> —J'y étais d'un cran, repartit Bixiou; mais avec ton juron, tu me
> mets au dénouement. (337)

> *"Oh, by the blessed name of the Stockholder," said Couture, "just tell us your story?"*
>
> *"I was just a hair away from it," rejoined Bixiou; "but with your curse, you push me up to the dénouement."*

Couture displays an even sharper perception later in the text, with his succinct reaction to Bixiou's description of the wealthy, naïve, young aristocrat, Beaudenord:

> —Bref, un *moutard* qui tenait ses dix-huit mille livres de rente à la disposition des premières actions venues, dit Couture.
>
> —Ce diable de Couture a tellement l'habitude d'anticiper les dividendes, qu'il anticipe le dénouement de mon histoire. (347)
>
> *"In short, a pigeon holding his 18,000 pounds a year out for the first shares that came along," said Couture.*
>
> *"That devil Couture is so much in the habit of anticipating dividends, that he's anticipating the dénouement of my story."*

One can almost hear Couture's regret of his inability to find enough *moutards* like Beaudenord.

But Couture is more than just a perceptive and insightful listener. Like Blondet, he also provides an important piece of information to Bixiou's scattershot narration. Nucingen is known to all of the men present, but as Couture points out, the other three can only see the tip of the financial iceberg:

> [. . .] pour le bien connaître, il faut être dans les affaires. Chez lui, la banque est un très petit département : il y a les fournitures du gouvernement, les vins, les laines, les indigos, enfin tout ce qui donne matière à un gain quelconque.[1] Son génie embrasse tout [. . .]. La Banque envisagée ainsi devient toute une politique, elle exige une tête puissante, et porte alors un homme bien trempé à se mettre au-dessus des lois de la probité, dans lesquelles il se trouve à l'étroit. (339)

---

[1] This list of commodities that Nucingen trades in recalls the goods accumulated by Gobseck after his decline has begun and is a capitalistic abstraction of the miser's hoard.

. . . to really understand him, one must be in business. For Nucingen,
banking is just a small department: there are also government con-
tracts, wine, wools, indigo, in short anything that can offer the chance
of any kind of profit. His genius embraces everything. The Bank under-
stood this way becomes a sort of politics all by itself, it requires a pow-
erful mind, and drives a well-forged man to place himself above the
laws of probity, in which he finds himself a bit squeezed.

Bixiou's story will prove the accuracy of Couture's description of *la Banque* according to Nucingen, especially the last part. This display of expertise highlights what is Couture's most important function as a narratee; the presence of this moneyman reinforces the verisimilitude of Bixiou's account of Nucingen's operations. We have already seen an example of this brazen technique—of Balzac using one of his fictional characters to bear witness to the novelist's own reliability—in Derville's affirmation that reality is far stranger than those things that novelists think they invent. That observation from *Le Colonel Chabert* rings true throughout *La Comédie humaine*, but Couture's observation is especially important here because of the complexity and technicality of the story Bixiou tells. The reader is inclined to accept the reliability of the story because the narratees do so, especially Couture, who is "dans les affaires."

Taken as a group, these four "*condottieri*" (330) form the perfect assembly for the story of Nucingen's great financial swindle. Blondet and Bixiou are *mystificateurs;* like Nucingen, they are actively engaged in deception, although on a much smaller and far less profitable scale. Also like Nucingen, these two understand perfectly the new society of the Restoration and July Monarchy—which makes Nucingen possible. Couture, again, responds to the financial nature of the story and guarantees the *vraisemblance* of Bixiou's (Balzac's) account of high finance. Finot serves a double purpose: he is himself something of a swindler—as Lucien de Rubempré learns the hard way in *Illusions perdues;* at the same time, his limited intelligence makes him a target for Bixiou during his narration, offering an excuse for the long digressions that surely amuse the narrator (and the author) as much as the audience(s). There is also one characteristic that these men share that makes them well suited for this analysis of society: they are all essentially outsiders, as the term *condottieri* suggests. None of these men quite fit in with any of the different social milieus that are depicted in the story Bixiou tells. This position, on the outside looking in, makes them ideal observers. As they have no sympathy for any of the people described in the story, they do not side with Nucingen, Beaudenord, or even the widow d'Aldrigger and her orphan daughters; everyone is a target for Bixiou. At the same time, the absence of any specific class sympathies must not be confused with objectivity, and their status must shade our evaluation of them as observers. As readers, we must be alert to ironies and double meanings in the things these characters say.

Most obviously, they are excluded from the nobility, and a consciousness of this distance can be seen in the simultaneously mocking and envious way that Bixiou describes Beaudenord: "D'abord il se nommait Godefroid de Beaudenord. Ni Finot, ni Blondet, ni Couture, ni moi, nous ne méconnaîtrons pas un pareil avantage" [*First of all, his name was Godefroid de Beaudenord. Neither Finot, nor Blondet, nor Couture, nor I will ever fail to understand such an advantage*] (340). This classically aristocratic name is only the first of Beaudenord's many advantages, and the four men in the dining room can only resent that all their native intelligence cannot get for them the advantages that this former "fleur du dandysme" received merely for having taken the trouble to be born. This sense of jealousy and exclusion vis-à-vis the aristocracy can be seen in several asides in the text. For example, when Bixiou speaks of the *comptes de tutelle* presented to Beaudenord by his uncle, the marquis d'Aiglemont: "des comptes de tutelles comme nous ne serions jamais capables de présenter à nos neveux" [*trustee accounts such as we would never be capable of presenting to our nephews*] (346). Whether this incapacity stems from a lack of ability, a lack of virtue, or simply from a lack of funds to be managed is unclear, but we see again here a certain mocking recognition of the dignity and privileges of the upper classes. The *nous* in both of these examples refers, obviously, to the four men present in the dining room, but we can also take it to refer to a larger group, the social group to which these four men belong, irremediably beneath the aristocracy.

Still another of Bixiou's ironic observations sheds light on the distance between these four men and the aristocracy and on their awareness of that distance. Speaking of Rastignac's having developed a repugnance for being financially supported by Delphine de Nucingen, the men each confess that they would have no compunctions about such an arrangement for themselves—Couture even proposes that such an arrangement should be the chosen role of any woman with heart (336). Bixiou sarcastically explains Rastignac's scruples as a question of class: "C'est un gentil-homme fort dépravé, voyez-vous, et nous sommes de vertueux artistes" [*He's a quite depraved gentleman, you see, and we are virtuous artists*"] (337). The irony of this observation is double-edged, cutting both the nobleman and the artists. First of all, the question of exactly what constitutes Rastignac's depravity is not easily answered. Obviously, Bixiou is jokingly referring to Rastignac's desire to be financially independent of his mistress, but his relationship with Delphine could also be seen as *dépravé* (or at least disreputable) according to the social code of his class. Others might say he is less dishonored by his arrangements with Delphine than by those he develops with her husband, which eventually lead to his independent (a debatable adjective, all things considered) fortune. As for the *vertueux artistes* themselves, all of them, with the probable and logical exception of Finot, benefit from a woman's loving generosity at some point in their careers: Blondet's lover is the comtesse de Montcornet, whom he will marry when she becomes a rich widow at the end of *Les Paysans;* it is very likely that Bixiou indirectly benefits from Crevel's attachment for Héloïse Brisetout (*La Cousine Bette,* 7:123, 158); and Couture will only narrowly miss becoming the beneficiary of the considerable financial acumen of Mme Schontz, mistress of the marquis de Rochefide (*Béatrix,* 2:904-5). This is not to say that these men are totally excluded from the *monde.* Blondet obviously has the strongest link, and all of them seem to be friends with, or at least acquainted with, Rastignac. Yet class still counts for a great deal in Balzac's world, and even the son of an impoverished *hobereau* family has a clear advantage over these clever Parisians. As much as society has changed since 1789, certain prejudices remain strong in 1836.

The force of such prejudices is apparent throughout *La Comédie humaine* as we see bourgeois families try to push their way into the nobility, even as that class deteriorates and diminishes in importance. This sort of ambition can be seen in *La Maison Nucingen* as the d'Aldrigger family, with their Imperial title, attaches itself to the old line pedigree of Beaudenord, himself on his way to ruin, along with the rest of his caste. This alliance will be mirrored, later in the evolution of Balzac's world, as the baron de Rastignac marries the daughter of the house of Nucingen. As Blondet says, "La Banque cherche la noblesse par instinct de conservation, et sans le savoir, peut-être" [*The Bank seeks out the aristocracy by an instinct of conservation, and without being aware of it, perhaps*] (340). Although Balzac does not say so here, it is clear from *La Maison Nucingen* and other texts that the reverse is also true. It is unlikely that the Nucingen family is unconscious of the advantages they acquire through their association with Rastignac. Delphine uses him to gain access to Mme de Beauséant's ball in *Le Père Goriot,* and Nucingen uses him first to keep his wife amused (333), and later as an accomplice ("compère") in his final, triumphant swindle (381). The eventual marriage of Eugène and Augusta will formalize—if not exactly legitimize—the ties that bind Rastignac and the Nucingens, giving his title wealth and their fortune a still useful social standing.

The social world of the bankers, where "la maison Nucingen" is "le haut bout de la société financière" [*The House of Nucingen is the high end of financial society*] (360), is clearly a notch below the nobility. The fact that single young men like Beaudenord amuse themselves "chez les banquiers" is merely tolerated by the indulgent elders of the faubourg Saint-Germain (341). This *société financière* occupies a sort of middle ground between the aristocracy and the bourgeoisie; the different classes meet at Delphine's balls, and the d'Aldriggers' *salon* is described by Bixiou as having been "un endroit unique à Paris" (363), a place where one could enjoy the genteel refinements and comforts provided by wealth without the restrictive manners that come with noble birth. That said, our four *condottieri* are as much excluded from the rich bourgeoisie as from the aristocracy, as is demonstrated by Bixiou's account of his failed attempts to, as he himself puts it, cultivate the Matifat family—rich, retired druggists with a daughter to marry off. Bixiou, invited to dinner at Matifat's country house, relieves his boredom by spinning an endless "aventure à tiroirs" which puts his uncomprehending bourgeois audience to sleep. When Bixiou pushes his cultivation too far, attempting to initiate the Matifat daughter in the "grand mystère de la vie," he finds the Matifat door closed to him for good. The plan was doomed to fail in any case; both the soporific story and the failed attempt at seduction prove the essential truth of Bixiou's final observation on the Matifats: "les bourgeois et moi nous ne nous comprendrons jamais" [*the bourgeoisie and I will never understand each other*] (368). Besides a lack of mutual understanding, the Matifats and Bixiou are separated by another all-important factor: money.

Bixiou and his kind can visit, amuse, and be secretly amused by, the bourgeois as well as the aristocrats, but they can never really join either world. They lack the essentials that would allow them to make a permanent connection, a secure fortune, and the social consideration that such a fortune almost automatically confers.

The spectacle of these marginal citizens commenting on the spectacle of Nucingen's swindle, and the different people caught up in it, is doubled in the text by the narrating *je,* who sits on the periphery of this act of narration and comments on it, and the characters involved in it, as he relays it to us. This is a first example of a *mise-en-abyme* in *La Maison Nucingen.* Taking this literary term in its broadest sense, as distilled by Gerald Prince in his *Dictionary of Narratology,* this *nouvelle* offers several examples of "a textual part reduplicating, reflecting, or mirroring (one or more aspects of) the textual whole" (53). This doubling has the further effect of reproducing the act of reading *La Comédie humaine,* as both Bixiou and the narrating *je* resemble the Narrator, telling us what has taken place in the world that Balzac created. The effects of this doubling of narrators are multiple and fairly complicated, and I will discuss them in more detail further on, but first I think it is useful to comment on the other examples of the *mise-en-abyme* in this text.

Another, perhaps more easily grasped, example of the *mise-en-abyme* is to be found in the episode of the "aventure à tiroirs" that Bixiou invents to play with the Matifats. As he describes this verbal construction, speaking specifically to Blondet, who would especially understand such a game:

> Blondet, un jour ils ont voulu me faire poser, je leur ai raconté une histoire depuis neuf heures du soir jusqu'à minuit, une aventure à tiroirs! J'en étais à mon vingt-neuvième personnage (les romans en feuilletons m'ont volé!)... (367)
>
> *Blondet, one day they wanted to put me on display, I told them a story from nine o'clock till midnight, an "aventure à tiroirs!" [literally, a story with drawers] I was on my twenty-ninth character (the serial novels robbed me!)*

This nonreproduced story, with its disparate parts and numerous digressions and large number of characters, is an unseen reflection of the story

Bixiou is telling about Rastignac, Nucingen, and others. The ever-perceptive Couture picks up on this and challenges Bixiou:

> —Je ne vois, dans toutes ces toupies que tu lances, rien qui ressemble à l'origine de la fortune de Rastignac, et tu nous prends pour des Matifat multipliés par six bouteilles de vin de Champagne, s'écria Couture. (369)
>
> *"I don't see, in all of these tops that you set spinning, anything that resembles the origins of Rastignac's fortune, and you're taking us for a bunch of Matifats multiplied by six bottles of Champagne," cried Couture.*

This is, of course, exactly what Bixiou is doing, playing with his bourgeois audience with an impossibly complicated story; but Couture, adept at piecing things together, announces to Bixiou that he will not be taken for another Matifat or Finot, and he rejects membership in the dull bourgeoisie that Bixiou and Blondet—and Couture—scorn and envy at the same time.

A more subtle use of the *mise-en-abyme* is perceptible only to the *lecteur initié,* because it involves Bixiou's history from another text, *Les Employés.* In that novel, which is named in the text, Bixiou is one of the minor bureaucrats who conspire to bring down a talented colleague, Xavier Rabourdin. Bixiou refers briefly to this episode in *La Maison Nucingen:*

> Dans le ministère où j'ai fait sept ans de galères, accouplés avec des bourgeois, il y avait un employé, un homme de talent, qui avait résolu de changer tout le système des finances. . . ah bien, nous l'avons joliment dégommé. La France eût été trop heureuse, elle se serait amusée à réconquérir l'Europe, et nous avons agi pour le repos des nations. J'ai tué ce Rabourdin par une caricature (voir *Les Employés*). (375)
>
> *In the ministry where I spent seven years as a galley slave, chained up to a bunch of bourgeois, there was an administrator, a man of talent, who had resolved to change the whole system of finances. . . ah, well, we fixed him good. France would have been too happy, she would have amused herself by reconquering Europe, and so we acted for the repose of nations. I killed this Rabourdin with a caricature. (see* The Clerks*)*

Again we see that Bixiou's sarcasm hides some real regret and bitterness, the bitterness that the narrating *je* alluded to in his introduction of this "diable enragé d'avoir dépensé tant d'esprit en pure perte" [*this devil enraged at having spent so much wit at a pure loss*] (331). Bixiou's talents were exploited not in the name of Continental peace, but rather in defense of the status quo. Rabourdin's great plan for reform threatened the comfortable positions of many titled men and great names *posés comme des vers à soie sur les feuilles du budget,* to paraphrase *Le Bal de Sceau* [*settled like silkworms on the leaves of the budget*] (1:113). And so those men unleashed Bixiou like an attack dog and dismissed him when he had served his purpose. This exploitation is reflected in *La Maison Nucingen* by the banker's exploitation of not only Rastignac, but also of Beaudenord, the d'Aldriggers, and others. Just as Nucingen appropriates their social standing or financial capital for his own profit, so did the shadowy powers-that-be of *Les Employés* exploit Bixiou's capital, his talent, for their own benefit. Just as Beaudenord is reduced to scribbling in a ministry after Nucingen's rout, so is Bixiou reduced to putting on a show for Finot. Bixiou's brief reference to Rabourdin and *Les Employés* is a nugget that contains, for the *lecteur initié,* a reflection of both his own story and the story he is telling.

We can also find in *La Maison Nucingen* an example of the literary *mise-en-abyme* that is linked to the original meaning of the term. In heraldry, a *mise-en-abyme* is the placement of a coat-of-arms within another coat-of-arms. This usually occurred when a woman of great rank married a man of lower rank, or when a great family had *tombée en quenouille* [fallen to the distaff]. There is at least one example of this sort of *mise-en-abyme* in *La Comédie humaine,* when the Lenoncourt family name, whose last descendant is Mme de Mortsauf, is preserved when Madeleine de Mortsauf is married to the younger son of the Chaulieu family, creating the ducal family of Lenoncourt-Chaulieu. At the request of the duc de Chaulieu, the Chaulieu arms are placed *en abyme* of those of the Lenoncourt (*Mémoires de deux jeunes mariées,* 1:535). This seems to be an unremarkable case of the *mise-en-abyme,* but *La Comédie humaine* also contains a number of irregular examples of the heraldic process. In *Béatrix,* Calyste du Guénic places the des Touches arms *en abyme* on his own, in recognition of Félicité's de facto financial adoption of himself and his wife. In *Albert Savarus,* we learn that the Watteville coat of arms was placed *en abyme* on those of the de Rupt family when Monsieur de Watteville married the redoubtable Mlle de Rupt. As Wayne Conner pointed out in his study of *Albert Savarus*, "[t]his is the opposite of the usual practice—also illustrated in Balzac—in which the wife's arms were placed in the center (abyme) of her husband's shield" ("*Albert Savarus* and 'L'ambitieux par amour,' " 259). I strongly suspect that this was not a mistake, but rather a subtle and ironic commentary on the Wattevilles' marriage, meant to underline the weakness of Monsieur de Watteville in the face of his formidable wife. The illustration of the "usual practice" that Conner alludes to is found in *Les Paysans,* where Louis XVIII grants the imperial count Montcornet the right "d'écarteler son ridicule écusson avec les armes des Troisville" [*to quarter his ridiculous escutcheon with the Troisville coat-of-arms*], the ancient noble family that Montcornet's huge fortune allows him to buy his way into (9:152).

There is a definite pattern in *La Comédie humaine* of men who are weak in one way or another—be it in terms of wealth, social status, or personal character—married to women who have some sort of advantage over them. In the case of the Wattevilles and Montcornets, this pattern is exemplified by the *mise-en-abyme.* An analogous case is to be found at the end of *Modeste Mignon,* when Charles Mignon de la Bastie preserves his name by marrying his daughter to Ernest de La Brière. The couple then become officially known as the vicomte and vicomtesse de La Brière-La Bastie (1:714). With time however, that name reverts to simply La Bastie, as we see in *Béatrix* (2:910). While not precisely a *mise-en-abyme*—as Ernest de La Brière has no arms to place *en abyme*—there is in this case a similar commentary on the relative social status and character of the persons involved. Though not a comic figure like Watteville, Ernest is one of Balzac's many androgynous young men; he is referred to as Mlle de La Brière in *Modeste Mignon* (1:575), and he displays an excessive sensitivity and an indisputable weakness of character in the novel. The evolution of names underlines Ernest's inferiority vis-à-vis his spirited and intelligent wife and especially his father-in-law—who is something of a Balzacian superman—in much the same way that the Watteville coat of arms does. Still another parallel can be seen in the alliance between the Popinots, the Camusots, and the Marville property discussed in the first chapter. While nothing indicates that either Popinot *père* or *fils* is weak in the way that

Watteville or La Brière are, they do seem willing to accept a disagreeable marriage in return for a nominal upgrade.

In *La Maison Nucingen,* we can see another example of this ironic and uniquely Balzacian twist on the *mise-en-abyme.* I have already alluded to the ties between Rastignac and the Nucingens, which grow increasingly complex as the *longue durée* of *La Comédie humaine* unfolds. These ties and the relative positions of the two families suggest a *mise-en-abyme* in the way that the story of Rastignac's fortune is enveloped in the story of Nucingen. Rastignac, who is born to the title of an ancient but impoverished barony, becomes a count under the July Monarchy—a title that in Balzac's eyes surely counts for less than even an imperial barony. It is only as his fortune grows, a direct result of his ever-strengthening ties to the *maison Nucingen,* that Rastignac will become "comte et pair de France," a change in title that is at once an elevation and a derogation. This not quite hostile takeover of the *maison de Rastignac* by the *maison Nucingen* is reflected, in the text, by the way that the story of Rastignac's fortune is presented as only a part of the story of Nucingen's fortune, the title of the *nouvelle* eliminating all doubt as to which story—and which fortune—is the more important. Nucingen's story contains Rastignac's story, just as Nucingen's fortune contains Rastignac's fortune, just as the Nucingen family will eventually take over Rastignac himself. His marriage to Augusta will cement the merger between *la Banque* and *la noblesse* that Blondet alludes to in the text. The name and the arms of the Rastignac remain intact, of course—after all they are far more respectable, and the Nucingens paid good money for them.

The similarity between the enveloped stories of Rastignac and Nucingen in the *nouvelle,* and their relationship in the larger *Comédie humaine* suggests another important instance of mirroring in *La Maison Nucingen.* As Armine Kotin Mortimer pointed out in her article "*La Maison Nucingen,* ou le récit financier," the substance of Bixiou's narration is reflected in the style in which he narrates; to borrow Genette's terms, Bixiou's *discours* mirrors his *histoire.* Bixiou weaves together the seemingly disjointed fragments of his narrative—the stories of Beaudenord, the d'Aldriggers, the Matifats, etc.—into one story, the story of Nucingen, just as Nucingen weaves the individual fortunes of those characters into his own great fortune. These parallel compositions of parts into wholes reflects the composition of *La Comédie humaine* from the fragments of *Le*

Père Goriot, Louis Lambert, La Maison Nucingen, etc. Within this reflection, discourse again parallels story, as *La Maison Nucingen* reveals itself to be in many respects a miniature of *La Comédie humaine;* this is true not just in terms of structure, but also of content.[2] Beyond the dominant theme of capitalism and Nucingen's fortune, the various subplots of this *nouvelle* suggest, in microcosm, many of the major themes and important milieus of the larger text. Beaudenord and his cousin d'Aiglemont, losing their money in Nucingen's scheme, reflect the decline of the aristocracy in an era that has passed it by; the Matifat family, losing money but still extremely rich, show the vulgar bourgeoisie in relentless ascent; the love story of Godefroid and Isaure comes close to a happy ending, which is in the end undone with the author's usual cruel irony; Malvina, on the other hand, fails altogether at love and becomes, with her dark looks, in some sense a precursor of the spinsters Lizbeth Fischer and Rose Cormon; the preposterous baronne d'Aldrigger and her daughters exposed to the rapacity of the thankless protégé Nucingen recalls the melodrama that sometimes colors Balzac's works. In this and other small ways, the structure and content of *La Maison Nucingen* suggests a textual part that reflects the textual whole.

Also worth mentioning is the fact that deception is used in all three of these combinations to bring the different parts together. Bixiou as a narrator appears to be meandering aimlessly, when in fact his seemingly incoherent narrative strategy is leading him to a logical conclusion and resolution of the central enigma. Nucingen, with his succession of fraudulent bankruptcies, uses deception, massive financial fraud in fact, to amass his pile of money. Balzac, obviously, uses the inherently deceptive mode of fiction writing to paint his portrait of his own era. The similarities between story and discourse lead us back to the principal example of *mise-en-abyme* in this *nouvelle*, namely the way that *La Maison Nucingen* reflects *La Comédie humaine* as a whole, as both are stories composed of stories.

Implicit in this sequence of reflections is a parallel between Nucingen's massive fortune, a whole composed of formerly independent frag-

---

[2] This parallel is reflected yet again, highly ironically, by Bixiou's *roman à tiroirs*. The key difference is that the good Balzacian reader, no dull bourgeois like Matifat, does not doze off at the introduction of the twenty-ninth character of *La Maison Nucingen*.

ments, and Balzac's massive text, like the smallest and the largest of Chinese boxes. The comparison is significant, because Nucingen—his wealth, his bank, and his financial genius—is an important image in *La Comédie humaine.* Just as the text is meant to reflect the time and place that Balzac lived in, Nucingen reflects one of the most important aspects of that society: the early and destructive triumph of nascent capitalism. Nucingen is as important a symbol within *La Comédie humaine* as Rastignac or Claës. His name is a sign that signifies much more than just the character who is a financier, a Peer, a deputy, etc.; the word *Nucingen* signifies a force, both moral and historical, at work in Balzac's world. Like his spiritual cousin Gobseck, Nucingen and all he represents can only be completely understood after having been considered in his starring role, so to speak. In other texts of *La Comédie humaine,* Nucingen is portrayed as merely a vulgar and cruel banker (*Le Père Goriot*) or even a buffoonishly comic figure (*Splendeurs et misères des courtisanes*), but in *La Maison Nucingen,* we see both the true genius and the true cruelty of the character as he spins a fortune as if out of thin air ("la création mystérieuse, on dirait presque magique, de l'argent par Nucingen" Mortimer, 66), coldly calculating the ruin of a large number of people, including the widow of his benefactor, along the way.

Perhaps the most intriguing, challenging, even confounding aspect of this *nouvelle* is the presence of the twin narrators and the multiple possibilities they suggest to an alert reader. If both resemble the Narrator, it can just as easily be said that both resemble Balzac. Bixiou knows things that others do not, and he shares that privileged information; he is both the keeper and teller of secrets. Superficially then, he resembles the Narrator, but in all those things that make Bixiou an interesting character, he resembles his creator. This similarity has not, of course, gone unnoticed. Balzac was well known to his friends and contemporaries as a lively raconteur (Pierrot, *Balzac,* 177) and Pierre Citron has pointed out the similarity between the gathering depicted in *La Maison Nucingen* and the *repas de garçons* that Balzac was extremely fond of (Introduction, éd. Pléiade, 318). One scene in particular from the *nouvelle* suggests another from Balzac's own life: One of the most entertaining parts of Bixiou's performance is the representation of d'Aldrigger's funeral, where Nucingen and his *compères* conduct business during the service itself. Bixiou becomes a one-man play, reproducing Nucingen's celebrated *baringouin,* using words to vividly represent the scene at the church, right down to the beggars at the door and the *chantres* singing the funeral service (357). This very theatrical bit earns the heartfelt approval of his sometimes impatient audience: "—Quelle verve! » dit Couture . . .—Il me semble entendre parler ce vieux Robert Macaire de Nucingen! dit Finot" [*What verve, said Couture. . . . It's like I'm hearing that old pirate Nucingen*] (358). As Citron reminds us, this fictional scene recalls the famous one, reported by Théophile Gautier, in which Balzac, acting alone, gave a lively and dramatic reading of one of his own plays, giving each character a different voice and personality (Pierrot, *Balzac*, 355). As dangerous as I think it usually is to look for Balzac's self-portrait in every character he draws,[3] I think we can reasonably conclude that Balzac put much of himself into Bixiou. The similarities do not necessarily end with their comparable style of storytelling, for if Balzac loaned Bixou some of his talent, we should ask ourselves if Bixiou's bitterness is not another trait he shares with his creator. A lively wit is not the only point of comparison between Balzac and this artist who is talented, who knows the society he lives in like the back of his own hand, who goes everywhere and amuses everyone, but who is never quite able to succeed in that society, who is always just on the edge of real success.

Like Bixiou, the narrating *je* teasingly resembles both Balzac and his Narrator, existing at one remove from the recurring characters, separated only by a thin wall from these people he knows so well. The setting for the act of narration creates an irresistible desire to see, in that thin wall, the line in Balzac's mind between the world he lived in and the world he created. This temptation is only strengthened by the fact, pointed out by Mortimer, that this narrator casts himself as the recording secretary of this gathering—the story is "sténographiée" in his memory (331)—just as Balzac assigned himself the role of secretary of Society in the *avant-propos* of 1842 ("*La Maison Nucingen,*" 60-61). However sophisticated we may be as readers, it is almost impossible for us, when contemplating the spectacle of this eavesdropping man, not to form a mental image of Balzac gathering the stories he will relate to us in *La Comédie humaine*. This temptation is reinforced by the fact that this narrator, as Allan Pasco observed, seems to be blessed with that same *science divinatoire* that so

---

[3] I believe that all of Balzac's characters, as they relate to real-life models, are composites; even Félicité des Touches differs, and in important ways, from George Sand.

many of Balzac's narrators have, and this *seconde vue* recalls the powers of observation and perception that Balzac displays in his novels (*Balzacian Montage,* 106).

The undeniable and undoubtedly intentional resemblance between Balzac and the narrating *je* is what makes the last sentence of this *nouvelle* so fascinating, and so frustrating:

> —Tiens, il y avait du monde à côté, dit Finot en nous entendant sortir.
> —Il y a toujours du monde à côté », répondit Bixiou qui devait être aviné. (392)
> *"Say, there was someone right next door," said Finot, hearing us leave.*
> *"There's always someone right next door," replied Bixiou, who must have been drunk.*

Bixiou's final comment is the most glaring reflection yet, and the narrator's hasty and unnecessary explanation for it, ostensibly meant to undermine Bixiou's words, only serves to heighten our interest, to ensure that we speculate as to the true meaning of the last sentence. On a purely diegetic level, the narrator's remark is perfectly innocent. Bixiou's remark makes no sense contextually; he has been drinking for hours, and so the narrator's explanation for it seems a perfectly logical response. But because we know we are reading a work of fiction, we know that in fact there is always someone *à côté,* namely us, the readers of the text. We also know that behind the fiction lies Balzac, and that neither Bixiou's remark nor the narrator's dismissal of it are innocent. Bixiou's remark is a crack in the fourth wall of fiction. It suggests to us that Bixiou is conscious of the fact that he does not really exist, and that logical impossibility is exactly what makes this passage so tantalizing. Balzac then pushes his bold game one step further, encouraging this impossible interpretation by having the narrating *je,* his alter ego, react as if he wants to cover up Bixiou's drunken indiscretion. The final result is the suggestion of a fascinating and impossible—fascinating because impossible—tension between a fictional character and his creator. The remark rivets our attention, grabbing hold of us just as the story ends, and leaves us hanging without any explanation.

One final question to be addressed seems rather simple compared to the confusion caused by Bixiou's (Balzac's) insolent *clin d'œil* to the reader: exactly who is the *monde à côté* that Bixiou refers to? Remaining within the fictional structure of *La Comédie humaine,* we could see this remark as an allusion to the connected individual stories of the larger text. As Pasco suggests, this would mean the structure of *La Maison Nucingen* reflects the way information moves around Balzac's fictional world, how the different recurring characters learn each other's stories (*Balzacian Montage,* 107). Going one step further, the *monde à côté* could be seen as the Narrator and the Narratee, who are constantly observing this world and all that goes on within it. The next logical step takes us to the author and the reader, who are likewise always present, always standing on the periphery of that world. For Armine Mortimer, this *monde à côté* is the critic, who not only observes but comments on what is observed ("le récit financier," 65). This interpretation suggests yet another doubling within this text, for the critic is also represented in the dining room with Bixiou, as Blondet, the brilliant writer who is too lazy to write, offers constant commentary on his friend's story and style.

La Maison Nucingen is an incredibly complicated, even confusing, text, and it does not become simpler as we reread. If anything, the text only becomes increasingly complicated with more careful consideration— a final example of how the whole is reflected in this fragment. Mortimer suggested that the confusion caused by Bixiou's style of narration is a reflection of the confusion created on the Parisian *Bourse* by Nucingen's *puff* ("le récit financier," 64-65): when the dust settled, the banker had already made his big grab. Everyone then knew that Nucingen had won, but very few people could figure out how. Even some of Nucingen's victims were unaware of what he had done to them. The situation is similar for Bixiou's listeners, as the question of Rastignac's fortune is finally resolved, the riddle answered, albeit after many twists and turns. But for the reader the dust never settles, there is no final resolution. The last words we read are perhaps the greatest enigma in an enigmatic text. *La Maison Nucingen* is like the hall of mirrors in a fun house, where every thing is at once reflected and distorted, and that destabilization both amuses and disturbs. The one important difference is that it is not our own images that we see reflected, so we have no fixed center from which to look at the different mirrors. The reflections are all the more unsettling, because we are never exactly sure of what we are looking at. Bixiou's final comment and the narrating *je*'s seemingly uncomfortable reaction to it are a final distorted reflection, a blinding flash from the depths of the abyss, that completes rather than cures our sense of disorientation.

Many Voices Speaking, Many Things Left Unsaid: Polyphony and Silence in *Autre étude de femme*

In *Autre étude de femme*, we find another dinner party, very different from the raucous *dîner de garçons* depicted in *La Maison Nucingen*. After a ball at the Parisian hôtel of Félicité des Touches, selected guests are invited to stay for an intimate late supper. Only the most desirable people are invited to remain for this *soirée* within a *soirée*, which is, as our narrator Bianchon assures us, the "véritable soirée." This smaller gathering is described to us as a wonderful anachronism, an island of wit and elegance worthy of the *ancien régime* amid the dull vulgarity of the July Monarchy. What is of interest to us is not the meal, but the conversation that follows it. If the verbal fireworks display of Bixiou and his friends was full of "verve et mordant," this more elegant exchange is marked by "verve" and "grace" (675). This is not to say that the conversation is without its own *mordant*—Bianchon at one point describes it as a joust—but the atmosphere of Mlle des Touches's dining room lends itself to a far more subtle, far more restrained tone. This restraint and subtlety is not only found on the part of the *devisants,* but on the part of Balzac as well. By using, at least for the majority of the text, a character narrator, Balzac is able to create an ambiguous text, where meanings are like buried treasures, discernable only to the *lecteur initié.*

Balzac establishes a narrating *je* in the first pages of the text, and it is not until almost the middle that this narrator is identified as Bianchon (725). In any case, as the conversation develops, the narrating *je* is overshadowed by the dinner guests; like a good servant, our narrator is always present, but unobtrusive. The effect of this subtle and constant presence is that we are able to forget that what we are reading is not direct, but rather reported discourse. Every story we hear told, every commentary or remark the characters round the table make during their conversation, is filtered through the naive voice of Bianchon; this relatively muted voice enables Balzac to relate to us everything that is said at this imagined feast of his

Olympians, while at the same time freeing him from the obligation of explaining every remark, of reporting every detail of the relevant history of each speaker through the authoritative voice of the Narrator. The result is a polyphonous text, marked by silences perceptible only to the *lecteur initié*. As these stories and quips are related to us by our narrator, the experienced reader is able to read between the lines, looking behind what Bianchon tells us to see the rich material that Balzac has placed there for us. This is a text to be read on two levels. Superficially, we read it for what it pretends to be, a *soirée mondaine* where stories are told and commented on. On the second, more subtle level, what we see is a *soirée balzacienne,* where carefully chosen characters use carefully chosen words to say much more to each other than what Bianchon explicitly reports to us.

Structurally, *Autre étude* is composed of four main parts: de Marsay's narration, which I refer to as *Premières armes d'un lion,* already discussed in the first chapter; a long discourse by Blondet on the *femme comme il faut;* General de Montriveau offers the tale of *La femme de notre colonel,* a brutal tale of adultery and revenge, that is also a *scène de la vie militaire;* and finally, there is *La Grande Bretèche,* Bianchon's tale, also discussed in chapter 1. Two smaller fragments are an *éloge* of Napoleon by the poet Canalis and the story of the death of the Duchess Charlotte, "la première de M. de Marsay" (709), witnessed and recounted by Bianchon. It is this last fragment above all that causes so much consternation among readers and critics of *Autre étude de femme,* since it describes the death of a woman described as very much alive only a few pages earlier. This discrepancy, which cannot be resolved even by the most indulgent and creative of critics, is especially irritating because the death scene is, to be bluntly concise, boring. It adds very little to the text as a whole and exposes a flank to critics who find the text lacking for other reasons. There is another flaw in the text, perhaps less obvious but equally irreconcilable, which should be mentioned right away: toward the end of the *nouvelle,* Bianchon's first-person narration, suddenly and without explanation or even changes in punctuation, switches to a third-person narration, as the Narrator takes over. These errors and what many perceive as a lack of unity among the different parts of the text lead many people to dismiss *Autre étude de femme,* considering the whole text to be merely a frame for *La Grande Bretèche.* This attitude is best summed up by the judgment rendered by Nicole Mozet in her introduction to the *Pléiade* edition of *Autre étude;* for Mozet, this is a text full of "incohérences," "difficilement lisible, et effectivement peu lu" [*difficult to read and in fact, infrequently read*] (670).

Those who ignore this text, or who choose to view it as no more than a loosely compiled collection of stories too short to be published as independent *nouvelles,* deprive themselves of one of the greatest pleasures of *La Comédie humaine.* The text may require a bit of indulgence, but the reader of *Autre étude* who is willing to make some allowances for "les hasards de la conversation" (Zélicourt, 259) is in a position to reap the benefits of this diamond in the rough. This is not merely the advice of overly indulgent critics. Balzac himself, through Bianchon, warns us of these *hasards* in the opening pages of the text. In this *préambule,* Bianchon prepares us for what we about to read, whetting our appetites for this glimpse into the most rarified circle of Balzac's Parisian society. This is a select company, and the reader is privileged to be admitted to "le salon de Mlle des Touches . . . dernier asile où se soit réfugié l'esprit français d'autrefois" [*the salon of Mlle des Touches, the last asylum where the old style French wit had taken refuge.*] (674), and to be allowed to attend this "soirée où, comme sous l'ancien régime, chacun entend ce qui se dit" [*a soirée where, as under the Old Régime, everyone understood what was said.*] (673). What we behold in this refuge of wit and understanding is the very French—and now very rare—art of conversation, unsullied by the influence of the increasingly *embourgeoisée* society of the July Monarchy. The rarity of the conversation is underlined by the setting. The first *soirée,* the *raout*—which is superficial, all about posing, seeing, and being seen— is English, a crass import, "une de ces inventions anglaises qui tendent à mécanifier les autres nations" [*one of those English inventions that are mechanizing other nations*] (674). The *souper,* with its select company, is French, at once more natural and more refined; there *l'esprit* takes precedence over *le paraître.* As readers, we must be prepared to look beyond what we can see, using some *esprit* of our own, in order to be worthy of the privilege we have been accorded.

Having established that we readers are privileged to be allowed to witness this second *soirée,* Bianchon informs us that what we are reading is not literature. One of the most important reasons for the quality of this conversation is that the guests feel at ease; no one sees the hideous skeleton of literature behind their fellow guests (674), and so no one holds back for fear of seeing their words reproduced in some vulgar piece of fiction. What we are reading, then, is better than literature, since the oral phenomenon clearly triumphs over the written. Such a conversation need not obey the strictures of literature, here seen as a rather crass bourgeois phenomenon. We should not necessarily look for such things as linearity, coherence, and unity. These things are all to be found in the internal stories, but the conversation itself is above such laws. French wit is by nature "capricieux" and gives a conversation "je ne sais quelle allure fluviale qui fait facilement serpenter cette profusion de pensées" [*I don't know what fluvial pace that allows the profusion of thoughts to flow in an easy, serpentine way*]. Because the conversation is as effortless as it is elegant, what we find are "causeries légères et profondes [qui] ondoient, tournent, changent d'aspect et de couleurs à chaque phrase" [*light and profound conversations that float, turn, change its nature and color with every sentence*] (675). The conversation at Mlle des Touches's, the most bewitching that Bianchon has ever witnessed, is no exception to this free-form style:

> La conversation, devenue conteuse, entraîna dans son cours précipité de curieuses confidences, plusieurs portraits, mille folies, qui rendent cette ravissante improvisation tout à fait intraduisible.
> *The conversation, turning toward stories, brought along in its precipitous wake curious confidences, several portraits, a thousand pleasantries, all of which made this ravishing improvisation utterly impossible to translate.*

All these twists and turns in the conversational flow are necessary if we are to truly understand the magic of this evening and of this conversation:

> mais, en laissant à ces choses leur verdeur, leur abrupt naturel, leur fallaciuses sinuousités, peut-être comprendrez-vous bien le charme d'une véritable soirée française. (675-76)
> *but, by leaving these elements their freshness, their natural abruptness, their deceptive sinuosity, perhaps you will understand the charms of a truly French soirée.*

This preamble, which Bianchon assures us is essential to our understanding of this text that is not literature, is too often overlooked by critics, just as in general they overlook the importance of the interplay between the characters gathered around the table. It is in this aspect of the *nouvelle* that the reader must look for the unity of the text, which comes, paradoxically, from the ununified conversation—capricious, sinuous, and serpentine—of the *devisants*.

In *Contre Sainte-Beuve,* Proust compared the profusion of recurring characters in this *nouvelle* to a certain memorial ceremony at the *Comédie française,* during which each actor would step forward, deliver a line by a playwright more-or-less at random, and retire to the wings (286). This impression of randomness is encouraged both by the large number of recurring characters named, and by the fact that so many of them have only one line, to continue Proust's theatrical analogy.[4] Yet Balzac seems to have anticipated this objection in his essential preamble: in the joust that is a Parisian conversation, "chaque nature d'esprit se condense par un trait [. . .] chacun dit sa phrase et jette son expérience dans un mot" [*Each nature of wit condenses itself into a line, each one says his phrase and puts all of his experience into one word*] (675). For the members of this spirited and *spirituel* assembly, one line is enough. This sentence is also interesting because, in the suggestion that a single *mot* can reflect the whole history of the speaker, it hints at what I feel is the key to understanding *Autre étude de femme.* For the naive reader, the names Blondet or Mme de Montcornet mean no more than the anonymous titles "un ministre étranger" or "un prince russe," but for the experienced reader, the first is the talented but lazy writer and the second is the high-born wife of an Imperial general, and the two have been lovers for most of their adult lives. While this particular example does not especially enrich our understanding of *Autre étude,* it does serve to remind us that the name of a recurring character can often mean much more than it appears to do. This is frequently the case in this text, in which the names resonate with the *lecteur initié,* creating a possibility of polyvalence in what might seem a perfectly innocent, even inconsequential remark. Each name brings with it a history that, when combined with our own Balzacian baggage, allows us to

---

[4] A list of the characters named in this *nouvelle* is provided at the end of this chapter. By my count, there are at least twenty-seven individual characters, not all of them named or recurring. It must be acknowledged that Mlle Des Touches has an unusually large dining room, with exceptional acoustics.

speculate on possible double meanings in each character's story or remarks, on those undercurrents that the Narrator is not present to explicitly clarify for us. By using Bianchon—a naive voice compared to the almost omniscient Narrator—Balzac is able to make *Autre étude de femme* one of the most richly ambiguous texts of *La Comédie humaine.*

One example of such a speaking silence is a case that Mozet cites as one of the *incohérences* of the text. The aristocratic poet Canalis offers a brief but emphatic praise of Napoleon. Mozet expresses some surprise that this character should make a speech in praise of the *usurpateur,* especially in public: "Pourquoi Canalis? Pourquoi avoir choisi l'amant de la duchesse de Chaulieu, le poète légitimiste et religieux, pour prononcer cet hymne à la gloire de Napoléon?" [*Why Canalis? Why choose the lover of the duchesse de Chaulieu, the legitimist and religious poet, to proclaim this hymn to the glory of Napoleon?*] (Introduction, éd. Pléiade, 660). For Mozet, the apparent contradiction between the character of the *énonciateur* and that of the *énoncé* confirms that this passage is merely an "emprunt pur et simple, qui ne se justifie par rien d'autre que par le désir de remplir" [*pure and simple graft, which is in no way justified by anything other than the desire to fill up space*]. It is true that the passage has little to do with the study of woman, but a nostalgic gaze back at the Empire fits in with a subjacent theme in this text, the general decline of French society. As far as the contradiction between Canalis's political position and his remarks on Napoleon, a closer examination of the character suggests that this contradiction is not so illogical as it first appears to be. In *Modeste Mignon,* where Canalis is most completely portrayed, it is made clear that the versifying baron is above all ambitious; every aspect of his life, his title, his principles, his love for the regal duchesse de Chaulieu, even his poetry, is put in service of his ambition. Given Canalis's dual qualities of opportunism and ambition, it is not necessarily contradictory that this character should harbor a great admiration for Bonaparte. And even if his royalism is sincere to some degree, this does not necessarily preclude a recognition of Napoleon's gifts on his part. Especially in Balzac's world, a writer who expresses both legitimist sentiments and a cult for Napoleon is hardly an unresolvable contradiction.

I have already proposed another possible case of hidden meaning, with the suggestion that de Marsay's Duchess Charlotte is actually a mask for Lady Dudley. That theory—which I admit is tenuous and which incidentally is utterly shattered if we accept Bianchon's account of that lady's death—came to me only after considering another interesting silence in this text regarding de Marsay and the grotesquely fascinating Dudley family. There is of course the omission of any explicit reference to Paquita Valdès, which was thoroughly discussed in the first chapter. If one reason for de Marsay's silence regarding *la fille aux yeux d'or* is, as I maintained, that the story reveals a part of his nature and history that he prefers to keep hidden, another plausible and probable explanation is proposed by Nicole Mozet in her introduction: Lord Dudley, the father of Paquita's other lover and killer, the marquise de San-Réal, is also present at Félicité's dinner; "on comprend très bien que [de Marsay. . .] par respect humain et par politesse mondaine, ne fasse aucune allusion" [*one can understand quite well that de Marsay, out of human respect and social courtesy, would make no reference*] to the bloody tale of his half-sister and their shared lover in front of the old man. What Mozet does not include in this observation is that this possible solution, like the problem itself, is yet another of those elements that could only be perceived by a reader familiar with *La Comédie humaine* as a whole. There is no explicit reference to either Paquita or her killer in *Autre étude,* there also is no direct reference to the fact that Lord Dudley is de Marsay's father. This illegitimate relationship is hinted at, however, in de Marsay's story, when he refers to Sultan, a beautiful horse that Dudley had sent to his son from England. What the naive reader would make of this gift is hard to say; it would perhaps seem merely an act of noble generosity among the rich and titled, perhaps suggesting a strong friendship between the two men. While the connection between the two men is not an absolute secret—Félix tells Natalie about it in *Le Lys*— we do not know exactly who knows about it, so Bianchon's silence is perfectly understandable.

This unspoken relationship is important in *Autre étude* because of another character, Lady Barimore, Lord Dudley's daughter. We know almost nothing of this character, other than the fact that she loves to shiver; "j'aime tant à frémir," [*I do so love to shiver*] she cries in anticipation of a frightening story. What is interesting about this banal exclamation of yet another *jeune personne, amie du fantastique* is the response it provokes: "—C'est un goût de femme vertueuse, répliqua de Marsay en regardant la charmante fille de lord Dudley" [*"It's the taste of a virtuous woman," replied de Marsay looking at the charming daughter of Lord Dudley*] (703).

What probably seems to a naive reader to be nothing more than mildly flirtatious banter is fascinating to the *lecteurs initiés*. We know that de Marsay is flirting with his half-sister—as Balzac doubtless intends us to see, as he recalls the relationship for a second time in this exchange—but we do not know who else at the table knows it. Is Bianchon unaware of their kinship, or does he merely gloss over it for reasons of taste or *bienséance?* Are de Marsay and Lady Barimore aware of it? Or is the depraved old Englishman Dudley, who is not in the habit of revealing to his children the "parentés qu'il leur créait un peu partout" [*the relatives he created for them more or less everywhere*] (*FYO*: 5:1054), amusing himself by watching his two bastards flirt with each other? If the Duchess Charlotte is indeed a mask for Lady Dudley, and if de Marsay has just avenged himself against his stepmother by telling their story in front of her, is his knowing flirtation with her stepdaughter (possibly even her daughter) a way of twisting the knife? The more we study this aspect of *Autre étude,* the more we see new possibilities, new questions that the text raises; and yet our closer study does not reveal answers to those questions. We see again how the use of a naive narrator has liberated Balzac from the need to respond to the questions he playfully raises by his choice of characters and the lines he assigns them. De Marsay's teasing banter with Lady Barimore is a reflection of the tantalizing wink that Balzac is making in the same passage to his loyal readers, and *Autre étude* is full of such *clins d'œil*, made over the heads of Bianchon and the other characters present.

Appropriately enough, the dissembling politician de Marsay is assigned a large number of such enigmatic phrases in the text. One such case comes just after the story of the Duchess Charlotte, which prompts a discussion on the decline of French women since the Revolution. Part of this discussion is an interesting bit of dialogue that incidentally reminds us of the importance of aristocratic titles in Balzac's cosmology:

> Quelque terribles que soient ces paroles, [dit de Marsay] disons-les : les duchesses s'en vont, et les marquises aussi! Quant aux baronnes, j'en demande pardonne à Madame de Nucingen, qui se fera comtessse quand son mari deviendra pair de France, les baronnes n'ont jamais pu se faire prendre au sérieux.

—L'aristocratie commence à la vicomtesse, dit Blondet en souriant. (689)

"However terrible these words may be," said de Marsay, "let's say
them: Duchesses are on their way out, and marquises as well! As for
baronesses, I beg the pardon of Madame de Nucingen, who will make
herself a countess as soon as her husband becomes a peer of the realm,
baronesses have never been able to make themselves be taken seri-
ously."
"Aristocracy begins with the viscountess," said Blondet with a smile.

Again, the naive reader would probably see nothing significant in these remarks, but for the *lecteur initié* another interpretation suggests itself. It is
possible that what seems like a polite excuse on de Marsay's part is actually a gratuitous dig at his former lover, since his remark is after all what
guarantees that his listeners will remember the baroness's presence and
rank. This is a case where our knowledge of *La Comédie humaine,* which
very often exceeds that of the characters, comes into play; we know that
Delphine will in fact never succeed in making herself a countess, even after her husband has become a peer. In *Les Parents pauvres,* as the curtain
falls on Balzac's world, Nucingen is richer than ever, a peer and a senator,
and still a baron. He has never made the ascension that so many others in
Balzac's world can and do: the baron de Rastignac becomes a count, in
part because of Nucingen's money; even the preposterous cuckold du
Bruel makes this leap, with far less money and influence than Nucingen
has. The baron de La Baudraye, who in so many ways resembles Nucingen, also manages to become *comte et pair.* Nucingen's social immobility
in the churning world of the July Monarchy is a curious anomaly, and the
key to the enigma may just concern Delphine. Nucingen and his wife have
a complicated relationship; she seems at various points to be his victim (*Le*
Père Goriot), his amused tormentor (*Splendeurs et Misères*), and his more
or less witting accomplice (*César Birotteau* and *La Maison Nucingen*).
One wonders if the banker holds himself back in order to hold his wife
back, keeping her from the social advance that would doubtless mean so
much to her—we should never forget the terrible rivalry between the two
filles Goriot, and the comtesse Anastasie outranks her sister. In either case,
the *lecteur initié,* who can see farther than the characters in the text, is able

to discern in de Marsay's remark the possibility of a double meaning, a riddle that Balzac's narrative technique hides from the naive reader.

A passage that precedes de Marsay's comments on the relative merits of duchesses and baronesses lends support to the idea that Mme de Nucingen may be the butt of a joke in the text. After hearing the story of de Marsay's *première*, Delphine announces her sympathy for de Marsay's second lover, forgetting, rather surprisingly, that she herself followed the Duchess Charlotte in de Marsay's affections:

> —Combien je plains la seconde! » dit la baronnne de Nucingen.
> Un sourire imperceptible, qui vint effleurer les lèvres pâles de de Marsay, fit rougir Delphine de Nucingen.
> « *Gomme on ouplie!* » s'écria le baron de Nucingen.
> La naïveté du célèbre banquier eut un tel succès que sa femme, qui fut cette *seconde* de de Marsay, ne put s'empecher de rire comme tout le monde. (688)
>
> *An imperceptible smile, which came fleetingly to the pale lips of de Marsay, made Delphine de Nucingen blush.*
> *"How one forgets," cried the baron de Nucingen.*
> *The naïveté of the famous banker was so successful that his wife, who was that very "seconde" of de Marsay, could not stop herself from laughing along with everyone else.*

I think it is reasonable to wonder if Nucingen's remark actually reflects naivete or frank indifference, given the way Bixiou describes Nucingen's attitude toward his wife's infidelities in *La Maison Nucingen* (352-53). This passage is ambiguous for another reason. On the one hand, if we take this moment at face value, as a moment of shared good humor among friends, it could confirm the idea, suggested in the preamble, that all of the guests present have met on a "pied d'égalité." On the other hand, it could be seen to put that very same idea into doubt. We can reasonably ask ourselves if Delphine laughs out of good humor or merely to save face in front of her august dining companions.

This question of the *pied d'égalité* is an important one, given the variety of characters who are found at the table, where the lions (de Marsay, Lord and Lady Dudley, Mmes de Cadignan and d'Espard) have sat down with the lambs (Adam Laginski, Mmes de Portenduère and de Vandenesse). The disparity of the personalities present could lead some to conclude that this is just another sign of the text's incoherence, that Balzac indifferently scratched in whatever name came to mind as he wrote and rewrote. It is true that some of the characters are simply too young to have been tested by the "commerce de quinze années" that Bianchon cites in the preamble, but, again, I think it can be demonstrated through an examination of the dialogue that the names used were anything but randomly chosen. For example, Adam Laginski's youth, worldly inexperience, and the fact that he is a foreigner make him a logical choice to act as an uncomprehending narratee for Blondet's discourse on the very French creature that is the *femme comme il faut;* the *naïf Polonais*'s questions give Balzac an excuse to draw out this section, refining and expanding his study of this new species. In a similar vein, it is Mme de Vandenesse—almost certainly Marie de Grandville—who hopes that women can be known for other reasons than a lack of virtue (703). I think that these younger characters serve to make *Autre étude de femme* a scene of transition between the old guard of *La Comédie humaine* to the second generation, between the high society of the Restoration to that of the July Monarchy. Félicité's dinner party seems to be in some sense a social education for that second generation, who, as Rose Fortassier accurately remarked, will never quite live up to the example set by their high-flying predecessors (*Les Mondains de "La Comédie humaine,"* 138).

There are many other textual indications that the dinner party represents a carefully composed group. To begin with, Balzac shifted the scene from the marquise d'Espard's home to Mlle des Touches's; as Mozet pointed out, such an eclectic company is far more plausible at the home of the generous and genial artist than in that of the arrogant marquise (674, nb. 1). Other indications of great care in composition are to be found in the reactions of the female characters to the judgments that the various narrators—all male—make on women. When de Marsay coldly and somewhat crudely states that all women are "des poêles à dessus de marbre," [stoves with marble tops] Mme de Camps replies with a smile: "O! faîtes-nous grâce de vos horribles sentences?" ["*O! spare us your terrible condemnations?*"] (678). The *lecteur initié* knows that the virtuous ex-Mme Firmiani has the right to protest, and that the lady does not protest too much. In a similar vein, but from the other side of the moral spectrum, the princesse de Cadignan takes up the defense of her sex (and her class) after hearing Blondet and others lament the decline of the French woman from the *grande dame* to the *femme comme il faut:*

> —Sommes-nous donc si réellement diminuées que ces messieurs le pensent? dit la princesse de Cadignan en adressant aux femmes un sourire à la fois douteur et moqueur . . . Je sais d'admirables dévouements, de sublimes souffrances auxquelles manque la publicité, la gloire si vous voulez, qui jadis illustrait les fautes de quelques femmes. Mais pour n'avoir pas sauvé un roi de France, on n'en est pas moins Agnès Sorel. (701-2)
>
> *"Are we really so diminished as these gentlemen think?" said the princesse de Cadignan, addressing the other women with a smile at once skeptical and mocking. "I know of admirable devotions, sublime sufferings that have lacked publicity, glory if you like, which once illuminated the faults of some women. But for not having saved a king of France, one is not less an Agnes Sorel."*

Again, it is perfectly logical that Diane should protest the denigration that catches her in its broad sweep. In virtually all her appearances in *La Comédie humaine,* especially in *Les Secrets de la princesse de Cadignan,* this character benefits from the obvious affection of her creator. She is a debauched libertine, hypocritical and almost pathologically selfish, and yet almost always retains the readers' sympathies because she always has Balzac's. Not the least of the reasons that Diane keeps our sympathy is her remarkable intelligence. She and several of the other women to whom she addresses her skeptical smile clearly do not fit into the model traced by Blondet and the other men at the table.

In this study of women, it is the men who offer the analyses, while the women are left the role of respondents. As the preamble indicates, the women present are more than equal to the task, holding their own quite well in this joust of words and wit. Arguing from positions of strength (Mmes d'Espard, de Cadignan, Lady Dudley), virtue (Mmes de Portenduère et de Vandenesse), or some combination of the two (Mlle des Touches, Mme de Camps), the ladies do not give the gentlemen the last word on women, until the end of the conversation. The dominant theme of the conversation, found in all three of the main stories, is feminine inconstancy—de Marsay, Montriveau, and Bianchon all tell tales of men's vengeance on unfaithful women.[5] The women present hold their own, until Bianchon's story, *La Grande Bretèche*. Neither de Marsay's tale of psychological cruelty nor the horrific physical cruelty decribed in Montriveau's can achieve the effect of Bianchon's story—which combines both—that is, the silence of the listeners, the end of the conversation. At the close of *Autre étude de femme,* the Narrator appears out of nowhere to give us an enigmatic ending that is the final silence in this text, and which even the most experienced of readers has no keys with which to uncode. The only course left to us is sheer speculation.

Balzac builds to this ending with great care, which is undermined by an apparent flaw in this same construction. *La Grande Bretèche* is Bianchon's second internal narration; it is immediately preceded by the problematic depiction of the death of "la première de M. de Marsay." I have already alluded to my belief that this contradiction is due less to carelessness than to the fact that this text was unfinished at the time of Balzac's death. The final pages of *Autre étude de femme* as we now know it were added on to the text following a handwritten note in Balzac's own copy of *La Comédie humaine,* the famous "Furne corrigé." It is reasonable to assume that Balzac would have addressed this contradiction in the text had illness and then death not prevented him from doing so. That said, the lines that introduce the death scene again raise questions about the possible identity of the Duchess Charlotte. As the company discusses the horrible death of Rosina, Lord Dudley asks "en souriant," "Et quelle sera la punition de la première de M. de Marsay?" [*he asks "with a smile: and what will be the punishment for M. de Marsay's* première?]. The question is a rather abrupt *retour en arrière,* even for Balzac. To the naive reader, it might seem to be an author's clumsy device, but for the *lecteur initié,* aware of the secret bond between Lord Dudley and de Marsay, there may be an undercurrent to the remark. Is Lord Dudley teasing his son by implicitly casting him in the role of Rosina's sheeplike husband, who in the

---

[5] Montriveau tells the story of Rosina. Briefly, she is an Italian countess, wife of a captain in Napoleon's Russian army, who becomes a camp follower and the mistress of her husband's commanding officer. The complacent cuckold is finally shamed when the young Montriveau laughs at him in front of their fellow officers. Driven to act, he locks his faithless wife and her lover in an old house and sets fire to it. As de Marsay says, "Il n'y a rien de plus terrible que la révolte d'un mouton" [*There is nothing more terrible than the revolt of a sheep*].

end took his revenge in a far more spectacular manner than de Marsay? If
Charlotte is really Lady Dudley, her husband's comment is a swipe at her
as well, the future tense indicating that the lady in question is very much
alive, and has some punishment in store for her—however hypocritical it
may be for Lord Dudley to be making warnings about karmic retribution.
Again, no definite answers can be given to the questions raised. And
again, I admit that I may be reading too much into the text, but such
speculation is one of its pleasures.

Returning to the death scene itself, I have already given my wholly
subjective opinion that this is a boring passage that, in the end, adds little
to the text as a whole. That said, I do think there is a logical reason that
Balzac chose to include this soft segment amid the harsher ones that overshadow it. This reason is suggested in the transition given in the text, after
Bianchon has told the story of the death of a kind and selflessly loving
woman who bears precious little resemblance to de Marsay's Charlotte,
and whose death seems less a punishment than some sort of redemption:

> —Les histoires que conte le docteur, dit le duc de Rhétoré, font des
> impressions bien profondes.
> —Mais douces, reprit Mlle des Touches.
>
> *"The stories the doctor tells," said the duke de Rhétoré, "leave
> profound impressions."*
> *"But sweet ones," replied Mlle des Touches.*

The sweet story has temporarily and deceptively changed the tone of the
evening; the sharply witty, occasionally even caustic, atmosphere of the
joust has suddenly become soft and sentimental. The narratees, textual and
extratextual, are thus set up for an emotional fall, for a story that will leave
deep but hardly sweet impressions. Bianchon, in vain, warns his audi-
ence(s) that not all his tales are so gentle as the first, responding to Mlle
des Touches:

> —Ah! madame, répliqua le docteur,[6] j'ai des histoires terribles
> dans mon répertoire; mais chaque récit a son heure dans une conversa-

---

[6] This marks the sudden appearance of the Narrator, as Bianchon is named in the third
person for the first time.

tion, selon ce joli mot rapporté par Chamfort et dit au duc de Fronsac:
« Il y a dix bouteilles de vin de Champagne entre ta saillie et le moment
où nous sommes. »

> *"Ah!, madame," replied the doctor, "I have some terrible stories
> in my repertoire; but every tale has its time in a conversation, accord-
> ing to the bon mot that Chamfort reports someone once saying to the
> duc de Fronsac: "We are ten bottles of champagne away from an out-
> burst like yours."*

This warning only serves to sharpen the appetites of Bianchon's listeners
who, *en bons amis du fantastique,* clamor for just such an *histoire terrible.*
Perhaps this is precisely the intention of Bianchon the talented storyteller;
this may be his, and Balzac's, way of setting the mood for his tale. After
the gentle portrayal of the death of the noble and kind lady has in some
sense neutralized the atmosphere, lulling the listeners around the table into
a sense of calm and well-being, the good-natured pleading of the guests
helps to create a sense of anticipation in the audience, listeners and readers
alike.

> —Mais il est deux heures du matin, et l'histoire de Rosine nous a
> préparées,[7] dit la maîtresse de maison.
> —Dites, monsieur Bianchon!. . . » demanda-t-on de tous côtés. À
> un geste du complaisant docteur, le silence régna. (710)
> *"But it's two o'clock in the morning, and the story of Rosine has
> prepared us," said the mistress of the house.*
> *"Tell it, monsieur Bianchon!" was the cry from all sides. At a
> gesture from the agreeable doctor, silence reigned.*

That silence of the company will remain unbroken. The last word at the
souper will be Bianchon's, and the Narrator will close the *nouvelle.*

The tale of Mme de Merret, the virtuous adulteress, will bring a
sudden end to the conversation and to this *étude:*

> Après ce récit, toutes les femmes se levèrent de table, et le charme
> sous lequel Bianchon les avait tenues fut dissipé par ce mouvement.

---

[7] It is worth noting, I think, that Mlle des Touches's *nous* refers to the women present.

Néanmoins quelques-unes d'entre elles avaient eu quasi froid en entendant le dernier mot. (729)

> *After this tale, all the women got up from the table, and the spell
> under which Bianchon had held them was broken by this movement.
> Nevertheless, some of them were almost cold (*quasi froid*) hearing the
> last word.*

This last fragment has a greater effect than the other two stories of feminine inconstancy and masculine revenge—and this seems to prove true not
only for the textual narratees, but for readers and critics as well. I believe
this has to do with the fact, mentioned earlier, that *La Grande Bretèche*
combines the psychological cruelty of *Les Premières armes* with the physical brutality of the story of Rosina. De Marsay's story takes place in the
world of *salons* and *boudoirs* with which all of these characters are quite
familiar, and it involves a fairly banal question of infidelity. If the narratees all recognize de Marsay's skill at this sort of social *escrime* as exceptional, there is nothing terribly unfamiliar in this story. Montriveau's story
contains much that is unfamiliar and terrifyingly brutal, but it is set against
the backdrop of Napoleon's Russian campaign, specifically the events surrounding the crossing of the Bérézina, an episode for which Balzac had a
specific and horrific fascination (cf. *Adieu,* and also *Le Médecin de campagne*). The horror of the death of Rosina and the colonel is further at-
tenuated by the fact that they are foreigners, Italians, people subject to
unreasonable passions. *La Grande Bretèche* is something quite different;
whereas Montriveau's story takes place in a faraway place, difficult to
pronounce, Bianchon's tale of illicit love and cruel revenge takes place in
a handsome provincial house, among people who are not so different from
those gathered around this table—Mme de Merret even bears a distinct
resemblance to Mme de Mortsauf, although of course *la Vierge de Clochegourde* died from *not* giving in to illicit passion. As romantic, even gothic,
as Bianchon's tale might be, it is not fantastic; rather it is terribly realistic,
and this violence hits close to home.

The last paragraph, which describes only the women's reaction to
the story, refocuses the reader's attention on the title. We should never
forget that the title of this work is *Autre étude de femme,* and not *Autres
études de femme.* It is logical, even necessary, to infer that Balzac intended
us to draw some general conclusions about women from the whole of the

text, and not merely from the diverse fragments and stories. By including very different female characters in his conversation scene, Balzac presents women as a highly diverse group rather than as a uniform species. This diversity further complicates the already ambiguous last paragraph. All the women are profoundly moved by the tale, all recognize that the spell is broken; but apparently not all of them are moved in the same way: "*quelques-unes* d'entre elles avaient eu quasi froid en entendant le dernier mot." We do not know which of the women experienced this sensation of *quasi froid.* For that matter, we can reasonably ask exactly what *quasi froid* means. On a most superficial level, we can take it to be a somewhat idiosyncratic expression of a very common sensation, a shiver inspired by a frightening story, the kind that thrill *jeunes personnes* like Lady Barimore. In a similar vein, perhaps virtuous and naïve young brides like Mmes de Portenduère and Vandenesse see Mme de Merret's fate as a cautionary tale, a warning about what horrors adultery may bring. In *Le Conseil,* the work where Balzac first used the story of *La Grande Bretèche,* it had just such a didactic purpose. Mmes de Montcornet and de Sérisy are neither so young nor so virtuous as the two *jeunes mariées.* Perhaps for these two flagrant adulteresses *quasi froid* implies a shudder of guilty recognition or fearful premonition as they contemplate Mme de Merret's fate. Finally, we should consider those women whose careers surpass adultery into frank *libertinage.* Perhaps *quasi froid* implies that Lady Dudley or Mme de Cadignan have enjoyed the story and feel the superficial shiver of pleasurable fear that such a story causes, but without feeling any real sympathy. Neither of these powerfully intelligent and utterly ruthless women would ever allow themselves to be placed in such a position—especially not by their husbands.

Turning again to the title, its deceptive simplicity belies the complexity of one central question underlying the text, namely, Balzac's view(s) of women. Balzac is generally thought to have fairly reactionary views on women and their role in society, but *Autre étude de femme* demonstrates that this view is both too vague and too simplistic. We do find in the text at least one of Balzac's (in)famously condescending generalizations about women, placed in the mouth of de Marsay, but confirmed by the reaction of his *auditrices:*

Il y a toujours un fameux singe dans la plus jolie et la plus angélique
des femmes! »

À ce mot, toutes les femmes baissèrent les yeux comme blessées
par cette cruelle vérité, si cruellement formulée. (682)

"There's always quite a monkey beneath the prettiest and most angelic
of women!"

At this, all the women lowered their eyes as if wounded by this
cruel truth, so cruelly expressed.

This remark is rather ham-fisted and more than a little out of place in this
elegant conversation. It can be challenged on other grounds as well; the
merit of the observation is undercut by the women present at the table,
their histories and their comments. It is unlikely that Diane de Cadignan or
Félicité des Touches or the ex-Mme Firmiani would see themselves in this
strange description. Mme de Camps dismisses another of de Marsay's in-
sulting remarks about women with a smiling but absolute self-assurance;
the joyous libertine Diane de Cadignan asserts her right to be counted
among the greats of her kind going back to the Middle Ages; Lady Dudley
implicitly rejects men's right to judge her; and Balzac's most singular female character, the genial rebel Félicité des Touches, is given her due by
her creator, who makes her the *présidente* of this assembly of some of his
greatest creations.

It is important to remember, when considering the title of this work
and the various portrayals of women that it contains, that in the arts the
term *étude* often refers to a series of sketches with which an artist attempts
to arrive at the perfect representation of a given subject. Viewing the work
through the prism of the varied women around the table, examining how
they react not only to the stories of adultery that they hear, but also how
they engage their fellow narratees in conversation, defend themselves or
their sex, etc., shows us perhaps Balzac at work on different varieties of
the model of *la femme*. This flawed text shows us in microcosm how varied, complex, and nuanced the image of women was for this artist who is
accused of painting only types, and of doing so with overly broad strokes
and stark colors. The Balzacian sketchbook that is *Autre étude de femme*
shows us varieties of tone and sophisticated play of shadow and light in its
portrayal of women.

In the end, it must be acknowledged that this *étude* raises more questions than it resolves. Perhaps more than in any other single text of *La Comédie humaine,* the reader of *Autre étude de femme* is required to be a producer rather than merely a consumer of text. By using Bianchon as his principal narrator, Balzac achieves a paradoxical end, at least with his loyal readers: he draws us closer into his world, giving us an illusory feeling of familiarity and self-assurance as we meet in these pages characters we know so well; at the same time, he obscures much of the detail that usually comes from the Narrator's garrulous voice. The many voices in this text are subtly altered because filtered through the naive voice of Bianchon, forcing us to read not only between the lines, but between the multiple layers of text. And we are rewarded handsomely for our effort.

The Self-Realization of a Departmental Muse in *Un Prince de la bohème*

Like *La Maison Nucingen, Un Prince de la bohème* contains a doubly framed object story. The story of Charles-Edouard Rusticoli, comte de La Palférine and "prince" of Balzac's Parisian Bohemia, is presented to us as part of a *nouvelle* being read to the playwright and author Raoul Nathan by Balzac's *femme-auteur,* Dinah de La Baudraye, protagonist of the novel *La Muse du département.* The curious thing about this recitation is that Dinah's *nouvelle* is actually her transcription of a story she had heard Nathan himself tell only a few days earlier. Further complicating this rather strange situation is the fact that Dinah has included Nathan's original act of narration in her story, so that a second frame surrounds the object story about La Palférine. In Balzac's *nouvelle,* Dinah tells the object story to Nathan, while in Dinah's *nouvelle,* Nathan tells the story to the marquise de Rochefide. At the end of Dinah's reading, Nathan approves her version of his story, asking only that the names be changed before publication. As I stated earlier, this is an example of the false fictions within *La Comédie humaine—all is true!* Beyond the multiplicity of narrators and narratees and the complexity of their various relationships, this work is further complicated, as always with Balzac, by the threads that run in and out of the text, both affecting and being affected by the textual whole.

Before discussing the frames, a word about the object story itself: the portrait of La Palférine and his bohemian milieu is presented chiefly through the story of the one-sided love affair between the proud and impoverished young count and Claudine du Bruel, better known in Balzac's world as Tullia, formerly a lead dancer with the Parisian Opera and one of the queens of Balzac's demimonde during the Restoration. In 1833, when Nathan's story begins, Claudine has retired from her career of quasi-prostitution and is aspiring to a life of dull bourgeois respectability as the wife of du Bruel, a member of the minor Norman gentry, a former government clerk (voir *Les Employés*), now a successful writer of Vaudeville plays under the name of de Cursy. The still beautiful and increasingly respectable Claudine has the misfortune to fall in love with the arrogant and much younger count, and continues to pursue him in spite of his cruelly and relentlessly degrading treatment of her. In one of his many tests of the strength of Claudine's attachment, La Palférine coldly tells the former *fille d'opéra* that she is not good enough to be his lover:

> Eh bien [. . .] si tu veux rester la maîtresse d'un La Palférine pauvre, sans le sou, sans avenir, au moins dois-tu le représenter dignement. Tu dois avoir un équipage, des laquais, une livrée, un titre. Donne-moi toutes les jouissances de vanité que je ne puis pas avoir par moi-même [. . .] Je suis fait comme cela, moi! Ma femme doit être admirée de tout Paris. Je veux que tout Paris m'envie mon bonheur! (82-84)
>
> *If you want to remain the mistress of an impoverished La Palférine, without a penny or any prospects, at least you must represent him in a worthy manner. You must have horses and a carriage, lackeys, livery, a title. Give me all the pleasures of vanity that I cannot afford for myself . . . I'm just that way! My woman must be admired by all of Paris. I want all of Paris to envy me my happiness!*

A combination of several factors—the most important of which are the remarkable power of Claudine's will and the generally degraded state of society under the July Monarchy—has startling results: within three years, the comtesse du Bruel triumphantly arrives at La Palférine's apartment in a carriage decorated with her husband's arms.

The object story stands well on its own, an amusing and revealing portrait of a fascinating milieu, shedding light on Balzac's demimonde and giving a more humorous than usual perspective on the author's contempt for his own times. Tullia (Claudine), du Bruel, and La Palférine are all recurring characters, giving the object story all the links it needs to the larger whole. There is also a thematic connection, beyond the very general one of the disdain for the society and government of the July Monarchy. As Patrick Berthier pointed out, this tale, with its reflections on the waste of talented youth of France, represented by the highly intelligent but parasitic La Palférine, serves as a comic pendant to the tragic *Z. Marcas* (Introduction, éd. Pléiade, 7:797). Marcas even appears, fleetingly but significantly, in the object story.

What is unusual about the frames of this text is that they actually weaken *Un Prince de la bohème* as a unit, even while enriching it as a part of the whole. As many critics, Anthony Pugh first among them, have pointed out, the metadiegetic frame, in which Nathan tells the story of La Palférine to Mme de Rochefide, tends to make this *nouvelle* seem like a displaced chapter from *Béatrix* ("Note sur l'épilogue de *Un Prince de la Bohème*," 358). The reader of *Un Prince* who has not read that novel will almost certainly be left confused by the references to the marquise simultaneously falling in love with La Palférine and deciding to return to her husband, Arthur, and would have no idea who Mme Schontz might be. Only the reader of the novel understands that Nathan's act of narration is a second-hand seduction; that, as narrator, he is part of a conspiracy, acting on the orders of the duchesse de Grandlieu and her most unlikely ally, Maxime de Trailles. Toward the end of *Béatrix,* the very devout and aristocratic Mme de Grandlieu—whose daughter is in danger of losing her husband, Calyste du Guénic, to Mme de Rochefide—turns to the thoroughly disreputable de Trailles, who in turn bribes La Palférine, a younger version of himself, to seduce Béatrix in order to free Calyste from her clutches. Nathan's role in this scheme is to arouse Béatrix's interest in La Palférine. He does so, successfully, with the story of Charles and Claudine.

It is also interesting, for the (re)reader of *Béatrix,* to note that Charles-Edouard drives Béatrix back to her husband with almost the same words that drive Claudine to make her husband *comte et pair.* After La Palférine has succeeded in driving a wedge between Béatrix and Calyste, Mme de Rochefide joyfully and prematurely declares that she and Charles are "liés à jamais. . ." [*forever joined together*]:

"—Madame, répondit froidement le prince de la Bohème, si vous
me voulez pour ami, j'y consens; mais à des conditions. . .

—Des conditions?

Oui, des conditions, que voici. Vous vous réconcilierez avec M.
de Rochefide, vous recouvrerez les honneurs de votre position, vous
reviendrez dans votre bel hôtel de la rue d'Anjou, vous y serez une des
reines de Paris, vous le pourrez en faisant jouer à M. de Rochefide un
rôle politique et en mettant dans votre conduite l'habileté, la persistance
que Mme d'Espard a déployée. Voilà la situation dans laquelle doit être
une femme à qui je fais l'honneur de me donner. . . (2:938)

*"Madame," the Bohemian prince responded coldly, "if you want
me for your friend, I consent; but with certain conditions. . ."*

"Conditions?"

*"Yes, these conditions. You will reconcile with M. de Rochefide,
you will reclaim the honors of your position, you will return to your
beautiful house in the rue d'Anjou, where you will be one of the queens
of Paris, which you will be able to do by having M. de Rochefide play
some part in politics, and in putting some skill in your own conduct, the
sort of persistence that Mme d'Espard has shown. That is the position
that a woman must hold in order for me to honor her by giving myself
to her.*

Béatrix, of course, fulfills every condition to the letter, just as Claudine
did before her. It is interesting to note the difference in tone and in language
that La Palférine uses in these two otherwise similar cases. Most
evident is difference in tone, between the *tutoiement* of Claudine and the
formality with which Charles addresses the marquise de Rochefide. Also,
Claudine's goal, stated by her would-be lover, is to be "la maîtresse d'un
La Palférine," for Béatrix, it is a much more discrete question of having
him "pour ami." Charles can be reasonably confident that the course he
prescribes will succeed, since it is exactly the one that Claudine had followed
some time earlier. The count tells the marquise that she should follow
the path set out by Mme d'Espard, but in reality she is walking in the
footsteps of the *courtisane* Tullia, right down to manipulating her nonentity
of a husband into politics.

It is also important to remember that when Béatrix receives these
orders from Charles, she has already, and quite recently, heard Nathan's

story, including the very similar orders given to Claudine. This instance of intertextuality brings up yet another problem with the narrative chronology of *La Comédie humaine.* If we follow *Un Prince de la bohème,* it seems that Béatrix decides within a matter of days to return to her husband, according to Lousteau's announcement at the end of the *nouvelle.* In *Béatrix,* it is clear that this process takes several weeks, which is far more logical, and which also explains in part that Béatrix does not realize that she has been implicitly cast in the role of an easily manipulated courtesan. Some might see this repetition as an oversight on Balzac's part, a clumsy bit of self-plagiarism. This is extremely unlikely however, given the fact that Balzac explicitly names Charles "le prince de la Bohème" at the beginning of this passage. The repetition is obviously deliberate, and very probably meant to emphasize the similarity between the proud marquise and the preposterous new countess. Doubtlessly drawn to La Palférine because she believes that they are two of a kind, this skilled seductress finds herself overmatched, and ultimately reduced to the same position as the former *fille d'Opéra.*

Sarrasine provides yet another intertext for *Un Prince de la bohème,* where we see Mme de Rochefide again in the role of narratee. Clearly this woman enjoys stories and is greatly affected by them. Another common thread between *Sarrasine* and *Un Prince* is that Béatrix is described in both texts as a child. In 1830, the young bride is described as a *femme-enfant,* to borrow Barthes's term; in 1841, the mature woman compares herself to a child, saying to Nathan as she waits for his tale to begin: "—Vous avez la parole, je vous écoute comme un enfant à qui sa mère raconterait *Le Grand Serpentin vert*" [*"You have the floor, I'll listen to you like a child whose mother is telling him the tale of* Le Grand Serpentin vert"] (808). Allan Pasco has analyzed in detail the significance of this specific reference in *Un Prince (Balzacian Montage,* 111-13), but what interests me is that Balzac has this character describe herself as a child specifically in relation to the act of storytelling. The implication is that, as a narratee, this woman is especially vulnerable, she is as susceptible to stories as men are to her charms. The connection is strengthened by the echo, in *Un Prince,* of the famous conclusion to *Sarrasine:* "Et la marquise resta pensive" [*And the marquise was left in a pensive state*] (6:1076). Béatrix becomes pensive while listening to Nathan's tale as well, as we see when a part of the story does not elicit the expected response: "La marquise, trop pensive pour rire dit à Nathan un « Continuez! » qui lui prouva combien elle était frappée de ces étrangetés, combien surtout La Palférine la préoccupait" [*The marquise, too pensive to laugh, told Nathan "Continue!" which proved to him how deeply she was struck by this strange tale, and especially how much La Palférine preoccupied her thoughts*] (825). The thoughts that each story inspires in her are obviously quite different—the story of Zambinella and Sarrasine disgusts her, while the disgusting behavior of La Palférine seduces her—but in both cases, we see an intense and active psychological and emotional reaction to storytelling.

If the second—that is, metadiegetic—frame links *Un Prince de la bohème* to *Béatrix,* the primary frame links the *nouvelle* just as tightly to another novel, *La Muse du département.* At the end of *Un Prince*, after Dinah has finished her reading and promised Nathan to change the names before publishing it, she confides in him that she knows of "un autre ménage où c'est la femme qui est du Bruel" [*another household where it is the woman who is du Bruel*] (838). For the *lecteur initié,* this is a clear reference to Dinah's own personal life: she is living with her adulterous lover, the writer Lousteau, and just as du Bruel loves his wife more than she loves him, so too does Dinah give more love than she receives. The similarity is underlined by Lousteau's entrance just as Dinah whispers her confession to Nathan. None of this, however, is evident to the naive reader of *Un Prince.* There is no specific allusion to Dinah's domestic arrangements in the *nouvelle,* and Lousteau's presence is completely unexplained; there is no suggestion that he is closer to Dinah than is Nathan. Just as the metadiegetic frame ties the *nouvelle* to *Béatrix,* the diegetic frame makes *Un Prince de la bohème* almost a chapter of *La Muse du département.*

The link between *Un Prince* and *La Muse* was a late addition to the former text. Originally, an anonymous narrator read Nathan's tale to Nathan and the baronne de Rastignac. This original narrative situation is quite interesting in and of itself, not least because of the curious twist of having Nathan listen to his own story being read back to him; this somewhat convoluted structure was not, as one might assume, invented to form stronger links between *Un Prince* and the larger *Comédie humaine.* As Berthier points out, the anonymous rewriter of this early version suggests Balzac, copying a story from a seemingly real situation, which will then be published as fiction after the names are changed (801). As with the anonymous eavesdropper of *La Maison Nucingen,* there is a teasing allusion created here for the reader, Balzac strongly suggesting himself within his own fiction to make it seem more real. Also interesting is the presence of Rastignac's wife, in what was her only truly significant appearance in *La Comédie humaine*, independent of her husband or her parents. In this early version of the text, it is Augusta who tells Nathan that she knows another household where the woman is du Bruel, an obvious reference to her own quasi-incestuous marriage. Pugh sees this change from Augusta to Dinah as an unqualified mistake, a diminution of the text. I disagree; while it is true that this reference would have provided an ironically satisfying closure to Rastignac's career,[8] it is also true, as Berthier pointed out, that this analogy is not without its own problems: Rastignac is not so weak as Tullia, and Delphine is a poor match for the master manipulator La Palférine (802-3). That said, I do not at all agree with Berthier when he states that "il est impossible de comprendre cette phrase dans la bouche de Mme de La Baudraye" [*it is impossible to understand this phrase in the mouth of Mme de La Baudraye*] (803).

It is true that Dinah and Lousteau's relationship is not directly parallel to the one described in the object story either—since Lousteau does not have an acknowledged lover who would correspond to La Palférine. However, there are other ways in which the analogy works quite well. If Lousteau has no (second) *maîtresse en titre,* it is strongly suggested in *La Muse* that he is unfaithful to Dinah. Even more importantly, in the context of *Un Prince,* Dinah supports her unfaithful partner through her own literary work, just as du Bruel's plays help provide Claudine with the money she tries to give La Palférine, and the means to satisfy the count's impossible (he thinks) demands. In *Un Prince,* Dinah hopes to publish Nathan's story in order to pay "notre loyer" (her and Lousteau's rent). In fact, Dinah takes this sacrifice one crucial step further in *La Muse,* allowing Lousteau to publish her work under his name.

There is, however, a more important reflection in the object story for Dinah, who hears this story and then claims it as her own. On a superficial level, it is Dinah's need for money that leads her to do this. In a larger sense, however, Dinah has a right to this story, since it is already in

---

[8] It is also true that one of the compelling aspects of *La Comédie humaine* is that Rastignac's career (and so many others) remains open-ended. We imagine him and other characters continuing on into the Second Empire.

some ways her own story. There are two images in the story of the count
and the showgirl in which she sees herself reflected, not only in the blindly
loving and betrayed writer, but also in the quasi-prostitute who betrays her
husband and degrades herself for the sake of an unworthy lover who does
not return her feelings. Again, this is not a parallel that has escaped the
notice of critics, but perhaps precisely because it is so obvious, critics have
neglected just how detailed and how carefully constructed the resemblance
is. The similarity between Claudine and Dinah is reflected in several examples of intertextuality between *La Muse du département* and *Un Prince
de la bohème*. In addition to their similar adulterous relationships, both
women have a convenient uncle whose timely death and generous legacy
helps to advance their affairs. In Claudine's case, it is only fitting that her
uncle Chaffaroux should leave her his 40,000-franc income (836), since it
came in large measure from favors Claudine obtained for him from her
former lover, the duc de Rhétoré (826). This enormous fortune is instru-
mental in Claudine's scheme, as it is shortly after this windfall that du
Bruel becomes a deputy, moving her closer to obtaining the dignities she
needs in order to humiliate herself before La Palférine. Dinah has no such
moral claim to the fortune bequeathed to her by her uncle Silas Piédefer,
who suddenly and unexpectedly leaves her a fortune earned in America.
This *coup de théâtre* allows Dinah to remain in Paris with her lover, after
she essentially uses it to bribe her husband. In return for control of Dinah's
fortune, the thoroughly and delightfully unprincipled baron de la Baudraye
allows his wife to remain in Paris, and even provides her with an income
(*MD*, 4:768-69).

An even more direct and more interesting point of comparison
between Claudine and Dinah involves the letters they write to their indifferent lovers. After Lousteau has seduced Dinah during a visit to her provincial home, the *femme-auteur* writes the cynical Parisian a number of
letters, some of which he shares with his bohemian friends, including his
mistress Mme Schontz, but most of which he does not even bother to read.
Claudine also writes to La Palférine, who uses the unread letters to wipe
his razor. The young count's friends, however, find the letters to have
some merit because of their sincerity. Nathan calls the letters "bien supé-
rieure[s] aux lettres factices que nous tâchons de faire, nous autres auteurs
de romans" [*quite superior to the facile letters that we, as novelists, try to
create*] (823). The admirable Marcas quietly reads one in a corner of the

room, a significant tribute to the former dancer's talents as a writer, or at
least to the poetry of true feeling. This parallel degradation is all the more
interesting because Dinah is almost certainly unaware of it. Whatever aspects of her own life she may see reflected in the story of Claudine and La
Palférine, there is no suggestion that Lousteau, as callous as he is, ever
told Dinah that her letters were used to amuse his friends. I suspect that
this similarity is one that Balzac intended for only his most alert readers to
discern, confirming to us that Dinah is correct in identifying herself with
Claudine. The connection is in fact stronger than even Dinah herself can
guess.

It is also significant that Balzac uses a comic tone in presenting the
two women; Dinah is the object of a sharply satirical portrait of the
femme-auteur, "une femme comme il n'en faut pas," [the kind of woman
we don't need] as Blondet caustically puts it in *Autre étude de femme* (7:
706). It is this character and Balzac's treatment of her that inspired Nicole
Mozet's observation that the pretension to authorship was the one trans-
gression that Balzac could not forgive in a woman (*Balzac au pluriel*,
166). We must always bear in mind that there was a marked difference in
Balzac's mind between bluestockings like Dinah and the *femme-artiste*, a
distinction that was reserved for the genius of Camille Maupin (and even
this author, always treated with respect and sympathy by her creator, in the
end repents her eccentric career and existence). If Dinah is the object of
a satire, Claudine is the main character in a farce. The comedy is broader
in this portrayal, perhaps because Balzac saw social climbers and even
prostitutes as less of a threat than Dinah and her kind. Yet in spite of the
comic overtones in both portraits, neither character is presented in a completely unsympathetic light. In each work, there is a broadly comic scene,
humiliating for the desperate lovers, and containing undertones that remind us that these women are victims; whatever their faults, however ridiculous their creator may make them appear, each deserves some degree
of sympathy.

In *La Muse,* when the pregnant Dinah suddenly arrives at Lousteau's doorstep—her impending arrival having been announced in an unread letter—her presence threatens a financially and socially advantageous
marriage that the enterprising Mme Schontz had arranged for him. The
callous Parisian sends an urgent request for help to his friend Bixiou. The
plan is for Bixiou to present himself "en vieillard de Molière, gronder ton

neveu Léandre sur sa sottise," [*like one of Molière's old men, come to scold your nephew for his folly*] with the hope that the provincial muse will sacrifice herself to her beloved's future and return to her husband. This farce within a satire does have a more serious subtext, however, as Lousteau instructs his friend: "il s'agit de la prendre par les sentiments, frappe fort, sois méchant, blesse-la" [*We've got to grab her by the sentiment, hit hard, be cruel, wound her*] (4:745). As Anne-Marie Meininger observed, this passage suggests the cruelty that lies beneath the ludic nature of the scenes that follow, and the drama underneath the comedy of *La Muse du département* (745, nb. 1). These scenes have a parallel in *Un Prince de la bohème*, as Claudine, feeling physically threatened by La Palférine, recoils, falls, and hits her head on a hearthstone. Nathan says that Claudine fell because she did not understand "la plaisanterie" in La Palférine's threats. It should be noted that the humor in that threat is not immediately evident to the reader either. This scene is melodrama presented as farce, it is true, but it also underlines for us La Palférine's cruelty; Claudine's very real physical danger following her fall shows us that his mistreatment of her goes beyond mere snobbery and crude sexual exploitation.

La Palférine is moved by Claudine's physical danger, but only temporarily; the episode quickly reverts to dark comedy as La Palférine's cruelty manifests itself again. This sequence is mirrored at the end of the object story, when the force of Claudine's genuine emotion impresses even the unfeeling La Palférine. When the comtesse du Bruel arrives with her liveried servants, La Palférine coldly informs her that he has added a new task to the herculean ones she has already accomplished: She must get him the Southern Cross, Claudine's simple response is: "Je te l'aurai" [*I'll get it for you*]. La Palférine laughs at her ignorance, but Nathan— himself quite capable of shabbily exploiting a devoted woman, as we see in *Une Fille d'Eve*—witnesses this scene and is "[s]aisi d'admiration pour cette intrépidité de l'amour vrai" [*seized with admiration for the intrepid quality of true love*]; he explains to the former courtesan that the Southern Cross is a constellation visible only from the South Seas. Again, Claudine's response is eloquent in its simplicity: "Eh bien . . . Charles, allons-y?" [*So Charles, shall we go?*]. This response even impresses the insolent bohemian prince: "Malgré la férocité de son esprit, La Palférine eut une larme aux yeux; mais quel regard et quel accent chez Claudine!"

[*In spite of his ferocity of spirit, La Palférine had a tear in his eye; what a tone of voice, what a look in Claudine's eye!*] At the end of the story, the force of Claudine's genuine emotion, which has made her the victim of La Palférine's hard, cynical wit, elevates her, giving her a moment of superiority that even the arrogant bohemian prince acknowledges, however briefly. The comic tone is quickly taken up again as we return to the meta-diegetic frame: Mme de Rochefide, who knows a few things about women and men, gives Claudine her due, pointing out that her cuckolded husband should be grateful for his wife's illicit ardor: "sans les fantaisies de sa femme, du Bruel serait encore de Cursy, un vaudevilliste parmi cinq cents vaudevillistes; tandis qu'il est à la Chambre de pairs . . ." [*without his wife's fantasies, du Bruel would still be just another vaudeville writer, one among five hundred; as it is, he sits in the Chamber of Peers*] (837).

By claiming this story as her own and thus identifying herself with Claudine, Dinah claims for herself a part of that dignity that comes from the sincerity of emotion, from the purity of a love that survives in the face of indifference. Dinah also earns the right to our sympathy because of her lucidity. In seeing herself in the story she heard from Nathan, Dinah shows that she is aware of the absurdity of her own humiliating domestic arrangement, and thus merits, in *Un Prince de la bohème*, a certain sympathy that Balzac does not allow her in *La Muse du départment*. It is in this regard that the differences between Dinah and Claudine become important. If they resemble each other as faithless wives and victimized lovers, they are very different in terms of their social background. For both of them, their adulterous love affair leads to a significant change in social status, but the respectably *bourgeoise* Dinah's social trajectory is, ironically, directly inverse to the former prostitute Claudine's. Before Lousteau, Dinah is a wealthy, provincial baroness. By following her lover to Paris, entering his world, she becomes a de facto member of the demi-monde, as is illustrated by the scene in which respectable society spurns her at the opera.[9] Claudine, on the other hand, climbs steadily up the social ladder, hiding her past in plain sight and resolutely committing herself to respectable conduct. She succeeds to the point where she attains the stamp

---

[9] Béatrix de Rochefide, linked to Dinah through *Un prince de la bohème*, receives the same treatment after her affair with Calyste becomes public knowledge. La Palférine comes to Béatrix's rescue, just as M. de Clagny comes to Dinah's.

of approval from the mixed world of the bourgeoisie and the petty nobility where she and her husband now live. The tacit approval of her new peers is explicitly expressed by none other than the very virtuous Mme Anselme Popinot: "Je ne peux pourtant pas me persuader que Mme du Bruel, la jeune, ait montré ses jambes nues et le reste à tout Paris, à la lueur de cent becs de lumière!" [*I just cannot believe that Mme du Bruel, the younger, showed her naked legs and the rest to all of Paris, by the light of a hundred stage lamps!*] (828) Whereas Dinah abandons all social respectability for the sake of her lover, Claudine's social status increases dramatically as a result of her affair with La Palférine—she becomes a countess, wife of a peer. Dinah will eventually achieve the same status, but only after abandoning her lover and returning to her husband.

Dinah also suffers in comparison to Claudine as regards their respective choice of lover. Both are treated disgracefully by their lovers, but Claudine's at least is a handsome young count—he is described as "le vivant portrait de Louis XIII" (817)—several years her junior. The beautiful, twenty-nine-year-old Mme de La Baudraye gives up her social status and security for an impoverished writer several years older than she is, who is only very ironically compared to Lord Byron:

> Lousteau [. . .] usé tout autant par le plaisir que par la misère, par les travaux et les mécomptes, paraissait avoir quarante-huit ans, quoiqu'il n'en eût que trente-sept. Déjà chauve, il avait pris un air byronien en harmonie avec ses ruines anticipées, avec les ravins tracés sur sa figure par l'abus du vin de Champagne. (*MD*, 4: 667)
>
> *Lousteau, worn out as much by pleasures as by poverty, by work, and by misfortunes, seemed to be 48, although he was only 37. Already bald, he had acquired a Byronian air in harmony with his own inevitable ruins, with the ravines created by overindulgence in Champagne.*

The distance between Claudine and Dinah, the inversely parallel distance between Lousteau and La Palférine, and the similarity between the two couples' relationships accentuate Dinah's fall. Not only does she implicitly compare herself to a courtesan, in some sense, she has fallen below that courtesan on a moral and social level. Speaking in narrow terms, Claudine does not have very far to fall; Dinah, an educated and affluent woman, should know better than to land in the place she does.

Stepping back from the individual texts to look at these two characters in the context of the larger *Comédie humaine,* the parallels between
Dinah and Claudine are interestingly underlined by the way in which Balzac plays with their names. The importance of names in Balzac's worldview is illustrated in several different texts. One that can be frequently
observed is the bourgeois' quest to abandon their common names in favor
of more aristocratic ones, such as the Camusot, who buy an expensive
piece of real estate in order to be known as M. et Mme de Marville. This is
obviously meant to reflect a social reality of the time. An even better
known example is found in the case of Lucien Chardon, who quickly re-
names himself M. de Rubempré. The duchesse de Langeais's refusal to
correctly name old Goriot (cf. chapter 1) is another illustration of the im-
por-tance of names, both in Balzac's text and in the world he (re)created.

    Un Prince de la bohème offers perhaps one of the best examples of
the importance of names in Balzac's text. For Denis Slatka, "la sémiologie
et la grammaire des noms propres fondent l'économie formelle du récit et
lui confèrent sa portée social [et] sa force critique" [*the semiology and
grammar of proper names forms the basis of the formal economy of the
story and confers to it its social import and its critical strength*] ("Sémiologie et grammaire du nom propre dans *Un Prince de la bohème,*" 235).
To illustrate his argument, Slatka points to—among many other things—a
scene in *Un Prince* that suggests the same aristocratic and anachronistic
attitude toward names as the duchess's game in *Le Père Goriot.* Among
the anecdotes with which Nathan paints his portrait of La Palférine is the
story of how the insolent count put an end to a duel between a noble friend
of his and a *bourgeois* by refusing to recognize the rights of someone *qui
n'est pas né* to a code of honor that rightly belongs only to the class of La
Palférine and his friend:

    "Un instant, dit La Palférine [. . .] monsieur est-il né? —Com-
ment, monsieur? dit le bourgeois. —Oui, êtes-vous né? Comment vous
nommez-vous? —Godin. [. . .] Godin! Cela n'existe pas, vous n'êtes
rien, Godin! Mon ami ne peut pas se battre en l'air. (811)
    *"Just one moment," said La Palférine, "was the gentleman born?"
"I beg your pardon, sir?" said the bourgeois. "Yes, were you born?
What is your name?" "Godin" "Godin! There's no such thing, you're
nothing, Godin! My friend can hardly fight with the air."*

As Slatka says, this brief comic scene illustrates the "mépris du nom obscur, anonyme" which is "un des fondements du discours polémique postrévolutionnaire" [*That contempt for the obscure and anonymous name which was one of the foundations of the post-revolutionary polemic discourse*] (242). This is merely one example of the importance of names in this text, where, as Slatka points out, almost every significant character has at least two names. Charles-Edouard Rusticoli is also the comte de La Palférine, du Bruel publishes his *vaudevilles* under the name de Cursy, and, most significantly, Claudine Chaffaroux, formerly known as Tullia, who becomes the respectable Mme du Bruel, and finally, in her *dernière incarnation*, Mme la comtesse du Bruel.

It is this last character's dual identity, as Claudine and as Tullia, that leads me to see an onomastic connection between this character and Dinah de La Baudraye. This connection is based on a pattern in *La Comédie humaine* that is wholly idiosyncratic, independent of any cultural reality outside of Balzac's fictional universe. The key to this parallel is the syllable *-ine* in the names of many of his courtesans: Florine, Florentine, Carabine, Jenny Cadine. The pattern is not limited to actresses and *filles d'opéra*. When the former Rose Chapotel, whom Chabert had once "prise, comme un fiacre," [*hired, like a hansom cab*] in the Palais-Royal (3:371), manages to rekindle some tenderness in the heart of her husband, Chabert begins to call her "Rosine" (359). The Italian camp follower Rosina of *Autre étude de femme* is gallicized into Rosine by the *devisants* around the table. Even the character who would seem to be the strongest exception to an imperfect rule, the noble Honorine de Bauvan, protests that she would be no better than a prostitute if she returned to a husband whom she does not love (578).[10] Finally, it is amusing to note that La Palférine—whose name, along with his physical appearance, suggests a certain androgyny—fits the rule: at the end of *Béatrix,* he seduces Mme de Rochefide in return for 20,000 francs and other implied favors, essentially prostituting himself to the duchesse de Grandlieu and Maxime de Trailles (2:914-16).

Returning to the courtesans, the names by which they are known in Balzac's fictional world, and thus to the readers, are often invented names,

---

[10] The rule is imperfect. Balzac's two Paulines, de Villenoix of *Louis Lambert* and de Witschnau of *La Peau de chagrin,* in no way suggest the courtesan. Another female character who absolutely breaks this rule is the saintly Joséphine Claës.

noms de guerre. This is relevant to this discussion because Dinah, who
implicitly compares herself to a prostitute by making Claudine's story her
own, has what could be called a *nom de guerre* of her own. Lousteau, for
whom this woman abandoned all social status and respectability, calls her
"Didine." We can say that this name represents the degraded, exploited
aspect of the character. Toward the end of *La Muse du département,* after
Dinah has finally grown tired of her adventure in the Parisian demimonde,
she tells Lousteau: "Il n'y a plus de Didine, vous l'avez tuée, mon ami
[. . .] Et je vous donne la première représentation de Mme la comtesse de
La Baudraye . . ." [*Didine is no more, you killed her, my friend. And I offer
you the first public appearance of Madame la comtesse de La Baudraye*
(4:779). Claudine's appearance as *la comtesse du Bruel* marks, or so the
former dancer hopes, the beginning of a new phase in their relationship—her dream is that Charles will at last return her love. Showing another inverse parallel between the two characters, the metamorphosis of
Didine into the *comtesse de La Baudraye* marks the end of her illicit relationship, bringing to its logical end—in 1842—the beginning of Dinah's
prise de conscience, which we saw in the whispered confession of *Un
Prince de la bohème,* in 1840.

Pursuing the idea that the syllable *-ine* is a sememe that frequently
connotes prostitution—or at least a lifestyle of degraded exploitation—in
Balzac's text, Mme du Bruel herself presents an interesting case. This
character's professional name, as a dancer and as a courtesan, is of course
Tullia. Her years as a courtesan are her period of great strength. Like the
resourceful Mme Schontz and the formidable Josépha Mirah, who to a
great extent follow in her footsteps, Tullia as a dancer/prostitute displays a
sharp business sense and a clear-eyed lucidity about the demi-monde and
her place in it. Aware that at the age of thirty she is becoming "un peu
grasse" [*a bit fat*] for the stage, "Tullia se retira dans toute sa gloire et fit
bien" [*Tullia retired at the height of her glory and was wise to do so*]. The
gifts she has received from her lovers, most especially the duc de Rhétoré
and perhaps also his father, the duc de Chaulieu, are the basis of a small
but adequate fortune: "Danseuse aristocratique [. . .] Claudine avait de
beaux souvenirs et peu d'argent, mais les plus magnifiques bijoux et l'un
des plus beaux mobiliers de Paris" [*As an aristocratic dancer, Claudine
had beautiful memories and little money, but the most magnificent jewelry
and some of the most beautiful furnishings in all of Paris*] (826). This

fonds de boutique is what allows Claudine to begin her slow but determined climb to respectability after she has taken du Bruel as a husband. It is after she has retired from her career as a courtesan, after Tullia has become Claudine, that this character becomes truly exploited through her relationship with La Palférine. As she acknowledges in a letter to her callous lover, La Palférine has become to Claudine what Tullia once was to other men. She contrasts her golden years with her life after she has come under La Palférine's spell:

> je souffre tout de toi; moi si impérieuse, si fière ailleurs, moi qui faisais trotter des ducs, des princes, des aides de camp de Charles X, qui valaient plus que toute la cour actuelle, je te traite en enfant gâté. (821)
> *I tolerate anything from you, I once so imperious, so proud, I who once commanded dukes, princes, even the aides-de-camp of Charles X, who were worth more than all of today's court, I treat you like a spoiled child.*

Taking the role of the wheel of fortune that sometimes seems to amuse him, Balzac turns the tables on the once proud courtesan, who becomes a humiliated countess.

Toward the end of *La Muse du département,* Dinah makes a conscious choice to return to respectability, rejecting the weakened position that passion had placed her in. Again, she reclaims a bit of sympathy by showing that she is aware of the absurdity of her degraded position. Balzac does not hold Dinah in that sympathetic position—the final pages of *La Muse* put Dinah back in a comic light—but, the whole of the character, by that I mean the character studied as a part of *La Comédie humaine* and not as a character in one or two individual works, is more complicated than a reading of *La Muse du département* as a unit would suggest. Like so many other major characters, if not the majority of them, Dinah is portrayed from multiple perspectives. While making her the emblematic *bas-bleu* of his fictional world, mocking both her work and her intellectual pretensions in *La Muse,* Balzac seems to take her more seriously in *Un Prince.* Not only does the *nouvelle* reveal that this befuddled woman is actually almost tragically lucid, but Balzac also allows this *femme-auteur* to make some observations about literature that are not undermined in any way by the sort of mockery that is nearly constant in *La Muse.*

As a portrait of the Parisian bohemia, *Un Prince de la bohème* shows us not only the world of courtesans, renegade ladies, and indebted young noblemen, but also of petty *littérateurs*. Dinah and Nathan are the obvious examples, Lousteau's presence is significant to the *lecteur initié*, as is that of du Bruel, the *employé* turned *écrivailleur* [*clerk turned scribbler*]. A number of other recognizable names—Finot, Bixiou, Blondet— affirm for us that Balzac's *bohème* is the land of letters as well as of sex. The presence of these literary characters is complemented by a literary discourse that playfully manifests itself on every level of the text. Most obviously, this discourse is present on the metadiegetic level, that is in Nathan's telling of the story to Mme de Rochefide. While painting La Palférine, Nathan playfully launches into an exaggeratedly baroque speech that a confused Mme de Rochefide, herself something of a literary marquise, characterizes as a "galimatias [*babble*]." Nathan responds that he is speaking in the fashionable new language, "le Sainte-Beuve, une nouvelle langue française." Nathan ironically defends his "galimatias" as "phrases précieuses," a transparent double meaning that allows Balzac to take a measure of revenge against the man now mostly remembered as the uncomprehending nemesis of a great novelist. Denis Slatka maintains that "[si] le pastiche de Sainte-Beuve est intégré *dans Un Prince de la bohème*, c'est que Sainte-Beuve est l'expression accomplie de cette médiocratie bourgeoise" [*if the pastiche of Sainte-Beuve is integrated into Un Prince, it is because Sainte-Beuve is the ultimate expression of that bourgeois mediocracy*] that disdains and wastes aristocratic talent like La Palférine's, and by extension Balzac's ("Sémiologie et grammaire," 255).

On the second metadiegetic level, La Palférine indulges in a bit of literary criticism of his own after he reads one of Claudine's letters to his bohemian friends. When the Bohemians defend the letters, the count responds that:

> toutes les femmes qui aiment écrivent de ces choses-là! s'écria La Palférine, l'amour leur donne à toutes de l'esprit et du style, ce qui prouve qu'en France le style vient des idées et non pas des mots. (823)
>
> *"all women in love write things like that" cried La Palférine, "love gives them all wit and style, which proves that in France style comes from ideas and not from words."*

Of course, this phrase is of doubtful sincerity. We can read between the lines and see La Palférine's sarcastic smirk; but even so the comment should not be completely dismissed, for it contains an echo of more serious views on literature expressed by more authoritative characters, such as Lousteau and Bianchon in *La Muse du département* or Daniel d'Arthez in *Illusions perdues*. Balzac himself often expressed similar ideas in defensive frustration at those who criticized his own style while ignoring the power of his ideas and observations.

Still another comment on the theory of literature is to be found in the diegetic frame. When Lousteau, coming in on the end of Dinah's reading, protests that the *nouvelle* lacks a dénouement, Dinah's response is quick and simple:

> —Je ne crois pas aux dénouements, dit Mme de La Baudraye, il faut en faire quelques-uns de beaux pour montrer que l'art est aussi fort que le hasard; mais, mon cher, on ne relit une œuvre que pour ses détails. (838)
>
> *"I don't believe in dénouements," said Mme de La Baudraye, "one must do a few pretty ones to show that art is as creative as chance, but, my dear, we only reread a book for the details."*

Nathan announces that there is in fact a dénouement, at least an extra-textual one: Mme de Rochefide "est folle de Charles-Edouard" and will soon return to her husband. And Dinah, in the course of time, will provide a similar dénouement to her and Lousteau's story as well. But what is of more interest is Dinah's contention that the act of rereading is more important than the act of reading. A first reading is for the end of a story, it's "wow" to borrow a phrase from Armine Mortimer ("Second Stories," 276); it is in rereading—which is not merely suggested but rather assumed—that we truly come to know and appreciate a text. It is the details that give a text, like any work of art, its lasting interest. This is very probably meant as a broad generalization about all literature, and the assumption of rereadings was probably a safe one among the reading classes of nineteenth-century France, but it is impossible not to consider this remark to be in some respect a self-reflexive aspect of the text. Balzac is telling us, through Dinah, that this work must be reread so that we can truly understand the character of La Palférine. Again, the beauty is in the details.

Of course, this counsel applies to the larger *Comédie humaine* as well. What we see here is a possible explanation for the "longue prépara-tion-dénouement rapide" structure that Dällenbach and others have dis-cussed ("Le tout en morceaux," 158). Dinah verbalizes and gives an exaggerated example of what was one of the central tenets of Balzac's views on fiction, that the details of a story, the evolution of a character or a situation, are more important than the final outcome. Pierre Barbéris of-fers *Le Père Goriot* as an example of a "roman sans dénouement" that il-lustrates the importance of detail as one of the innovations in Balzac's fiction; before Balzac, "le monde était l'accessoire et le décor; il est de-venu l'essentiel" [*the [real] world was accesory and décor, it became the essential feature.*] (*Le monde de Balzac,* 88). The essential truth of this statement as it regards the larger *Comédie humaine* is obvious—it is in fact one of the underlying assumptions of this thesis—but Balzac's opin-ions in this regard do not only apply to his own work. I think it is safe to say that any true lover of literature has several favorite texts that are read and reread many times, just as the cinephile can become fascinated by a specific film, watching it over and over. Books are not meant to be read only once, any more than a painting or sculpture is meant to be seen one time, or a piece of music to be heard once and then ignored. We do not return to these works of art because we have forgotten the ending, but be-cause we appreciate the details: plot points; descriptions or portraits; an author's (or filmmaker's) personal style or technique. However preposter-ous Dinah de La Baudraye may be as a departmental muse, in this case she seems to speak with a great deal of authority.

The complicated narrative configurations examined in this chapter reinforce the idea that Balzac's frames are much more than a hackneyed literary device. These highly ambitious structures are not separate from but rather integral parts of the artworks they surround. Even in *Un Prince de la bohème*—where the framework is at once overly complicated and underdeveloped, in the end undermining the work as a whole—there is significant evidence that Balzac's intent was to create reciprocal relation-ships between the *nouvelle* and the two novels that serve as its intertexts. The very elements that cause confusion for the naïve reader are a boon to the rereader, creating nuance and providing clarity for characters and situations both in and outside of the *nouvelle* itself. The flawed but still fascinating *Autre étude de femme* offers one of the clearest examples of how different a Balzacian text can be for different readers, at various points on the spectrum from naïve to expert. What the naïve reader would probably find the least interesting part of the text, the dialogue between the characters, is a rich terrain for the *lecteur initié*, ripe for interpretation and conjecture. Even the admitted debatability of my own conclusions shows how ambiguous a text the supposedly complete *Comédie humaine* can be. Finally, the complicated construction of *La Maison Nucingen* shows us Balzac, supposedly the most classical of novelists, at play with the conceits of his own work and of fiction in general. The fractured storytelling, the interweaving of numerous strands of narrative, and the repeated reflections of story and discourse in this enormously complicated text make it one the best examples of revolutionary writing in the work of this allegedly reactionary writer.

In the next chapter, I will explore those texts in which object stories are a part of a larger plot. In these cases, which I refer to as embedded narratives, the narrator and narratee roles are again more fixed, and motivations for storytelling and the effects of learning those stories are often explicitly given in the text. What is different about these structures is that the causes and effects of narration are often more complicated because of the way they figure into the plots.

Guests of Félicité des Touches in *Autre étude de femme*

Women	Men
Mlle des Touches	Emile Blondet
Mme de Nucingen	Joseph Bridau
Mme de Sérisy	Lord Dudley
Mme de Camps	Henri de Marsay
Mme de Cadignan	Nucingen
Lady Barimore	Félix de Vandenesse
Lady Dudley	Daniel d'Arthez
Mme de Rochefide	Rastignac
Mme de Vandenesse (Marie?)	Count Adam Laginski
Mme de Portenduère	Canalis
Mme de Montcornet	General Montriveau
Mme d'Espard	Duc de Rhétoré
	"un prince russe"
	"un ministre étranger"

Chapter IV

Stories within Stories:
The Embedded Narratives

ALL OF THE NARRATIVE STRUCTURES DISCUSSED up to this point have involved framed narratives, where the object story is the main story, and the frame a secondary part, of a given work. I draw a distinction between framed narratives such as these and embedded narratives, although the two terms are more commonly used almost interchangeably. For the purposes of this discussion, an embedded narrative is an object story that is a part of a larger plot line. In these cases, the act of storytelling is a plot event that advances a narrative, just like a murder or a seduction. The content of the embedded narratives is essential but secondary to the embedding text. As an example, consider the case of *Sarrasine*. If one were to follow the traditional approach, looking simply at the structure of the text and following the implication of Balzac's choice of title, one would say that the story of the sculptor and the castrato was the main story, and the framing story of the narrator's attempt to seduce Mme de Rochefide were a mere secondary appendage to it. *Sarrasine* would then be considered an example of framed narrative. If however one were to follow the approach laid out by Barthes in *S/Z*, that *Sarrasine* is the story of a contract (*S/Z*, 96)—specifically of the aborted exchange of story for sex between the narrator and Béatrix—the text would then be considered a case of an embedded narrative, the story in Rome informing and completing the primary story of seduction in Paris. The act of narration is thus placed on a level equal to that of

Béatrix's fascination with the portrait of Endymion. Both events move the reader toward the dénouement of the nouvelle, which is not Sarrasine's discovery of La Zambinella's secret, but rather Béatrix's rejection of the narrator. As this example suggests, it becomes necessary to establish a hierarchy between the two parts of a narrative structure, exactly as Barthes warned against doing. The texts studied in this chapter however are less ambiguous than *Sarrasine;* the examples discussed here offer fairly clear examples of internal narrations, instances of storytelling, used to advance still another story.

I should also explicitly distinguish between the embedded narratives I will discuss in this chapter and narrated exposition. A perfect example of narrated exposition is the duchesse de Langeais's recital of the history of the Goriot family, already discussed in the first chapter. Although the narrative situation in this scene is important to the larger novel, and quite interesting in its own right, the essential material in this narration is the background it provides Rastignac, and of course the reader, about the old man and his daughters. Everything the duchess says fits clearly and cleanly into the plot development of *Le Père Goriot.*

Again, I qualify as an embedded narrative any object story that is a part of a larger text, when the narration of that object story is a part of the plot of the surrounding text. In these cases, the act of narration—the fact that the material was exchanged, and the circumstances under which it was exchanged—is at least as important to the larger text and the advancement of the plot as the material itself. Within *La Comédie humaine,* I include in this category: the different *récits* from Lousteau and Bianchon's visit to the La Baudrayes' chateau in *La Muse du département;* the two narrations from the peasants' *veillée* in *Le Médecin de campagne;* the fictionalized autobiography that the princesse de Cadignan recites—really performs—for Daniel d'Arthez; and finally *L'Ambitieux par Amour,* the *nouvelle* that Albert Savarus writes as a coded message for his distant lover.

The embedded narratives in *Albert Savarus* and *Les Secrets de la princesse de Cadignan* might seem quite close to the sort of exposition that I said should be considered separately from embedded narratives, but both are at least to some extent metafiction. In the case of *L'Ambitieux par amour,* Savarus changes the names and some other important aspects of his own love story for his *nouvelle,* separating the fragment from the rest of the text, and opening it for independent interpretation. Moreover, that love story is of secondary importance to what I believe is the main plot line of *Albert Savarus,* namely the story of the romantic obsession and the demonic machinations of Rosalie de Watteville. In *Les Secrets,* when Diane tells the story of her life to d'Arthez, she is, to put it bluntly, lying. We readers know the truth; the Narrator gives it to us just before Diane begins her story. We can thus see that the changes she makes in her own life story are carefully calculated, and the narration can be dissected to reveal a number of important points within it that nuance the *nouvelle* as a whole, as well as our perception of Diane's relationship with Daniel.

In some ways, these narrative situations are easier to analyze than those in the framed stories, because the motivations of the narrators and their relationships with their narratees are more completely developed in the text surrounding the embedded narrative than in the briefer frames. These embedded texts are well worth examining independently, for although they are set apart from the stories that contain them, they greatly impact the texts in which they appear, affecting our reading of both the embedding texts and the whole *Comédie humaine* as much as any framed object story could do.

Seducing the Muse: Narration, Reception, and Noncomprehension in *La Muse du département*

Perhaps the easiest case to begin with is *La Muse du département,* where the act of storytelling is clearly more important to the novel than the content of the stories told, and where the motivations for and the effects of narration are explicitly stated. It is during a politically inspired visit to Sancerre that Étienne Lousteau first meets Dinah de La Baudraye. Stunned to find such a young and beautiful woman married to a (seemingly) preposterous "avorton" like M. de La Baudraye, Lousteau suspects that the baroness is having an affair with M. de Clagny, the *procureur du roi.* In order to test his theory, Lousteau proposes to two accomplices, his Parisian traveling companion, Bianchon, and Gatien Boisrouge, a local youth who is in love with Dinah, that they guide the evening's conversation to the topic of adultery by telling stories about adulterous lovers who come to an unhappy end. The sophisticated Parisian is convinced that a guilty conscience will cause Dinah or M. de Clagny to somehow betray their true feelings. In the end, this plan leads to nothing, for not only is Mme de La

Baudraye not guilty of adultery, she is, as the gifted diagnostician Bianchon detects, after four years of marriage, a virgin.

If the storytelling proves fruitless for Lousteau, Balzac uses the occasion rather profitably. During the storytelling evening at Anzy, the La Baudrayes' château, three stories are told. Lousteau begins the evening with the story of the *Chevalier de Beauvoir,* a *cape et épée* sort of story about a captured hero of the Vendée movement who escapes the murderous vengeance of his jailer, whose wife the young nobleman had seduced. Bianchon follows his fellow Parisian with a story from his repertoire (4:688). Finally, M. Gravier, another local official, attempts to preserve the honor of Sancerre by telling the story of *Un Grand d'Espagne,* the very gothic tale of the violent revenge taken by a Spanish nobleman against his unfaithful wife. Both Lousteau's and Gravier's stories are perfectly enjoyable if rather light tales that would not be out of place in a short-story collection. But the most interesting of the three stories told is the one that is not reproduced. This is *La Grande Bretèche,* told by Bianchon in circumstances very different from those of *Autre étude de femme.* Balzac explicitly refers to that first telling in *La Muse du département.* The Narrator tells us that Bianchon chooses this story from his collection of anecdotes, and that it is useless to repeat the story, which has become so well known since that first telling "chez Mlle des Touches." The cynical explanation for this reference to *Autre étude de femme,* the one that would suit the opinion that Balzac was merely a *faiseur de copie*, more capitalist of fiction than novelist, would be that he was merely indulging in a bit of intertextual, or intratextual, publicity, or that he was arrogantly assuming that the reader of the fragment was or at least aspired to be a reader of the whole.

This interpretation is not completely invalid, although I would argue that these assumptions on Balzac's part have more to do with his artistic vision than with his financial concerns, with his creative ambitions rather than his commercial ones. However, this somewhat superficial reasoning does not go far enough, for what we have here is more than just the usual parenthetical reference that is especially common in the later works, that is "(voir *Autre étude de femme*)." The passage deserves to be cited in its entirety, since it suggests a more complex motivation than mere self-promotional shorthand:

> l'illustre docteur choisit [l'anecdote] connue sous le nom de La Grande
> Bretèche et devenue si célèbre qu'on en a fait au Gymnase-Dramatique
> un vaudeville intitulé *Valentine* (voir *Autre étude de femme*). Aussi est-
> il parfaitement inutile de répéter ici cette aventure, quoiqu'elle fût du
> fruit nouveau pour les habitants du château d'Anzy. Ce fut d'ailleurs la
> même perfection dans les gestes, dans les intonations qui valut tant
> d'éloges au docteur chez Mlle des Touches quand il la raconta pour la
> première fois. (688)
>
> *the illustrious doctor chose the anecdote known under the name of "la*
> *Grande Breteche that has become so famous that the theater of the*
> *Gymnase-Dramatique made a drama out of it, called* Valentine *(see*
> Autre étude de femme*). And so it is perfectly useless to repeat the ad-*
> *venture here, although it was all new to the guests of the château*
> *d'Anzy. It was in any case the same perfection in gesture and intona-*
> *tion that earned the doctor such high praise at Mlle des Touches's*
> *when he told it for the first time.*

What is interesting about this reference is not merely the assumption that
the reader is familiar with *Autre étude de femme,* but, on a deeper level,
the assumption that the Narratee knows this story, is familiar with Bianchon's reputation as a storyteller, with the vaudeville play that *La Grande
Bretèche* has become, even with the evening at Mlle des Touches's house
where the story was first told. Between the lines of this seemingly straightforward passage, we can again see the great textual mobile in motion.
Since that first telling at Mlle des Touches's exclusive supper, the story
has been repeated, gaining a broader audience and eventually given a form
by that hideous skeleton of popular literature—in one of its most vulgar
forms too, *un vaudeville.* The story that was so powerful when told in the
right atmosphere and among the right company has become degraded by
its wider circulation. Again, things have happened in the fictional universe
of *La Comédie humaine* that are not explicitly presented in the text. Yet
even in this somewhat degraded state, the story is not without some
power: "Le dernier tableau [. . .] produisit tout son effet. Il y eut un moment de silence assez flatteur pour Bianchon" [*The last scene produced its
usual effect. There was a rather flattering moment of silence for Bianchon*]
(688).

The circumstances of this nonreproduced narration inform us about
the Narrator's opinion of this departmental gathering, and also tell us
something about our narrator, Bianchon. The first telling is valorized by
the social setting in which it occurs. It is there that we, the extratextual
readers, hear this story, during that première, along with the chosen company around the table. The telling at Anzy is a repetition, an exact repetition, right down to the gestures and inflections, but a mere repetition all
the same. When Bianchon tells the story in *Autre étude,* it is something
special, a rare thing that only the elite are privy to; in *La Muse,* the value
of the tale has been diminished by its circulation, by its theatrical adapta-
tion, by its becoming something generally known. Bianchon uses it now
for a lesser audience, and for a lesser purpose. In *Autre étude,* he was taking part in a discussion of the nature of woman; in *La Muse,* he is partici-
pating in a somewhat mean-spirited and juvenile game. These different
tellings of the same tale by Bianchon remind us, once again, of the complicated nature of a Balzacian character. Just as de Marsay is equal parts
dandy and member of *Les Treize,* Bianchon has one foot in the virtuous
and intellectual world of the *Cénacle* and one foot in the more equivocal
world of the Parisian *monde* of dandies and journalists. He is a friend of
Michel Chrestien and d'Arthez on one hand, and of Rastignac and Lousteau on the other. The narration at Mlle des Touches's reflects the more
admirable and elegant Bianchon, while the one at the La Baudrayes' is
part of his less attractive side. Balzac shows a similarly dismissive attitude
toward this provincial gathering by not bothering to repeat the story for the
reader—if Balzac had been truly interested only in selling pages of *copie,*
he surely would have exploited the opportunity to reprint the text of *La
Grande Bretèche* a second time.

The decision not to reproduce the tale in the text of *La Muse du
département* not only underscores Balzac's attitude toward the provincials
assembled at Anzy—and of course, most importantly, toward Dinah de La
Baudraye—it also preserves the integrity and effectiveness of *La Grande
Bretèche.* The power of this story in *Autre étude de femme* is due, in part
to the way that Balzac builds up to it, with Bianchon's hesitation and
warning that it is an *histoire terrible;* in part to its internal construction,
that is to say the detective novel-like revelation of the facts in the story
itself; and finally to the way in which he ends the tale, with the deafening
silence of the company around the table, as the author's extratextual audi-

ence—that is, the reader—is to a great extent manipulated by this reaction on the part of character-narrator's textual one. All of this would be greatly diminished, if not destroyed altogether, if the reader of *Autre étude* had first read the tale in *La Muse du département*. Not only would the ending of the story already be known, the tale itself would suffer somewhat by association with the far lighter stories that are reproduced in *La Muse*. Both are perfectly serviceable, but they lack the power of *La Grande Bretèche*. The story of Mme de Merret would especially suffer from association with *Un Grand d'Espagne*, which also touches on adultery, Spanish lovers, and a wronged husband's cruel vengeance. Lousteau, taking up the role of critic that Balzac's less-talented writers sometimes find themselves in, criticizes the provincial Gravier for attempting to pass off his story—a hackneyed cliché, according to the Parisian—as either true or very original:

> Il faut raconter cela, dit le journaliste, à des charbonniers, car il faut leur foi robuste pour y croire [. . .] cette manie de couper les bras . . . est fort ancienne [en Espagne], elle reparaît à certaines époques comme quelques-uns de nos canards dans les journaux, car ce sujet avait déjà fourni des pièces au Théâtre espagnol, dès 1570. . . (695-96)
>
> *"You ought to tell that," said the journalist, "to a few coalmen, because it would take their robust faith to believe it. That passion for chopping off arms is an old one in Spain, it comes back every few years like some of our old chestnuts in the newspapers, because that stuff had already inspired plays in the Spanish theatre, from 1570 on. . ."*

Tying the two stories together, especially given Lousteau's critiques, would minimize the most important difference between the two stories, which lies in their very similar endings. The brutal, violent revenge taken by the Grandee in M. Gravier's story lacks the subtle psychological cruelty of M. de Merret, who makes his wife's virtue the cause of her greatest sin. By making only a vague allusion to *La Grande Bretèche* in this case, Balzac allows the story to retain its full power in *Autre étude de femme*.

The three stories that are part of Lousteau's spitefully playful investigation are not the only embedded narratives in *La Muse du département*. On the next evening at Anzy, Lousteau performs again for a larger provincial assembly—more guests have come in anticipation of hearing a conversation, as if it were an arranged entertainment like a fireworks display (703); but his performance is more for his own amusement than that of his audience. Having received a parcel from Paris, Lousteau finds among the papers used as packing material the pages of a novel, *Olympia, ou les Vengeances romaines*, yet another story of an adulterous woman. Using only the fragments, Lousteau manages to (re)create a story for the guests assembled at Anzy. The improvised reconstruction of this *roman d'Empire* by a Parisian sophisticate for a mostly uncomprehending middle-class audience recalls Bixiou's *roman à tiroirs*, improvised for the bewildered Matifat family *in La Maison Nucingen*. The effects of narration are not dissimilar in the two texts; Lousteau's audience does not fall asleep, but they may as well for all that they understand in his performance. Lucien Dällenbach has thoroughly and brilliantly analyzed this portion of the novel and its import to the larger *Comédie humaine*. For Dällenbach, *Olympia* serves not only, by its content, to "redoubler spéculairement" [*redouble, as in a mirror*] *La Muse du département*, more interestingly, the form of the tale and its construction, a whole story drawn together out of fragments, constitutes a *mise-en-abyme* of *La Comedie humaine* ("Du fragment au cosmos," 426). Lousteau, who strings the pieces together, adding detail and supplementing the information given with his own knowledge of time, place, and genre, fills the role of both author and reader (Dällenbach, 426-27). It is from this example that Dällenbach makes his case for reading between the texts, the concept that I have so heavily relied upon throughout this study.

   This is of course a very rough summary of a far more detailed argument. For the purposes of this chapter, the important point is that the response to this curiously fragmented narrative is determined largely according to social origin. Dällenbach divides the assembly at Anzy into two groups, the sophisticated "Parisiens d'adoption" Lousteau and Bianchon, and the uncomprehending provincials (422), with Dinah serving as a sort of "trait d'union" between the two groups (423). This is true at the beginning of the performance, when Lousteau's only desire is to "mystifier les Sancerrois" (704), but as he progresses in his creative reading, he himself gets caught up in the interest ("l'intérêt") of the story, as do Bianchon and M. de Clagny. There are varying degrees of interest and comprehension, just as there are varying degrees of sophistication, or intelligence, among the listeners. Dinah is of course predisposed to surrender herself to this quasi-literature, both because of her literary pretensions and her growing romantic interest in Lousteau. We would think that the stolid M. de Clagny would be especially resistant to Lousteau's recital because of his antipathy for the Parisian, but he finds himself caught up in the story in spite of himself, as does Bianchon, who, although in on the joke, finds himself carried along with the others. Finally, Lousteau himself succumbs to the force of literature.

There is however one provincial listener who shows himself to be far more perceptive than his neighbors, whose constant refrain is "je n'y comprends rien." M. de La Baudraye cuts through the romantic and literary musings of his wife and her new friends, and pronounces, prophetically, that the heroine of the novel will not be happy, "car elle a un amant. . ." [*because she has a lover*] (719). This elliptically prescient pronouncement is one of the first indications that there is far more to this character than meets the eyes of his fellow characters, or those of the reader. Up to this point, it seems that La Baudraye's obsession with money has blinded him to everything else, in this case his wife's growing infatuation with another man. This observation suggests that, even though the greedy little man is indeed focused on his fortune, he remains well aware of what is going on around him. This impression is confirmed in the highly ironic final phrases of the novel, which indicate that La Baudraye has not been the victim, but the willing accomplice and happy beneficiary of his wife's infidelity.

Listening While Looking Down: *Le Médecin de campagne* and *"la veillée dans la grange"*

Le Médecin de campagne is a novel without a plot. Essentially a long portrait of a pragmatic utopia and the man who created it, this text is unusual in many respects. First and foremost is the fact that nothing really happens, which is unusual both for Balzac and the literary conventions of the time, as many contemporary critics noted (Rose Fortassier, Introduction; 9:352). Also unusual is the fact that this novel contains no recurring characters, which is true of very few of the individual works of *La Comédie humaine;* and *Le Médecin* is the only full-length novel that operates completely outside the system. This of course is not to say that the text does not have intertexts within *La Comédie humaine*. For example, Benassis's life in Paris, torn between fashionable society and a virtuous, devoted, and half-forgotten young girl, is very similar to Raphaël de Valentin's life before finding the *peau de chagrin*. The depictions of Napoleon's Russian campaign resonate with readers of *Adieu* and *Autre étude de femme,* and the abbey of the Grande Chartreuse and the motto "Aux cœurs blessés l'ombre et le silence" [*For wounded hearts, shade and silence*] play an important role in *Albert Savarus*. Most significantly, a similar Balzacian utopia is created, also in a remote provincial wasteland, in *Le Curé de village*. It is this last comparison that is the most interesting, because of key similarities and differences between the two texts. In *Le Curé,* Véronique Graslin is inspired to her good works as penance for her doubly criminal association with Jean-François Tascheron. In this case, the programmatic aspect of the novel is subordinated to, or at least mitigated by, a more traditionally novelistic plot.

This is not the case in *Le Médecin de campagne,* which is, as every introduction dutifully points out, a very programmatic text. As Bernard Guyon noted, Balzac conceived and wrote this novel, to some extent, as a vehicle to express his personal political philosophy: "Sans doute il l'avait conçu, dès l'origine, comme une œuvre à la fois d'édification et de propagande électorale" [*Without doubt he conceived of it from the first as a work of both edification and electoral propaganda*] (*La Création littéraire,* 157). It is in many respects a campaign pamphlet, as Balzac hoped that it would establish him as a leading thinker of the legitimist party and eventually secure his election as a *député*. This is not to say that the book should be regarded as no more than a piece of Balzacian propaganda. There are several elements of *Le Médecin* that 'novelize' the text, such as the stories of Benassis's Parisian life and Genestas's exploits in war, as well as the romantic figures of La Fosseuse and the *braconneur* [poacher] Butifer. Most interestingly novelistic—in the sense of *romanesque*—is the scene of the *veillée* in the barn, where a group of peasants gather together to listen to stories, two of which are reproduced in the text. Immediately preceded by the rather dry sociopolitical discourse of Benassis and the other notables of the village and immediately followed by the somewhat melodramatic recounting of the good doctor's Parisian experience, this lively passage is full of color and verve. It contains some fine storytelling, performed on a wholly different register than we find in the more sophisti-

cated settings that typically frame Balzac's narrations. The main focus of
this scene is the life of Napoleon as recounted by a former soldier, but we
are also treated to an ample fragment of a fantastic folktale about a hunchbacked old woman who—after some particularly grotesque prodding by
the ghost of the man she saw murdered—brings two *malfaiteurs* to justice. The second part of the *veillée* is the Napoleonic epic, recounted by
Goguelat, a veteran of *la Grande armée,* a former foot soldier who sur-
vived the Russian campaign and the crossing of the Bérézina. This *récit* is
in and of itself one of the most interesting fragments of *La Comédie humaine,* as Balzac uses classical, religious, and epic imagery, filtered
through a peasant's voice, to create a popular image of Napoleon that is
part myth, part legend, and part history.

    This scene is at first remarkable for that dramatic shift in tone
mentioned above. Even in a text that is already noteworthy for the disparate nature of its different parts, the whole *veillée* fragment stands out
from the rest of the novel. *Le Médecin de campagne* taken as whole has a
heavy, somber tone, even when Benassis is describing his successes; indeed, the overwhelming seriousness of this novel makes it almost grim.
The scene of the *veillée,* coming more or less in the middle of the text, is a
welcome relief. It also serves as a transition between the first part of the
novel, which is the most programmatic part, and the scenes of mutual confession between Benassis and Genestas, which are both more traditionally
novelistic and more typically Balzacian. What I call the programatic parts
of the text are the account of Benassis' work and his success in rejuvenat-
ing the *canton*, followed by a long oral dissertation of his political philosophy during the *dîner des notables.* It is very interesting to note that
this political discourse is found in the same chapter as the scene of the
veillée, implying a strong connection between the two very different
scenes. The link can be understood by studying the chapter through the
prism of its title, *Le Napoléon du peuple.* This title would at first seem to
refer most specifically to Goguelat's recounting of the life of Napoleon,
but looking to another level, we can see how this title suggests the common links between Goguelat's story, Benassis's politically oriented
speech, and even the tale of the *bossue* and the bandits.

    Starting at the very beginning of the chapter, Benassis's political
speech is a reflection of what are generally regarded as Balzac's own political views. To summarize briefly (and perhaps overly simply) these are:

A healthy suspicion of democracy, growing out of a deep mistrust of the average individual's ability to decide what is best for either himself or the country. Lack of confidence in the *peuple* and in political parties leads to a belief in the necessity of a strong, centralized power who can act with some degree of independence from a fractious, popularly elected legislature. To assist this strong central power in the task of governance, religion is necessary both to curb the baser instincts of the citizenry—including the impulse to resist that central power—and to enlighten the man who holds power. Benassis seems to believe, like his creator, in the necessity of those "deux Vérités éternelles: la Religion [et] la Monarchie" (*Avant-propos*, 1: 13). Significantly, this political philosophy is presented after we have seen its effects. This ordering gives the doctor's political views a strong basis of credibility. The *canton* that Benassis and his guest have spent the last two days touring is the effect of such a philosophy of unilateral action on the part of an enlightened despot, a microcosm of what France could (and should) be under a strong, competent government.

The setting for this political theorizing is, again, a gathering of the local élite in Benassis's dining room, *une réunion de robes noires;* the parish priest, the notary and the magistrate, and the adjunct mayor gather at the house of the physician-mayor and listen to him politely like the good acolytes that they in fact are. The chapter then switches to a markedly different setting, an old barn where Benassis has discreetly, almost underhandedly, arranged that a *veillée de campagne* should take place for the amusement of his guest. The doctor and the officer climb into a hay loft to observe unseen, so that the peasants will not lose their *naturel*. In an introduction he wrote for the novel (Folio edition, 1974), the historian Emmanuel LeRoy Ladurie wrote that this "grande veillée folklorique" is a classically *campagnard* event; according to LeRoy Ladurie the one depicted by Balzac is an excellent representation, "l'un des sommets de l'ethnographie balzacienne," as the women work, spinning and sewing, and the men do nothing while the stories are told (37). As readers, we observe this peasant phenomenon much as Benassis and Genestas do, as spectators to a spectacle. This aspect of the two friends as spectators, not merely as narratees, is emphasized by their physical situation in relation to the space where the act of narration actually takes place. The storytelling, the primary relationship between the two narrators and their audience/narratees, takes place on the floor of the barn. This de facto stage is lit up by lamps, as if for the benefit of Genestas and Benassis up in their loft, like spectators at a theatre. As readers, we follow the pair from their dinner, up the ladder and into the loft, so that we too are looking down on the act of narration.

Genestas and Benassis arrive after the story of the *bossue* [*hunchbacked woman*] has begun—like so many other stories in *La Comédie humaine,* it begins *in media res.* An old peasant woman, having sold her hemp at market, is obliged to ask for a night's lodging at a farmhouse. While she is there, she hears another lodger murdered, "le monsieur à la grosse valise" (9:517), whose property is stolen and whose body is then fed to the pigs. The woman feigns sleeps and the next day manages to escape. Returning home, she says nothing to her husband nor to the authorities, and is subsequently haunted by the dead man, who drops parts of his body down the chimney. After his head drops down, it bites the husband—who is chiefly bothered by these spectral apparitions because they delay his dinner—and then comes to the door to insist that the old couple avenge his death by going to the law. The reward for this reluctant virtue is an abundant hemp crop and a son, born to a woman whose skin was said to be tanned like leather by old age—"un enfant mâle qui devint, par la suite des temps, baron du Roi. Voilà l'histoire véritable de LA BOSSUE COURAGEUSE" [*a male child who became, with the passage of time, one of the king's own barons. This is the true story of THE BRAVE HUNCHBACK*] (sic, 520).

This thoroughly enjoyable tale receives relatively little attention from critics, overshadowed as it is by the Napoleonic epic that follows it. Rose Fortassier, in her notes to the Pléiade edition of *Le Médecin,* suggests that the tale is an homage to Nodier and Perrault, and also points out several elements that were typical of folktales, indicating that Balzac may be reproducing a tale that he had heard himself at some point (*nb* 2, 1489-90). It should also be noted that this seemingly atypical Balzacian story has at least two elements with echoes in other texts. The rich traveler killed for the contents of his "grosse valise" [big suitcase] recalls the victim of *L'Auberge rouge,* who carries his treasure in a "lourde valise" [heavy suitcase]; and the disembodied head biting the living who annoy it brings to mind the strangely comic ending of the rather bizarre *Élixir de longue vie.* In the context of the novel, the tale ostensibly shows the peasants in their natural habitat, part of the proto-ethnologic aspect of this novel that LeRoy

Ladurie and several other critics have noted. Both the teller—who is never named or even described—and his audience are portrayed as " des primitifs" (Fortassier, 1489); the peasants seem to unquestioningly accept walking, talking dead, and the legend, mentioned in passing in the tale, that nobles have (or at least once had) a taste for "les pâtés de chair humaine" (*pâtés of human flesh* 517), made from the flesh of murdered peasants. As we shall see in a moment, it is this aspect of the tale, and the scene of its telling, that makes it important in the larger context of the novel.

The folktale is followed by the peasant-epic telling of the life of Napoleon. This is the reason that Benassis and Genestas have come. Benassis, for whom this sort of eavesdropping is something of a habit, had promised this spectacle to his guest earlier in the day—"je vous donnerai le spectacle de cette scène" [*I will offer you the spectacle of such a scene.*] (417)— and taken steps to make sure his visitor is not disappointed. The country doctor has planted a sort of *claque* in the audience to ensure that Goguelat will tell the story of "L'Empereur": "j'ai quelques compères qui doivent faire jaser Goguelat [. . .] sur ce dieu du peuple" [*I have a few cronies who are to push Goguelat to carry on about that god of the common people*] (515). Before discussing the content of this *récit*, which I think proves worthy of its build-up, it is worth commenting on the setting and circumstances of this singular act of narration. Léo Mazet has enumerated the norms for the tale-telling scenes in *La Comédie humaine;* the keywords are: "Paris," "petit salon," "souper," "feu" ("Récit(s) dans le récit," 131). As Claudine Vercollier pointed out in a later article on this same subject—"Le lieu du récit dans les nouvelles encadrées de Balzac"—this list is slightly reductive, but generally sound. We can reduce the formula even further to two key words: elegance and intimacy. Even outdoor tale-telling (*Honorine*) and provincial soirées (*La Muse du département*) have some level of elegance or sophistication; even in *Autre étude de femme*, the large number of dinner guests notwithstanding, there is a certain intimacy that goes along with the act of storytelling. As I said earlier, Balzacian storytelling is generally found either in high society or the more equivocal but still relatively sophisticated milieu of the demi-monde. The *veillée* of *Le Médecin de campagne* is the glaring exception to this rule.[1] This is one storytelling situation that is typically overlooked even by critics studying the internal narrations of *La Comédie humaine*.

Again, similarities and differences speak volumes. Time is an important similarity; storytelling is an evening activity, meant for the shadowy time between the activity of the day and sleep. The most obvious difference is in the larger, more public and more plebian setting. This barn is as far from the Paris of *petits salons* as can be, much farther away, psychologically, than the La Baudraye salon at Anzy or even the hearthside where Benassis and Genestas will shortly hear each others confessions. The barn is obviously a much less exclusive place than the private dining room of *La Maison Nucingen* or the Grandlieu salon, yet it is not without a kind of intimacy. Just as the large number of guests in Félicité des Touches's dining room does not preclude a certain restrictive quality for the gathering that takes place there—the curtains have been drawn and the servants have been dismissed (Mazet, 138)—the peasants in the barn intend their evening only for their own kind. Benassis insists that he and Genestas hide their presence, so that the peasants will not put on airs: "Mais cachons-nous bien, si ces pauvres gens voient un étranger, ils font des façons et ne sont plus eux-mêmes" [*Let's hide ourselves well, if these poor folk see a stranger, they'll put on airs and won't be themselves anymore*] (515). Language (*langage*) is certainly a difference, as Balzac attempts, with varying degrees of success, to use a register consistent with the class and education level of the company he is representing in the text. As far as the content is concerned, this might at first seem to be a marked difference, but it is perhaps not so clear a distinction as we might think. None of the stories actually reproduced in *La Comédie humaine* resemble *La Bossue courageuse,* but the resemblance that others have seen between this story and Nodier's suggests that such topics were not unfamiliar to polite society of the Restoration. Marguerite de Navarre, La Fontaine, and Maupassant all portrayed the lower classes in their work, which was intended for the authors' social peers. As for the life of Napoleon, this subject had become quite fashionable in literature of all kinds in the early years of the July Monarchy, as Guyon points out (173). Balzac's efforts to

---

[1] The story of Cambremer and his son in *Un Drame au bord de la mer* is certainly a peasant's story, but Louis Lambert refines the language and denaturalizes the story when he writes it down for his uncle.

express this theme in a popular voice was perhaps less common, but the image of Napoleon haunts many texts and characters of *La Comédie humaine,* even inspiring admiration in the putatively royalist poet Canalis.

Our narrator, Goguelat, is yet another blend of the new and the very familiar. Lacking the maliciously sophisticated wit of a Bixiou or the respectable social position of Bianchon, the old *fantassin* seems nonetheless to have his own *petite reputation de conteur.* His story is familiar to all in his audience, with the exception of Genestas, but the peasants at the *veillée* clamor for its retelling. Like any good storyteller, including Bianchon and Bixiou, Goguelat resists at first, but popular demand is simply too strong:

> [. . .] Voyons, monsieur Goguelat, racontez-nous l'Empereur.
> —La veillée est déja trop avancée, dit le piéton, et je n'aime point à raccourcir les victoires.
> —C'est égal, dites tout de même! Nous les connaissons pour vous les avoir vu dire bien des fois; mais ça fait toujours plaisir à entendre.
> —Racontez-nous l'Empereur! crièrent plusieurs personnes ensemble.
> —Vous le voulez, répondit Goguelat. Eh bien, vous verrez que ça ne signifie rien quand c'est dit au pas de charge. J'aime mieux vous raconter une bataille. Voulez-vous Champaubert . . .?
> —Non! l'Empereur! l'Empereur! » (520)
> *"Come on, Mister Goguelat, tell us about the Emperor."*
> *"The night is too far along," said the mailman, "and I don't like to cut the stories short."*
> *"Tell us about the Emperor!" several people cried out at once.*
> *"If you like," replied Goguelat. "Eh, well, you will see that it's worth nothing when it's told too quickly. I would rather tell you the story of a battle. How about Champaubert. . .?"*
> *"No! The Emperor! The Emperor!"*

We can credibly attribute Goguelat's hesitation to several factors: part genuine reluctance; part false modesty; part tradition. Like the preemptive declaration that the story will not mean as much "dit au pas de charge," another declaration of dubious modesty, the narrator's reluctance to speak is a topos of the raconteur in literature.

And yet *raconteur* is not quite the right word to describe Goguelat as a narrator. It is not just the register of his language that separates him from Bianchon, Bixiou, and the other Parisian storytellers. His heroic, impassioned discourse has an almost religious quality, he is part bard and part preacher. These qualities distinguish him as much from the narrator who precedes him at the *veillée* as they do from the Parisians. To give just one easily isolated example of this somewhat intangible quality, consider the question that Goguelat repeatedly addresses to his audience. Having begun his story with a sort of preface about Napoleon's childhood, Goguelat addresses his listeners directly: "Maintenant, suivez-moi bien, et dites-moi si ce que vous allez entendre est naturel" [*Now, pay attention, and tell me if what you are about to hear is natural*] (521). This theme, that Napoleon was supernatural, more than a man, becomes a refrain repeated throughout his *récit*, recurring again and again in the form of slightly varied rhetorical questions: "Un homme aurait-il pu faire cela?" [*Could a man have done that?*] (522); "Ha ça, mes amis, croyez-vous que c'était naturel?" [*How about that, my friends, do you think that was natural?*] (525); and so on through to the end of his story. This oratorical device gives the whole scene of Goguelat's narration a quality markedly different from the more conventional social situations of the narrations in the rest of *La Comédie humaine*.

In the European literary tradition, this repetition suggests the oral literature of the early Middle Ages, such as the *chanson de geste*. Such an oral tradition seems wholly appropriate to the peasant society represented at the *veillée*, which if not necessarily illiterate was certainly nonliterary. The epic is suggested not only by the form but also by the content. Rose Fortassier called Goguelat's narration the "récit naïf de la geste napoléonienne" [*a naïve telling of the Napoleonic epic*] (352). As LeRoy Ladurie noted, the Napoleon portrayed in this narration stands between Charlemagne and the *poilus* of World War I, a military hero on a divine mission for the sake of France (39). Several other aspects of the text remind the reader of the medieval epic, and, as I mentioned earlier, other sorts of allusions are used to skillfully communicate to the reader how towering a figure Napeleon is in the popular imagination. Balzac does this very subtly and cleverly; the allusions are never so direct as to seem out of place in the peasant's discourse, but they are recognizable to a reader operating on or near the same level of sophistication as the author.

A first allusion is to be found in what I earlier referred to as the preface to the Napoleonic story. Goguelat tells us that Bonaparte was born in Corsica, which he portrays as a wild and violent place, frightening, but also appropriate for producing the sort of great warrior that Napoleon would become. We also learn that Bonaparte's mother, who is described as "une finaude," had dreamed that the world was ablaze just before her son's birth, and had thus had the good idea to commend him to God, "pour le faire échapper à tous les dangers de son enfance et de sa vie" [*in order that he might escape all the dangers of his childhood and his life*] (520). The idea that Napoleon's birth was announced in a dream, which in itself suggests a legendary hero, is complemented by the image of a great warrior granted invincibility through the pious actions of his devoted mother. The pattern recalls the myth of Achilles, but is even better, since Bonaparte, in this version, has no vulnerable heel. Also worth noting in this opening passage is the seed of an idea that becomes more pronounced and more important through the course of the narration: that Napoleon is divinely protected, that God is specially interested in the fate of this particular man who is more than a man.

The classical, epic, and religious themes are further developed as Goguelat tells the story of the Egyptian campaign. If this episode is today less strongly associated with Napoleon than the Russian campaign or Waterloo, it is a major theme in this novel and seems to have interested Balzac more generally (cf. *Une Passion dans le désert*). Like Goguelat, Genestas, listening in the hayloft, was also one of Bonaparte's *Egyptiens,* as he recalls during the brief story of the final exile that he tells for La Fosseuse at the end of the novel (591); Chabert, too, was an *Egyptien,* as were Boutin and Vergniaud, the old soldiers who recognize and aid the colonel during his return from the dead (*CC,* 3:331, 345). Goguelat sees Bonaparte's entry into Egypt as a point in common between Bonaparte and Christ; I suspect Balzac is deliberately putting a flawed analogy in the character's mouth to show both the peasant's enthusiasm for the *Empereur* as well as his ignorance. However, I believe we can see in this episode a common point between Bonaparte and the Crusaders. Much of the imagery in this portion of the story recalls that of the medieval epic, such as the *Chanson de Roland,* and the story of the French adventure in Egypt is clearly presented in terms of East and West. Egypt is depicted as "un pays de génies et de crocodiles," and these magical people had known that

Napoleon was coming—"ces gens-là, auxquelles Napoléon était prédit."
The Egyptians regard Napoleon with "une peur comme du diable."

> Alors, le Grand-Turc, l'Asie, l'Afrique ont recours à la magie, et nous
> envoient un démon, nommé Mody, soupçonné d'être descendu du ciel
> sur un cheval blanc qui était, comme son maître, incombustible au
> boulet, et qui tous deux vivaient de l'air du temps. (523)
>
> *So, the Great Turk, Asia, Africa all turned to magic, and sent us a de-*
> *mon, named Mody, said to be descended from heaven on a white horse*
> *that was, like his master, immune to cannonballs, and both of them*
> *lived off the air they breathed.*

A warrior so great as Napoleon cannot be faced with a mere mortal as an
enemy. Like the Saracens in the *Chanson de Roland,* the Turks who face
him must use devilish tricks to fight him. These mysterious ways are all in
vain, of course. Not even the anthropomorphized plague that the Arabs
send to defeat the French can stop Napoleon:

> le Mody s'arrange avec la peste, et nous l'envoie pour interrompre nos
> victoires. [. . .] Napoléon seul était frais comme une rose, et toute
> l'armée l'a vu buvant la peste sans que ça lui fît rien du tout. (524-25)
>
> *this Mody made a deal with the plague, and sent it to us to stop our*
> *victories. Napoléon alone was as fresh as a rose, and the whole army*
> *saw him drinking the plague without it doing him any harm at all.*

With his divine protection and superhuman qualities, Bonaparte is immune
to war and to pestilence. Only the need for Napoleon to protect the French
people from the incompetence and avarice of the government in Paris—
"des imbéciles qui s'amusaient à bavarder" [*imbeciles who love to babble*]
(525)—can put an end to the Egyptian campaign; and once "L'HOMME"
has returned to Europe, all is lost in the East.

When Goguelat describes the circumstances of Bonaparte's marriage to Marie-Louise of Austria, we can again detect certain elements that
suggest a classical subtext:

> . . . il lui fallait des petits, rapport au gouvernement. Apprenant cette
> difficulté, tous les souverains de l'Europe se sont battus à qui lui don-

nerait une femme. Et il a épousé, qu'on nous a dit, une Autrichienne, qu'était la fille des Césars, un homme ancien dont on parle partout, et pas seulement dans nos pays, [. . .] cet homme, qui paraît qu'a été, à Rome, parent de Napoléon d'où s'est autorisé l'Empereur d'en prendre l'héritage pour son fils.

. . . he had to have kids, for the government. When they heard about this, all the sovereigns of Europe fought for the right to give him a wife. And he married, so they tell us, an Austrian, that was the daughter of the Caesars, an old-time man that everyone talks about, and not just around here . . . this man, it seems was some kind of relative of Napoleon in Rome, that's why the Emperor could take his legacy for his son.

This marriage leads to other complications, however:

Mais voilà l'empereur de Russie, qu'était son ami, qui se fâche de ce qu'il n'a pas épousé une Russe et qui soutient les Anglais, nos ennemis (530)

But then the Emperor of Russia, who was his friend, got mad that he hadn't married a Russian girl and supported the English, our enemies.

This subplot about Napoleon's second marriage suggests the classical era not only in the direct references to Caesar, but also in the creation of a mythical heroic ancestry for both Bonaparte and his new bride. Even more so in the idea that great wars are caused by the petty personal jealousies of the mighty, whether that be the gods of Olympus or the kings of Troy and Greece. Of course, the imaginary connection between Caesar and Napoleon underscores for us the almost comical ignorance of our narrator.

These subtle classical and epic references color our perception of the peasant's image of Napoleon, but they do so in some sense directly from Balzac to the reader. It is unlikely that Goguelat knows the story of Achilles, or that he is very familiar with the *chansons de geste*. These points are yet another wink over the heads of the characters listening to the story, at least those on the floor of the barn. But perhaps more important than either of these themes is the religious one, which is explicit and deliberate on the part of Goguelat. The veteran does not stop at saying that Napoleon was sent by God—"Et la gale à qui ne dira pas qu'il a été envoyé par Dieu pour faire triompher la France" [*and damned be anyone*

who we'll say that he wasn't sent by God to bring triumph to France]
(530)—he goes so far as to directly compare Napoleon to Christ.[2] We saw
this first in the faulty comparison drawn between the two regarding the
journey into Egypt. At another point, the old infantryman expressly names
Bonaparte the "enfant de Dieu" (521). And when describing Napoleon toward the end of the Hundred Days, the most explicit comparison yet: "Il
avait l'idée de mourir [. . .] comme Jésus-Christ avant sa passion, il se
croyait abandonné de Dieu et de son talisman" [*He had the idea that he
was going to die, like Jesus Christ before his suffering, he thought that he
had been abandoned by God and his talisman*] (535). These explicit references strengthen a vague impression created at the very beginning, when
Goguelat tells the story of Napoleon's birth. No father is mentioned, only
the mother, the child, and God; Napoleon's conception and birth would
seem almost a doubling of Christ's.

We should not, however, read too much into these passages, as
significant and deliberate as I believe they are. Goguelat's enthusiasm
leads him to exaggerate the strength of connection between his *Empereur*
and God; the essence of this relationship is that Napoleon has divine protection, not paternity. If Bonaparte is not quite on the same level as Christ,
we can put him on an equal footing with such divinely inspired French
heroes as Joan of Arc or Saint Louis. A final possible point of comparison
to Christ can be detected in the peasants' refusal to believe that Napoleon
is dead. Goguelat and his friends firmly believe that Bonaparte is still alive
in 1829. The obvious implication is that there will be a second coming of
Bonaparte, the first being the return from Elba, just as Christ came back
from the tomb and will come again in glory. Again, we should nuance this
perception. The proper comparison is perhaps not Christ but King Arthur,
another warrior-monarch who, according to popular legend, will one day
return to save his people.

All in all, it must be acknowledged that Goguelat is a fine storyteller. The end of his narration is especially powerful, and not just for the
peasant audience on the floor of the barn. Goguelat vividly and poetically
describes the battle of Waterloo, the battlefield soaked in blood and lit-

---

[2] Frank Bowman pointed out that the image of Napoleon as a Christ figure was not unusual and would become increasingly common in later romantic literature (*French Romanticism*, 34-56).

tered with fallen eagle standards (536). Genestas, who lived through these events just as Goguelat did, finds himself compelled to jump down into the *veillée*, into the storytelling space. It is significant that Genestas should be literally moved by the story he has just heard, while Benassis, although surely appreciative, remains calm. First of all, as a matter of simple logic, we should remember that Benassis has heard this story before. On a more profound level, Genestas is much closer to the story and its teller than his new friend, most importantly in terms of his military service, but there is also a question of class. Genestas, the self-educated *enfant de troupe* (389), comes from the same level of society as Goguelat and the others at the *veillée;* while he is not a peasant (*paysan*), he is one of the *peuple* for whom Napoleon is a god. Benassis, son of a prosperous landowner and educated at the Parisian university, comes from the middle class. Genestas, through his own efforts and intelligence, has raised himself up to that class, an elevation which is reflected in his position during the telling of the story, up in the hayloft with Benassis. But the force of the story—which speaks to the old soldier on a different level than it does to the stoical doctor—is such that Genestas almost involuntarily jumps down to (re)join the people, with whom he shares roots and a veneration for Bonaparte. He seems a little embarrassed by his emotional reaction after rejoining Benassis: "J'ai fait des bêtises [. . .] Ces aigles, ces canons, ces campagnes! [. . .] je ne savais plus où j'étais" [*I acted like a fool. . . Those eagles, those canons, those campaigns. . . I forgot where I was*] (537). But Genestas does not completely revert to the popular level; he tells the peasants what they do not want to hear and what they refuse to believe, that their idol is in fact dead. The peasants, however, refuse to believe this, they seem to prefer to believe their own oracle, Goguelat, who tells them: "L'officier est encore au service, et c'est leur consigne de dire au peuple que l'Empereur est mort. Faut pas lui en vouloir, parce que, voyez-vous, un soldat ne connaît que sa consigne" [*The officer is still in the service, and it's their duty to tell the people that the Emperor is dead. Can't hold it against him because, you see, a soldier only knows his duty*] (537).

As I have already said, this whole interlude receives relatively little attention from critics. Guyon, who is of course an exception, cites two reasons for its inclusion in the novel, both of which I have already alluded to: "Raison que nous pourrions qualifier à la fois d'*esthétique* et de *commercial* [...] Il fallait a tout prix animer l'œuvre" and an "hors-d'œuvre" about

Napoleon "avait le plus de chance de lui valoir les applaudissments d'un public largement populaire" [*Reasons that we can describe as both esthetic and* commercial. *It was absolutely necessary to animate the work, and an "hors d'œuvre" about Napoleon had the greatest chance of winning him the applause of a largely popular public*] (173). This twin explanation seems to have satisfied most analysts of the novel, and while I agree of course that it is entirely valid, I think there is more to say about this *veillée*. Returning to the problem posed by the title of this chapter, *Le Napoléon du peuple,* it is worth discussing the possible reasons why Balzac would have included two such diffferent episodes as the *dîner des notables* and the *veillée des paysans* in one chapter, with such a significant title. The title, which would seem at first to refer only to the second half of the section, in fact acurately reflects, in different ways, the two very disparate parts of the chapter. François Paqueteau, in his article "Idéologies dans *Le Médecin de campagne,*" pointed out that the two halves of the chapter are tied together by "un lien politique" between the "histoires napoléoniennes" and "la discussion précédente [. . .] La seconde moitié plus anecdotique nous éloigne un peu de l'essai dans sa présentation habituelle, mais la signification en est toujours très proche" [*There is a political link between the Napoleonic stories and the preceding discussion. The second half, more anecdotal, removes us a bit from the essay form in its usual presentaion, but the meaning is still very close*] (158). While I certainly agree with Paqueteau that the two halves are linked by a political theme, the assertion that the scene of *veillée* is a slight change from the essay form of the dinner conversation is rather surprising; in fact, it is difficult to imagine how the difference between these two fragments could be greater.

Emmanuel LeRoy Ladurie detected a certain political dimension in both of the *veillée* stories. In the story of the *bossue,* the social order is protected, justice is served; the dead man goes into heaven, and the poor woman is rewarded with good crops and a son: "Que chacun occupe la place qui lui revient, mort ou vif: et tout le monde sera bien servi" [*Let each remain in his place, dead or alive, and everyone is well served*] (38). But underneath the "conservateur, réactionnaire" aspect of the text, there is also the grotesque humor and the "piqure d'épingle" of the story about flesh-eating nobles. This last point might be negligeable but for another fleeting reference to the callous nobility in the novel, in the person of the capriciously petty young noblewoman who dismisses la Fosseuse for a minor infraction, leaving the vulnerable young girl destitute and homeless. This slight swipe pales in comparison to the political import of the "second volet du diptyque" [*the second wing of the diptych*]; as LeRoy Ladurie notes, the Napoleonic legend, especially in this peasant version, which maintains that the emperor is still alive, is "la plus subversive des légendes" (39). The exaggerated praise of Napoleon is an oblique attack on the weak and ineffectual rulers who came after 1815, every bit as much as is Benassis's political discourse that precedes it. It is in this thematic sense that the peasant's lively tale rejoins the doctor's dry political theorizing.

Speaking again reductively, the thrust of Benassis's political discourse is that democracy does not work, that the people cannot be trusted to govern themselves. The scene of the *veillée* complements that theory by showing the people as superstitious and somewhat indifferent to facts, thus easily swayed by superficial, and potentially inflammatory, oratory. This is especially true of the first portion, as the peasants seem wholly persuaded of the truth of the story of the *bossue courageuse*. There is nothing in the *veillée* itself that necessarily suggests that the peasants are completely gullible, that they believe in ghosts and cannibalistic aristocrats any more than moviegoers today believe in space-aliens or unstoppable serial killers. In the larger text, however, the peasants are consistently painted in bleak shades, conveying a definite impression of superstitious ignorance. To begin with, in the story of the *crétins*, Benassis must force the people to accept what is in their own best interest. They are hostile to his hygienic improvements because of ingrained superstitions:

> Ici, comme dans les autres sphères sociales, pour accomplir le bien, il fallait froisser, non pas les intérêts, mais chose plus dangereuse à manier, des idées religieuses converties en superstition, la forme la plus indestructible des idées humaines. (404)
>
> *Here, as in other social spheres, in order to achieve good results, I had to go against, not just interests, but something more dangerous to manipulate, religious ideas turned into superstition, the most inde-structible of human ideas.*

This is just one example of the harsh view that Benassis, who serves to some extent as the eyes and ears of the readers, has about the peasantry;

they are an ignorant, suspicious, and sometimes hostile class. Even the doctor's own servants, Jacquotte and Nicolle, who should know him best, are prepared to believe the worst about him based on bits of an overheard conversation that they are not fit to understand. Having heard snatches of Benassis's discourse, the old housekeeper Jacquotte is stunned to hear her employer speaking so harshly of the people:

> —Qu'est-ce que dit donc notre maître? s'écria Jacquotte en ren-
> trant dans la cuisine. Ne voilà-t-il pas ce pauvre cher homme qui leur
> conseille d'écraser le peuple! et ils l'écoutent.
> —Je n'aurais jamais cru cela de M. Benassis, répondit Nicolle.
> (509)
> *"What is our master saying?" cried Jacquotte coming back into*
> *the kitchen. "Isn't the poor man in there telling them to crush the sim-*
> *ple folk, and they're listening."*
> *"I never would have thought such a thing of M. Benassis," said*
> *Nicolle.*

In a darker text such as *Les Paysans,* one can easily imagine this case of eavesdropping and miscomprehension having dangerous, even fatal consequences for Benassis. The focus of *Le Médecin de campagne,* however, lies elsewhere, and this thread is not pursued.

In this novel, the view of the peasantry is neither all black nor all white; as Benassis says: "Je n'ai point fait des idylles sur mes gens, je les ai acceptés pour ce qu'il sont, de pauvres paysans, ni entièrement bons, ni entièrement méchants" [*I have no illusions about my people, I have accepted them as they are, poor peasants, neither entirely good nor entirely wicked*] (415). The peasants in this story are brought round to good because Benassis is there and can lead them, by force if necessary. *Les Paysans,* again, offers a more pessimistic but completely consistent view on the peasantry. As far as the urban *peuple* is concerned, it is made clear that they are no better toward the end of *La Cousine Bette,* when the baronne Hulot makes her excursions into the moral wastelands of the proletariat *faubourgs,* and finds, along with her wandering husband, a bestial people prepared to sell their daughters, ignorant of the ways of the Church or moral society. The people not only need strong leadership, they actually seem to crave it. Goguelat and his friends have built up a cult around Napoleon, remembering only the glory and the pride that he brought to France. In their rose-colored recollections, there is no resentment of the man whose wars decimated a generation, recruited by force mostly from the lower classes. They even absolve him of the cost of his wars; in Goguelat's version, Napoleon "remplit ses caves d'or" [*filled his cellars with gold*] with booty and tribute from conquered countries and built arches and monuments "sans mettre d'impôts sur vous autres" [*without taxing any of you folks*] (528). The Napoleon painted during the *veillée* is both a benevolent despot and a man of action, and in this sense the *Napoléon du peuple* is not so different than the one lauded by the aristocratic Canalis in *Autre étude de femme:*

> Un homme qu'on représente les bras croisés, et qui a tout fait! qui a été le plus beau pouvoir connu, le pouvoir le plus concentré, le plus mordant, le plus acide de tous les pouvoirs [. . .] prodigieux phénomène de volonté [. . .] tout pensée et tout action (3:701-2)
> *A man who is always represented with his arms crossed, and who did it all! Who was the greatest known power, the most concentrated power, the most trenchant, the most acidic of all powers . . . a prodigious phenomenon of will . . . all thought and all action.*

The active, concentrated power described by Canalis was found not only in Napoleon, but also of course, in miniature, in Benassis. The doctor is also the *Napoleon du peuple,* who has devoted his energies to improving their lives. The philosophy that he expresses in the essay portion of the chapter is the intellectualized expression of what the peasants remember in the second part. Strength, organization, and compassion aptly summarize both what Benassis has done in the *canton* and what Napoleon did in the selectively remembered biography performed by Goguelat.

This difference between the hard but optimistic view of *Le Médecin de campagne* and the harsh pessimism of later works points out another important element of the story of Benassis's good works. Although chronology is often problematic in *La Comédie humaine*, I do not believe it is a coincidence that Balzac specifically placed this novel, written in 1833, in 1829. In order for Benassis to accomplish his recreation of the canton, it is necessary for him to act with a great deal of arbitrary authority: he has himself named mayor, he gets rid of an ignorant priest who resists his innovations, etc. (404). Symbolically, with a certain nostalgic license, all this is possible under the Restoration and would have been impossible under the constitution of the July Monarchy with its broad suffrage and weakened monarch. How much this corresponds to reality is difficult to say, but it is significant, I believe, that Benassis dies in December of 1829, like the death of hope, just before the new bourgeois monarchy is born.

Lies and Seduction and Genius and Love: Diane de Cadignan and Daniel d'Arthez

In her study of love and marriage in *La Comédie humaine—Le Mariage et l'amour dans l'œuvre romanesque d'Honoré de Balzac*— Arlette Michel famously observed that

> Balzac a toujours aimé les aventurières de haut-vol: Marie de Verneuil, Lady Dudley le séduisent. Diane de Maufrigneuse a toute son indulgence, il est en complicité avec elle. (2:1058)
>
> *Balzac always loved high-flying adventuresses: Marie de Verneuil and Lady Dudley fascinate him. Diane de Maufrigneuse has his every indulgence, he is in complicity with her.*

This attraction is surely strongest in the case of Diane d'Uxelles, the princesse de Cadignan. No other adventuress of *La Comédie humaine* achieves quite the same altitude as the former duchesse de Maufrigneuse. Mme de Sérisy has many lovers and Lady Dudley is also a highly intelligent libertine, but neither of these characters is drawn with the fullness that Diane is. The marquise d'Espard, who is very significantly and very deliberately placed in direct opposition to Diane in *Les Secrets de la princesse de Cadignan,* is a well-defined character; she is also very smart, manipulative, and politically powerful. She possibly has many lovers in her past as well. But she does not benefit from the affection that Balzac seems to have for her rival. Diane de Cadignan is one of those characters in *La Comédie humaine* that we probably should not like, but do. The capricious, duplicitous, and almost pathologically selfish Diane has one saving grace: her intelligence. Like Gobseck and Vautrin, two other characters who inspire equivocal, almost reluctant, appreciation on the part of the reader,

Diane is endowed with a clear-eyed lucidity that sets her apart from, really lifts her above, the majority of her fellow characters. As is often the case in Balzac's oeuvre, this intelligence manifests itself in humor. On several occasions, in different texts, Diane displays a fine and sometimes self-directed, if not exactly self-deprecating, wit. These qualities separate her from other aristocratic, romantic female characters; Lady Dudley and Mme d'Espard are not at all sympathetic, and Mme de Mortsauf's earnest virtue frankly becomes overbearing. Intelligence, humor, and an awareness of her own faults give this character a humanity that some of Balzac's characters lack, while at the same time the fact that she is aristocratic, beautiful, and a woman makes her more attractive, because less threatening, than Gobseck or Vautrin. Another point that suggests that Balzac found this character more humane than some of his other creations is the fact that she is frequently referred to by her first name; as someone once observed, no one ever thinks of the marquise d'Espard as Jeanne. Finally, we should consider the end of Diane's story—she is one of the few major characters in Balzac's vast tableau who can be said to find happiness.

Another clue to Balzac's affection for this character is her title. As I have already stated, I believe that aristocratic titles count for a great deal in Balzac's world, and I believe that it is quite significant that Diane has the highest rank of any fictional character in *La Comédie humaine*. In *Les Secrets*, Balzac gives a brief nod to the social and historical reality of his time by pointing out that the different noble ranks no longer mean much, and then undermines that observation by launching into a detailed description of the special privileges of princes in the feudal system:

> les princes de Cadignan avaient droit à un trône chez eux, ils pouvaient avoir des pages, des gentilshommes à leur service. Cette explication est nécessaire, autant pour éviter les sottes critiques de ceux qui ne savent rien que pour constater les grandes choses d'un monde qui s'en va, et que tant de gens poussent sans le comprendre. (6:950)
>
> *The princes de Cadignan had the right to a throne in their house, they were allowed to have pages, and gentlemen in their service. This explanation is necessary, as much to avoid the silly criticisms of those who know nothing as to attest to the grander aspects of a world which is fading away, and that so many people are pushing away without understanding it.*

Anne-Marie Meinenger, among others, has labeled this passage "saint-simonien." The reference to Saint-Simon is especially interesting when we consider that the original name of the character who became Diane de Cadignan was Carignan (Introduction, éd. Pléiade, 942), the name of a branch of the House of Savoy that appears fairly frequently in the *Mémoires* of Saint-Simon and those of the Cardinal de Retz as well. The link between Diane and the *Grand Siècle* is reinforced later in the text when she is compared to the heroines of the Fronde (955). If the princess's title is something of an anachronism, it is in keeping with her character (*caractère*); her regal arrogance, her sexual mores, and her personal grandeur tie her to the Golden Age of the French aristocracy.

In 1833, when *Les Secrets de la princesse de Cadignan* takes place, this elegant anachronism is living in genteel poverty—which she attempts to pass off as virtuous economy—and seeking to arrange a marriage that will allow her son, the young duc de Maufrigneuse, to live in the lifestyle that befits his title and ancestry. To this end, the reclusive princess has maintained a close relationship with the marquise d'Espard. This friendship is somewhat surprising, especially to those readers who come to *Les Secrets* after having read *Splendeurs et misères des courtisanes,* where these two intriguing *grandes dames* are rather fierce antagonists in the matter of Lucien de Rubempré's imprisonment. The action of the *nouvelle* begins when the lonely princess reveals to her friend that in spite of her many lovers, she feels that she has never known true love. All of her past lovers, the princess complains, were too dull to make her feel any real fulfillment. Diane nostalgically and fondly remembers the romantic obsession she inspired in a curious heart, that of the republican revolutionary Michel Chrestien. The marquise recognizes Chrestien as the friend of another man, whose politics and particule make him a more socially acceptable object of Diane's attention, the brilliant writer and conservative deputy Daniel d'Arthez. The marquise arranges a meeting between the two, and the princess sets out to inspire one last passion in a man worthy of her genius for seduction, and to see if she can finally find true love herself. She succeeds on both counts, and after what Balzac called "la plus grande comédie morale qui existe" has played itself out, Diane and Daniel ride off into Balzac's figurative sunset, a villa on the shores of Lake Geneva.

Many readers take this *nouvelle* at face value for a light comedy with a happy ending. Some of those who have studied it more closely, however, have found it disturbing that a man of genius appears to have been duped by the lies of a coquettish *grande dame*. These critics have discerned rather darker undertones in the text and conclude that the apparently happy ending is actually highly ambiguous. This interpretation has, in turn, inspired others to seek a justification for the ending, one that takes into account both Daniel's genius and the princess's lies. At the center of both the *nouvelle* and the controversy is the fictional autobiography that Diane performs for Daniel. Knowing that her past is far too well known to be completely hidden from her latest lover, Diane reinvents it. In this revisionist history, she casts herself as a victim, first of her mother, who married Diane off to her own lover, then of an indifferent husband, and finally of a society that painted her as a libertine when in fact, she merely had a number of platonic admirers, like a virtuous lady of the Middle Ages, surrounded by chivalric *serviteurs*.

As readers, we know this story to be false. The ultimate question is whether d'Arthez is Diane's dupe. In the end, she herself believes that he has fallen for her lies, as do those critics who see Daniel as her victim. In order to arrive at a conclusion, I believe that we must consider this narration as a part of Diane's larger scheme of seduction, and as a part of the development of d'Arthez's feelings for her. As I said at the beginning of this chapter, this narration seems like narrated exposition, but it cannot be considered as such because it is false. We find the truth not only in other parts of *La Comédie humaine,* but provided for us, by the Narrator, in the text of *Les Secrets* itself. Diane's *récit* is a careful blend of truth and fiction, and since we readers are provided with enough information about Diane's past to distinguish between the two, we are able to interpret her story with some degree of independence. We can evaluate the degree(s) of truth in different parts of Diane's tale, and we can speculate on her motivation for the specific lies and shadings that she adds to that truth, and the meaning that lies behind these additions and embellishments.

Diane's portrayal of her relationships with her mother, her husband, and her son offer us an opportunity to study the basis of truth in her carefully constructed tale, and how she maintains, alters, or distorts that truth to suit her own purposes. When Diane tells Daniel that her mother married her off to a former lover, we believe her. The Narrator has told us that this was in fact the main reason for Diane's marriage to the much older duc de Maufrigneuse: "Le duc de Maufrigneuse avait eu des liaisons avec la duchesse d'Uxelles. Vers 1814, au moment où M. de Maufrigneuse atteignait à trente-six ans, la duchesse, le voyant pauvre mais très bien en cour, lui donna sa fille qui posséda environ cinquante ou soixante mille livres de rente" [*The Duke de Maufrigneuse had had an affair with the Duchess d'Uxelles. Toward 1814, when the duke reached the age of 36, the duchess, seeing him poor but well-connected at court, gave him her daughter who had fifty or sixty thousand a year*] (983). When Diane paints herself as a tortured victim in this arrangement, however, we know that she is taking some poetic license; the duke, it is generally acknowledged, has been a perfect gentleman for his wife—according to the standards of Balzac's aristocracy—casting a benign eye on her peccadilloes and protecting her even during her most reckless adventures (983). We can legitimately ask ourselves, however, if there is not some grain of truth in Diane's self-flattering portrait of the circumstances of her marriage. Such quasi-incestuous marriages are of course not unknown in the world of *La Comédie humaine,* but Balzac was enough of a psychologist to realize that this was a profoundly unhealthy arrangement. We know that at one point he intended to show the scars that such an arrangement had left on Augusta de Nucingen, and Diane describes it to Daniel as an "horrible combinaison" that unfortunately "a lieu souvent" [*a horrible but fairly frequent arrangement*] (989). If the princess exaggerates the extent of her suffering resulting from her mother's method of rewarding a former lover, it is also an exaggeration to paint her mother, or even her husband, as victims of slander in Diane's portrait.

Another subtle blend of truth and fiction can be found in Diane's description of her relationship with her son. Seeking to cast herself as a virtuous and unworldly woman, Diane describes the joy she experienced as an attentive young mother whose only concern was her little son. We know this to be false. Like all of Balzac's *grandes mondaines,* Diane appears to have had little interest in raising her son; she only became interested in him when he was an adult. But when Diane is describing Georges to Daniel, she says that he is "tout moi-même" [*my very image*] (991). For d'Arthez, this is merely a doting mother's proud reflection on a genetic fact, and pointing out their physical resemblance is no doubt meant to underline their (supposedly) strong emotional connection. But once again the

reader has information, that Daniel does not, that puts a different light on
this seemingly insignificant remark. We know that by the time Diane married, her husband was impotent: "Dès l'âge de trente-six ans, il était par
force d'une aussi parfaite indifférence pour le beau sexe que Charles X
son maître; puni comme son maître pour avoir, comme lui, trop plu dans
sa jeunesse" [*From the age of thirty-six, he had been, of necessity, as
completely indifferent to the fair sex as his master, King Charles X; pun-
ished like his master for having been too successful in his youth*] (982).
There is a very good reason why the birth of an heir was, for the duke, "un
bonheur inespéré" [*an unhoped-for good fortune*] (983). We do not know
who the real father is, although de Marsay would seem a likely suspect; he
acts as something of a father in helping Diane to arrange Georges's marriage. This is yet another of the princess's secrets. This circumstance does
lend some ironic credibility to Diane's contention that she was driven to
other men by her husband. After all, it was her duty to produce an heir,
and her husband wasn't up to the job. In any case, when Diane says that
Georges is all her, the reader can perceive a double meaning in the seemingly innocent expression; it is much richer for us than for Daniel. Perhaps
the *spirituelle* princess is having a little joke to amuse herself during her
grand, melodramatic performance; no doubt Balzac is amusing himself
with this double entendre. As readers, we are in on the joke, d'Arthez is
not. The key difference between our interpretation of Diane's recital and
Daniel's is that, as narratees, we are prepared for it by the Narrator, while
Daniel is prepared for it by Diane herself. Even if we have come to share
Balzac's affection for the princess, we do not feel as strongly about her as
Daniel does. He is very probably in love with her before they are even
introduced.

Diane and Daniel have never met face to face before the marquise
d'Espard's dinner,[3] but d'Arthez has been aware of the princess for some
time. Blondet and Rastignac, sent by Mme d'Espard to lure Daniel to her
dinner party, regale him with the scandalous chronicles of the duchesse de
Maufrigneuse. As Daniel tells the two "corrupteurs" at this very early

---

[3] Both were present at Félicité des Touches's supper in *Autre étude de femme*, which
logically must take place before *Les Secrets*. We can either attribute this minor inconsistency to the problematic internal chronology of *La Comédie humaine*, or to the inordi-
nately large size of Félicité's dining room table.

point in the story, there is little that they can tell him that he does not already know about Diane, as he learned all about her many years earlier because of Michel Chrestien's obsession with her. Later, during their intimate conversation at Mme d'Espard's table, Daniel reveals to Diane that he was often at Chrestien's side when the Republican pursued his impossible ideal through the streets of Paris. As Daniel tells Diane this story, we can detect that the writer followed not only his friend's footsteps, but also his emotions as the two followed Diane about the city: "Combien de fois n'ai-je pas reçu la pluie en accompagnant votre voiture jusque chez vous, en luttant de vitesse avec vos chevaux, pour nous maintenir au même point sur une ligne parallèle, afin de vous voir. . . de vous admirer!" [*How many times was I drenched with rain accompanying your carriage to your home, racing against the speed of your horses to hold ourselves parallel to you, just to see you, to admire you*] (971). If Daniel was not actually in love with her at this time, clearly he was already fascinated. It is also clear to us readers by this point that Daniel is familiar with Diane's faults as well as her charms. Blondet and Rastignac make no effort to spare Diane's reputation; to the contrary, they take great pleasure in recounting every detail, but they do not succeed in diminishing her in d'Arthez's eyes: "La femme qu'ils traitaient si légèrement était sainte et sacrée pour d'Arthez, dont la curiosité n'avait pas besoin d'être piquée" [*The woman they were treating so lightly was sainted and sacred for d'Arthez, whose curiosity had no need of encouragement*] (967). But as Daniel is shortly to learn, and the reader along with him, what is important about Diane, what men find so irresistible in her, is precisely what cannot be known, but only felt on a level beyond knowing.

The princess begins creating an impression of honesty and simplicity from the moment she meets d'Arthez. Many of the small details of her conduct during this first meeting reveal a great deal to us about Diane's overall plan of seduction and the image she seeks to project to d'Arthez. To begin with there is her wardrobe. This is a tactic that Diane uses with great skill; according to the Narrator, Diane is "une des plus fortes sur la toilette, qui, pour les femmes, est le premier des arts" [*one of the most elegant of dressers, which is, for women, the first of all arts*] (968). Much to the amazement of her hostess, the princess brings her grown son as her escort. The marquise d'Espard, who in *L'Interdiction* holds her much younger sons at a distance for fear they will reveal her true age to acquaintances, offers herself a rather facile explanation: "Je vous comprends! En faisant accepter à d'Arthez toutes les difficultés du premier coup, vous ne les trouverez pas à vaincre plus tard" [*I see! In making d'Arthez see all the difficulties at first glance, you won't have to vanquish them later on*] (969). The marquise is partly right, but the princess's thinking goes deeper. Diane, who as the Narrator assures us dominates her friend "de toute une tête" [*by a whole head*] (998)—a significant description that has little to do with physical stature—realizes that her son's presence is an asset in her long-range plans: A woman known above all for her beauty who publicly acknowledges that she is old enough to be a grandmother (at 36) is one who can be trusted. Finally, there is the fact that she eats heartily at dinner. This seemingly most insignificant detail is important because it goes directly against the grain of Balzac's *grandes mondaines*. Again, this can be seen as a direct counterpoint to Mme d'Espard; in *L'Interdiction,* Bianchon detects that the marquise hides "un appétit de loup" beneath a veneer of feminine weakness (3:423). Diane's hearty appetite is another sign of a natural and honest woman who has abandoned the poses and pretense of the *monde*. Everything about her suggests modesty and indifference to her appearance and to the opinions of others.

Diane's most important strategy on this evening is her conversation. During their tête-à-tête at dinner, Diane and Daniel speak almost exclusively of Michel Chrestien. He is a both a common and sacred ground that allows them to meet on a higher plane, and the fact that they both admire Chrestien even while rejecting his politics is another bond between them. The subject of Michel Chrestien serves as

un admirable prétexte à Daniel comme à la princesse de parler à voix basse : amour, sympathie, divination; à elle de se poser en femme méconnue, calomniée; à lui de se fourrer les pieds dans les souliers du républicain mort. Peut-être cet homme d'ingénuité se surprit-il à moins regretter son ami?

an admirable pretext for Daniel as well as for the princess to speak quietly: love, sympathy, divination; for her to pose as a misunderstood woman, calumnied even; for him to place his feet in the shoes of the dead republican. Perhaps this ingenius man found himself missing his friend a bit less?

At the end of the meal, the memory of Chrestien allows Diane to open the door of her retreat to Daniel: "Je ne veux pas être inaccessible pour l'ami de ce pauvre républicain" [*I do not want to be unavailable for the friend of that poor republican*] (974). And when d'Arthez leaves the d'Espard house with Rastignac, the die seems to be cast: "Michel avait raison de l'aimer [. . .] c'est une femme extraordinaire" [*Michel was right to love her. . . she's an extraordinary woman*] (976). After having served to bring Daniel and Diane together, Michel Chrestien virtually fades out of the story. Apart from a brief—albeit essential—mention in Diane's autobiography, he no longer plays a major role in the story; his specter does not hang over the soon to be happy couple. This is not to say that the attachment that both have shown for his memory is insincere. Diane of course is especially vulnerable to accusations of insincerity, that she merely used Chrestien's name as a pretext to gain access to d'Arthez. We should remember, however, that Diane spoke lovingly of Chrestien before she even knew of his friendship with d'Arthez. The letter that Chrestien sent to Diane—"Cette lettre courte et terrible, me remue le cœur quand j'y songe" [*that short and terrible letter, that moves my heart when I think of it*]—is her only souvenir of an "amour . . . trop grand et trop saint" [*a love too great and too sacred*] to be exploited for any base purpose (961). The content of that letter is one of the secrets of the princesse de Cadignan; she refuses to show it to the marquise, and the Narrator does not share it with the reader.

Already after that first meeting, it seems that each is taken with the other. It is interesting to note that the Narrator expresses the first feelings of love in terms of surrender: "D'Arthez laissa l'amour pénétrer dans son cœur [. . .] sans faire la moindre résistance, il procéda par l'adoration sans critique, par l'admiration exclusive" [*D'Arthez allowed love to enter into his heart without the least resistance, he proceeded with uncritical adoration, with exclusive admiration*] (977). As for Diane: "En revenant chez elle, la princesse ne discuta pas plus avec elle-même que d'Arthez ne se défendit contre le charme qu'elle lui avait jeté [...] elle aimait avec sa science et avec son ignorance" [*Returning home, the princess did not argue with herself any more than d'Arthez defended himself against the spell she had cast upon him; she loved with her science and her ignorance*] (979). Their relationship proceeds slowly—too slowly for Diane's taste—until the moment she decides to speed things up with her grand performance.

Dressed, as always for d'Arthez, in shades of gray, a "demi-deuil" for this quasi-widow (980), she arranges the room and the lights to help her in her role of victim in what the Narrator calls "l'une des comédies inconnues […] entre deux êtres, dont l'un sera la dupe de l'autre" [*one of those hidden comedies between two people, one of whom must be the dupe of the other*] (979). Her stage set, she proceeds to ensnare the brilliant writer in "les lianes d'un roman préparé de longue main" [*in the snares of a novel long since prepared*] (989). The ground for the story of her martyrdom already having been prepared during the first tête-à-tête between them, during which Diane presented herself as a woman "méconnue [et] calomniée," the princess paints herself as an innocent slandered by a society in which vice and jealousy triumph over virtue. The notion of calumny, a word that is used repeatedly throughout the text, is essential to the understanding of Diane and Daniel's relationship, and I shall return to it a bit further on. When she finishes, Diane is convinced that she has won: "« Ah! je le tiens » pensa-t-elle; et, elle le tenait bien en effet" [*"Ah! I've got him," she thought; and she had in fact a good hold on him*] (996).

This relationship between Diane, Daniel, and this autobiography suggests another well-known situation in French literature, that of the marquise de Merteuil, Valmont, and the famous eighty-first letter of *Les Liaisons dangereuses*. In both cases, a manipulative, aristocratic libertine reveals to one man a version of her life that is in direct opposition to the one generally known and accepted by society. The difference of course is that while Merteuil reveals to Valmont the scandalous secrets of her life, which is completely disguised for those around her, Diane offers Daniel a pack of lies meant to distract him from the scandalous truth, which is known to everyone. Although there is little else about Daniel that suggests Valmont, they are both men of genius, albeit a very different sort of genius, whom strong and brilliant women believe they can, for very different reasons, confide in, and ultimately dominate. The connections between Diane and Mme de Merteuil are easier to see. Most obviously, they share an aristocratic rank and uninhibited sexual mores; most importantly, they are both supremely confident and have the intelligence to back up their self-assurance. Both of them seem to exercise, up to a certain point, complete control of themselves and those around them. The apparent perfection of Diane's manipulations is almost certainly one of the reasons that so many critics see d'Arthez as her dupe. Her manipulative skill is clear in her life story, for the brilliance of Diane's tale is not merely the way in which she rearranges the past, but the way she prearranges the future.

   To fully appreciate Diane's skill, we must examine not only her relationship with d'Arthez, but also her second important relationship in this novel, with Mme d'Espard. A comparison to *Les Liaisons dangereuses* is instructive in this case as well, as Rose Fortassier has pointed out; the "amitié armée" between these two women is not unlike the uneasy alliance between Merteuil and Valmont. Fortassier also cites Mme d'Espard's title and her coldly manipulative nature as similarities between Laclos's marquise and Balzac's ("Balzac et Laclos," 278-79). Two other points of comparison are illuminating with regard to the curious relationship between the princess and the marquise. One is the similarly arch friendship between Mme de Beauséant and the duchesse de Langeais as portrayed in *Le Père Goriot.* This is also a rivalry disguised as friendship, and in that situation as in *Les Secrets,* it is not difficult to discern on which side Balzac's sympathies lie. Through the prism of that comparison, we find another analogous relationship in *Le Misanthrope.* In *Le Cabinet des Antiques,* Diane is repeatedly compared to Célimène, and in the letter in which Balzac described *Les Secrets* to Mme Hanska, he referred to Diane as "Célimène amoureuse"; the brittle and duplicitous marquise d'Espard, like Mme de Langeais in *Le Père Goriot,* is thus cast as Arsinoé. This last comparison is further strengthened if we consider that d'Arthez, the solitary, intellectual aristocrat who largely shuns society, is not without certain similarities to Alceste. But in Balzac's version, Célimène falls in love, and she and Alceste leave Paris together.

   After Diane and Daniel have gotten acquainted, the princess tells the marquise that she fears that d'Arthez will represent merely one more conquest without a battle. Mme d'Espard proposes to make things more challenging by becoming the princess's rival: "Comme vous voudrez, répondit la princesse" [*"As you like," replied the princess*] (973). Like Valmont's assurance to Mme de Merteuil that he will retake Mme de Tourvel whenever he chooses, after having claimed his reward from the marquise, the dismissive confidence of this statement is wounding for its recipient. Later developments in the *nouvelle* put into question the princess's sincerity in this exchange with the marquise, but at the time, it seems to us that Diane has made her first blunder: "Mme d'Espard se jeta dans la conversation générale et ne parut ni blessée du *Comme vous voudrez,* ni curieuse

de savoir à quoi aboutirait cette aventure." [*Mme d'Espard threw herself
into the general conversation and seemed neither wounded by this 'As you
like' nor curious to know how this adventure would play out*]. Obviously,
the marquise is extremely interested in the outcome of the meeting, and
we can safely assume that she is deeply insulted by her friend's implicit
assumption of superiority. It seems that, as with *Les Liaisons,* the casual
confidence of a supremely self-assured libertine might drive a vindictive
marquise to lethal vengeance.

This impression is only strengthened at the end of the *nouvelle,*
when the marquise arranges another dinner for d'Arthez, where the guest
list just happens to include a number of Diane's former lovers, including
the caustic and ruthless Maxime de Trailles and the spiteful Victurnien
d'Esgrignon. Yet if this is Mme d'Espard's attempt at revenge for her
friend's high-handedness, then the marquise has underestimated the princess. Mme d'Espard's offense has been undermined by a preemptive defensive strike in Diane's autobiography. Among the general pettiness of
the *monde* as portrayed by the now-retired princess, de Trailles and
d'Esgrignon are singled out as especially perfidious. Both are named in
the list of men that make up Diane's "recueil des erreurs," her album of
portraits of former lovers, whom Diane retroactively assigns the (implicitly platonic) role of "admirateurs" (996). The "infâme de Trailles" is
described as "un coupe-jarret politique" [*a political cut-throat*]; while
Victurnien becomes "ce petit sot d'Esgrignon" [*that little nitwit
d'Esgrignon*] It must be acknowledged that, if Diane is less than candid
about the exact nature of her relationships, the descriptions of the men involved are accurate. D'Esgrignon fares especially poorly. Diane describes
him as "un jeune étourdi" with whom she ran away to Italy, but promptly
deserted when he began to talk of love. Again, as throughout Diane's
story, truth and fiction have been artfully, subtly blended. It is absolutely
true that Diane ran to save Victurnien after he had committed fraud for
her, and that she pulled him out of "l'abîme où il s'était plongé pour moi"
[*the abyss into which he had plunged himself for me*] (992). Diane accepts
just enough responsibility in this matter to make her claim of virtue be-
lievable. When d'Esgrignon later complains, at Mme d'Espard's second
dinner, that Diane is to blame for his marriage (1001)—a statement that
the reader of *Le Cabinet des Antiques* knows to be patently false—he af-
firms in Daniel's mind the image of himself as a selfish "étourdi" that

Diane sought to ascribe him, and further her own self-assigned role of
"vierge et martyre" (996).

Diane uses a similar technique to undermine the credibility of
Mme d'Espard. Complaining of the false reputation that the gossips of
Paris had created for her, Diane uses the following anecdote to illustrate
the viciousness of the *monde*, and of one *mondaine* in particular:

> Savez-vous le mot infâme qui m'a fait faire d'autres folies? Inventerez-
> vous jamais le sublime des calomnies du monde? "La duchesse de
> Maufrigneuse est revenue à son mari, se disait-on. —Bah! c'est par dé-
> pravation, c'est un triomphe que de ranimer des morts, elle n'avait plus
> que cela à faire", a répondu ma meilleure amie, une parente, celle chez
> qui j'ai eu le bonheur de vous rencontrer.
>
> —Mme d'Espard! s'écria Daniel en faisant un geste d'horreur.
>
> —Oh! je lui ai pardonné, mon ami. D'abord le mot est excessive-
> ment spirituel, et peut-être ai-je dit moi-même de plus cruelles épi-
> grammes sur de pauvres femmes tout aussi pures que je l'étais. (993)
>
> *"Do you want to know the infamous comment that pushed me to even
> further follies? Could you [novelists] ever invent the sublime of social
> calumny? The duchesse de Maufrigneuse has gone back to her hus-
> band,' someone said. 'Bah! Another depravity, it's a triumph for her to
> revive the dead, it's the only thing she hasn't done yet,' replied my best
> friend, a relative, the very one at whose home I had the good fortune to
> meet you."*
>
> *"Mme d'Espard!" cried Daniel with a gesture of horror.*
>
> *"Oh! I've long since forgiven her. First of all the remark is ex-
> tremely witty, and perhaps I myself have said even crueller things
> about poor women every bit as pure as I was."*

This anecdote offers still another point of comparison between the friendship of these two women and that of Mmes de Beauséant and de Langeais.
In *Le Père Goriot*, the duchess makes a similarly disparaging remark behind the back of her so-called best friend. Speaking of Mme de Beauséant's attempts to hold onto d'Ajuda-Pinto, the duchess says: "Au lieu de
sauter noblement par la fenêtre, elle se laissait rouler dans les escaliers"
[*Rather than nobly throwing herself out the window, she let herself roll
down the stairs*] (3:122). The key difference is that Mme de Langeais's

remark is related to us by the Narrator. In *Les Secrets,* Diane, more of a fighter than Claire de Beauséant, turns the verbal dagger back on her false friend. Most importantly, Diane is able to portray Mme d'Espard as poison-tongued and hypocritical; her words thus lose all value for d'Arthez. Diane is also able to play the part not just of victim, but of forgiving victim, even blaming herself for having committed similar crimes while caught up in the wickedness of the society she now, of course, rejects. As with her remarks concerning d'Esgrignon, the partial blame she places on herself only serves to further elevate her in Daniel's estimation. The impression that Diane is using the marquise in her strategy to win Daniel is confirmed in the text, when the Narrator tells us that the princess wants to use her friend as a "chien de chasse" [*hunting dog*]—a very significant term given Diane's association with the Roman goddess of the hunt. The *coup de grâce* comes when Diane sends Daniel into the lion's den, sending him to Mme d'Espard's house again, apparently sure that he will hear all sorts of "calomnies," but willing to bet that the brilliant novelist is so caught up in her fiction that he will reject the truth.

By the time Daniel goes to that second dinner at Mme d'Espard's, everything seems to have been so completely and successfully orchestrated by Diane that we are inclined to believe, as she does, that d'Arthez is her dupe. This impression is reinforced by the fact that most of the *nouvelle,* and especially the scene of the autobiography, is written in a point of view that heavily favors Diane and her own impressions. But a careful consideration of the whole text suggests that Daniel is not the dupe of the princess, but rather that she is the dupe of a brilliant writer, just as are the readers who from the beginning of the text are led to believe in Diane's invincibility. The portrayal of the princess and the text's point of view serve to overshadow the fact that d'Arthez is different from all the others who were such easy conquests for Diane. One of the first things that Diane, and the readers, learn about Daniel is that his intelligence is "toute rétrospective." Mme d'Espard tells Diane: "Sa pénétration [. . .] agit après coup et dérange tous les calculs. Vous l'avez surpris aujourd'hui, demain il n'est plus la dupe de rien" [*His penetration comes into play after the fact and upsets any calculations. You may take him by surprise today, tomorrow he will fall for nothing*] (967). This is before he meets Diane. After her seductive performance as an unjustly accused innocent, d'Arthez, who had known Diane from a distance for quite some time and whom Ras-

STORIES WITHIN STORIES: THE EMBEDDED NARRATIVES   223

tignac and Blondet had told everything there was to tell, finds himself dis-
oriented: "La perspicacité rétrospective de cet homme si naturel et si pro-
fond fut mise en défaut par le naturel de ce roman, par sa profondeur, par
l'accent de la princesse" [*The retrospective perspicacity of this so very
natural and profound man was thrown off by the simplicity of this novel,
by its depth, and by the tone of the princess*] (997).

   Whatever confusion Daniel might temporarily feel about Diane,
his retrospective understanding is surely put back into place by the conversation he finds at Mme d'Espard's second dinner, when the bare facts
of Diane's scandalous past are again laid before him. Daniel resolutely
takes Diane's side against those who seek to slander her with the truth. His
defense of her—which as the writer Nathan observes, is more vengeance
than defense—completely accepts all the charges against her as true. Ac-
knowledging both her sexual and financial dissipations (one wonders
which Balzac himself considered the greater sin), d'Arthez responds to
Diane's attackers:

> Mme la princesse de Cadignan a sur les hommes un avantage: quand on
> s'est mis en danger pour elle, elle vous sauve, et ne dit de mal de per-
> sonne. Pourquoi, dans le nombre, ne se trouverait-il pas une femme qui
> s'amusât des hommes, comme les hommes s'amusent des femmes?
> Pourquoi le beau sexe ne prendrait-il pas de temps en temps une re-
> vanche?. . . (1003)
> *Madame la princesse de Cadignan has one advantage over men: when
> one has placed himself in danger for her, she saves him and never
> speaks ill of anyone. Why should there not be, in all the world, one wo-
> man who amuses herself with men, just as men amuse themselves with
> women? Why shouldn't the fair sex avenge itself from time to time?*

This curious counterattack does not answer all our questions, but it shows
fairly clearly that Daniel has not fallen for Diane's lies. He protects her
and loves her "*quand même*" (*anyway* sic, 1003). As Balzac said in his
letter to Mme Hanska, love justifies the lying. But as Alexander Fischler
observed, it would be selling this work and these characters short to
assume that this story is no more than that of a rather naive man overwhelmed by the beauty and charms of a high society coquette ("Duplication and 'comédie morale,' " 259). As I said earlier, the challenge of this

nouvelle is to understand the ending while taking into account both Diane's lies and Daniel's genius.

I believe we can find the key to this enigma if we remember that the connection between the two lovers has its roots in the memory of Michel Chrestien, another man who towers above the ordinary. That this austere republican loved an aristocratic lady raises other questions, that Balzac answers at the beginning of the *nouvelle*. Before Chrestien's death, d'Arthez had, to the amazement of his friends, been involved in "la plus vulgaire et la plus incompréhensible liaison avec une femme assez belle, mais qui appartenait à la classe inférieure, sans aucune instruction, sans manières, et soigneusement cachée à tous les regards"[*the most vulgar and most incomprehensible liaison with a woman who was pretty enough, but who belonged to the lower class, with no education, no manners, and carefully hidden from all eyes*] (963-64). The admirable Chrestien had justified the equally admirable d'Arthez's strange liaison by explaining that for men of genius, love is not the same thing as for the rest of us:

> Michel Chrestien accordait aux hommes de génie le pouvoir de transformer les plus massives créatures en sylphides, les sottes en femmes d'esprit, les paysannes en marquises : plus une femme était accomplie, plus elle perdit à leurs yeux; selon lui, leur imagination n'avait rien à y faire. Selon lui, l'amour, simple besoin des sens pour les êtres inférieurs, était, pour les êtres supérieurs, la création morale la plus immense et la plus attachante. (964)
>
> *Michel Chrestien accorded to men of genius the power to transform the most massive creatures into sylphs, ninnies into women of intelligence, peasants into marquises: the more a woman is accomplished, the more she suffers in their eyes; according to Chrestien, their imagination had nothing to do with such women. For him, love, a simple emotional need for inferior beings, was, for the superior, the greatest and most endearing moral creation.*

Just as the brilliant d'Arthez falls in love with a vulgar woman, the virtuous Republican Chrestien sees an angel in the debauched *grande dame*. D'Arthez, who is Chrestien's *âme jumelle* [*twin soul*] (974), sees the same thing, that the woman who appears to be a model of feminine perfection is actually deeply flawed. In fact, because her moral flaws are, somewhat paradoxically, grander than the common faults of d'Arthez's previous lover, she is a more worthy object for the redemptive power of d'Arthez's genial love.

Unquestionably, Diane's considerable attractions have their effect on d'Arthez just as they do on the other men in her life, but it is her imperfections that make it possible for him, as a man of genius, to love her. His genial imagination compensates for her past and even for her lying. An *homme de génie* like d'Arthez can see more in Diane than can those *hommes d'esprit* who attack her, for as Blondet observes after Daniel's rout of Diane's detractors, "le génie est plus fort que l'esprit" [*genius is stronger than wit*] (1003). Genius can see in Diane what others cannot, perhaps even the essential truth of the princesse de Cadignan's original secret, that this woman has had many lovers, but never loved. Before he has even met her face to face, after Blondet and Rastignac have finished recounting the scandalous chronicle of her past, "D'Arthez leur dit qu'il en avait su plus qu'ils n'en pouvaient lui en dire sur elle par leur pauvre ami, Michel Chrestien" [*D'Arthez told them that he knew more about her than they could ever tell him from their poor friend, Michel Chrestien*] (966). This is a fascinating sentence; there is more to be known about Diane than can be said, much more than her beauty, her grace, or her faults. But only men of genius, like d'Arthez and Chrestien, can recognize that true worth.

All of that taken into consideration, there is still something disturbing about the fact that d'Arthez forgives Diane for lying, and that he allows her to go on believing that she had duped him. It is useful perhaps to remember that d'Arthez is a novelist. His genius is expressed through the subjective medium of fiction; his talent is related to the poetic, the nonrational. Allan Pasco has brilliantly identified, in a seemingly clumsy repetition of the name of Antinoüs in the opening pages of the text, a governing image—what Pasco calls a generative idea (*idée mère*)—of the whole *nouvelle* in an etymological deconstruction of that name: *anti*, meaning against and *noüs*, meaning reason (*Balzacian Montage*, 35). The fact that antirationality is linked to an image denoting physical beauty is also significant. Just as there is no logical reason for human attraction to physical beauty, there is no logical reason for Daniel to love the princess, or to forgive her for her lies. D'Arthez's love for Diane is not a rational but an emotional choice, and *le cœur a ses raisons que la raison ne connaît point*. Two comments from extremely authoritative voices in the text support Daniel's decision to love *quand même.* The first is Rastignac. At this point in *La Comédie humaine,* this aging dandy is on the point of succeeding the dying de Marsay—whose deteriorating condition is referred to in the opening pages of the text—as the elder statesman of *La Comédie humaine.* After Daniel silences Diane's detractors, Rastignac overhears Nathan and Blondet expressing their surprise at the virtuous author's nondefense of Diane, and sardonically replies: "Absolument comme si la princesse en valait la peine" [*Just as if the princess was worth the trouble*] (1004). Rastignac, who has always been extremely logical in his choice of lovers, who was in fact once dissuaded from pursuing Diane by the logic of the eternally calculating de Marsay [*Le Cabinet des antiques,* 4:117], and who is about to make a very rational marriage, recognizes that d'Arthez has won a very great prize by playing by different rules. The other voice is that of the Narrator, in what he calls an "opinion individuelle." It is of course not unusual for the Narrator to express strong opinions on a character or a situation; it is however rare that these opinions are explicitly presented as subjective. This is also one of those rare occasions where the Narrator's voice can be designated as masculine in its outlook, as he says of Diane's attempts to deceive d'Arthez: "S'il est permis de risquer une opinion individuelle, avouons qu'il serait délicieux d'être ainsi trompé longtemps" [*If one may be permitted to hazard an individual opinion, let us admit that it would be delicious to be deceived in this way for a very long time*] (989).

Daniel's love for Diane and his conscious decision to allow her to believe she deceived him would not rescue him from the status of victim if Diane did not return his love; and it would seem that the sincerity of her feelings could be called into question. If Daniel's love for Diane is the rejection of reason, her conduct, from minor details such as clothing and poses to the fictional autobiography, all seems rationally, almost coldly calculated. At the end of the *nouvelle,* however, it becomes clear that her love is genuine. Having sent Daniel to Mme d'Espard's, the master manipulator does not rest easy: "Pour la première fois de sa vie, cette femme souffrait dans son cœur et suait dans sa robe" [*For the first time in her life, this woman was suffering in her heart and sweating in her gown*] (1004). The use of such a crassly physical image (Diane sweating in her dress) used to describe such an elegant character, and placed in opposition to the romantic image of heartfelt suffering, seizes the attention of the reader.

This sentence—and most of the passage in which it is found—firmly establish the idea that Diane has actually fallen in love for the first time. I earlier said, half facetiously, that the brilliant surgeon and atheist Desplein had altered Pascal's wager to fit his own virtuous but unbelieving philosophy of life. In Diane's case, I think we can talk about not a *pari de Dieu*, (*wager of God*) but a *pari d'Eros (wager of Eros)*. Diane has decided that after a lifetime of sex, she wants to fall in love. By acting as if she really is in love with d'Arthez, she finds that she is experiencing emotions she never suspected were possible:

> Quand elle entendit le pas de Daniel dans la salle à manger, elle éprouva une commotion, un tressaillement qui l'agita jusque dans les principes de sa vie. Ce mouvement, qu'elle n'avait jamais eu pendant l'existence la plus aventureuse d'une femme de son rang, lui apprit alors qu'elle avait joué son bonheur. (1004)
> *When she heard Daniel's footsteps in the dining room, she felt a commotion, a trembling that shook her to the very principles of her life. This movement, that she had never experienced during the most adventurous existence ever lived by a woman of her rank, made her realize that she had risked her happiness.*

A large part of her anxiety derives from the fact that she knows she is lying, and thinks that d'Arthez has believed her: "elle aimait d'Arthez, elle était condamnée à le tromper, car elle voulait rester pour lui l'actrice sublime qui avait joué la comédie à ses yeux" [*she loved d'Arthez, she was condemned to deceive him because she wanted to remain for him the sublime actress who had played the comedy before his eyes*]. Lucienne Frappier-Mazur, in the camp that views the end of this story as ambiguous, considers that condemnation as a flaw in the happiness of the couple. Personally, I do not believe the sentence will hold, because, again, I do not believe that Diane has succeeded in deceiving d'Arthez. She has not outsmarted him, but only herself.

This misunderstanding on Diane's part is expressed in one of the last lines of the text. When Daniel finally returns from Mme d'Espard's, Diane says: "Daniel, on m'a calomniée et tu m'as vengée!" [*"Daniel, they slandered me and you avenged me!"*] (1004). If Daniel's surprise at this declaration shows that he has not guessed at the extent of Diane's manipulations, that is to say that he does not realize that she sent him to Mme d'Espard's for a specific purpose, Diane's words show that she does not understand exactly what happened there, either. The key to understanding this phrase lies in decoding the nuances of two pairs of related but distinct concepts. The first of these is the difference between that all-important word "calomnie" (with its variants) and "médisance" [*malicious gossip*]. It is Mme d'Espard herself who demonstrates the distinction, when speaking of Diane's past. It is rumored among the faubourg Saint Germain that Diane has had thirty lovers. "Ce nombre était une calomnie, mais, relativement à une dizaine, peut-être était-ce, disait la marquise d'Espard, de la belle et bonne médisance" [*"This number was a calumny, but, with regard to a good ten or so, perhaps it was," said Mme d'Espard, "just a good bit of gossip"*] (952). This difference, between a calumny, which is untrue, and *médisance,* which is an unpleasant truth, is essential to understanding Diane's view of her affair with Daniel. The second conceptual pair is established by Nathan after Daniel's performance at Mme d'Espard's second dinner: "Il est aussi habile que difficile de venger une femme sans la défendre" [*It's a difficult task, requiring a great deal of skill, to avenge a woman without defending her*] (1003). To defend Diane, to deny the truth of the *médisances* of de Trailles, d'Esgrignon, and the rest, would be impossible, and that is not what Daniel does. So when Diane welcomes Daniel back to her home, she is half right; she has not been the victim of calumny, but the subject of *médisance,* and the vengeance that her lover has taken in her name is surely not what she imagines it to be. Diane is happy to be duped, however; as she tells d'Arthez: "Ô niais illustre! ne vois-tu pas que je t'aime follement?" [*O illustrious naïf! Can't you see that I love you madly?*]. Diane's exclamation contains far more truth than she can possibly be aware of. As an arrogant *mondaine,* the supremely confident libertine assumes she has won the game; as she sees it, d'Arthez the illustrious writer is a social nitwit, who has fallen into her seductive web just like so many others. Again, Pasco's generative idea— *anti-nous* (anti-reason)—clarifies the situation for us. Beneath Diane's joyous and arrogant victory cry, we hear the voice of Balzac. Daniel is illustrious, because he has chosen to be a fool. By allowing Diane to believe she has won, by avenging her without attempting to defend her, d'Arthez has won the greatest match in the never-ending game played in Balzac's Parisian *monde.* The brilliant author has written his own rules and gained the greatest prize. And there can be no doubt that this prize is pure gold, for Diane's exclamation of crazy love—again, *anti-nous,* irrational—is not just a cliché: the calculating princess has fallen in love beyond reason. Daniel's love has justified Diane's lies, and her love has justified his forgiveness.

The *nouvelle* closes with one of those shifts to the present tense that create the illusion that the world of *La Comédie humaine* is ongoing, that these characters live on beyond the scenes that are described for us in the text:

> Depuis ce jour, il n'a plus été question de la princesse de Cadignan, ni de d'Arthez. La princesse a hérité de sa mère quelque fortune, elle passe tous les étés à Genève dans une villa avec le grand écrivain. (1004-05)
>
> *From that day on, there has not been much talk of the princesse de Cadignan, nor of d'Arthez. The princess inherited a small fortune from her mother, and she spends all her summers in Geneva, in a villa with the great writer.*

The happy couple receives a double benediction from their doting creator, not only the haven in Switzerland, but a fortune as well! The old duchesse d'Uxelles has made up for any sins she may have committed toward her daughter by dying at a most opportune moment. As for the extended honeymoon in Geneva, this of course is a Balzacian cliché of happiness, a flattering message for Mme Hanska in memory of the time that she spent there, also in the company of a great writer. There is one important distinction that must be made, however. In other texts, this time in Switzerland is always an interlude for lovers. For Gaston de Neuil and Mme de Beauséant, for Albert Savarus and his Italian duchess, even for Balzac and Eveline, the time spent in Switzerland is the apogee of the relationship, and is always followed by a decline and an ultimately tragic ending. Only Diane and Daniel end their story in this Swiss idyll. The switch to the present tense places their happiness in a suspended state, underlining its eternal quality; this couple did not live happily ever after, they are living happily ever after. A final demonstration of Balzac's affection for these characters, especially for the high-flying adventuress who is never forced to land.

If the story of Diane and Daniel remains open-ended, the text of
Les Secrets de la princesse de Cadignan must end, and Balzac closes it
with yet another insolent rupture of the fourth wall of fiction: "Est-ce un
dénouement? Oui, pour les gens d'esprit; non, pour ceux qui veulent tout
savoir" [*Is this a dénouement? Yes, for people of wit and intelligence; no,
for those who want to know everything*] (1005). Rather like Diane, Balzac
has included in his story a preemptive strike against those who might be so
perfidious as to try and undermine it after the fact. Given Balzac's well-
known problems with literary critics, I wonder if this sentence is not in
some regards a deliberate swipe at that feeble race. Still, if we are going to
qualify for the enviable title of *gens d'esprit*, we must search for a deeper
meaning. Pasco's generative idea yet again serves to illuminate this last
enigma in the text. Just as there is more to Diane than can be said, there is
more to this ending than can be known; just as a genius like d'Arthez or
Chrestien can see the angel in Diane de Cadignan, so too can clever people
see that we know all we need to know about the love of our protagonists.
Those who want to know everything, those who cling too tightly to reason—like the empiricist Desplein, whose genius is limited—will remain
unsatisfied. Those who possess the wit (*esprit*) to see beyond the merely
factual, the banal world of reason, will know all they need to know from
the last paragraph of the story.

A Hidden Message, An Unwanted Receiver:
Rosalie de Watteville and *Albert Savarus*

The title character of *Albert Savarus* is an ambitious, middle-class
Frenchman who is seeking to succeed (*parvenir*) in society through legitimist politics. The ultimate object of his ambition is not political power
and social status in and of themselves, but the fact that such standing will
allow him to marry the great love of his life—a beautiful and wealthy foreign aristocrat, married to a much older man—when she becomes a
widow. The fact that Savarus becomes a writer of (meta)fiction reinforces
the impression that this text is in many respects a *roman à clef,* that Balzac
has transposed his own situation vis-à-vis Mme Hanska to create the love
story of Albert Savarus and Francesca Soderini, duchess d'Argaiolo. The

strong and absolutely intentional resemblance between Albert's story and
that of his creator tend to overshadow the other points of interest in this
story. If we can imagine a wholly naive reader of *Albert Savarus*, one who
knew nothing either of Balzac's biography or the rest of *La Comédie humaine,* the romantic story of the virtuously restrained love affair of Savarus and his Italian duchess would almost surely seem secondary to the tale
of dark obsession that occupies a parallel place in the text, and the title
character—who remains somewhat one-dimensional throughout the
text—would surely be eclipsed by the repellent but fascinating Rosalie de
Watteville.

   Rosalie is the eighteen-year-old daughter of the leading citizens of
Besançon, where *Albert Savarus* takes place. The petty nobility of Besançon, one of those social circles that Balzac ironically dubbed the *faubourgs Saint-Germain de province,* is dominated by Rosalie's mother, the
baronne de Watteville, as are Rosalie and her father. The baroness, whom
the Narrator describes as "une des reines de la sainte confrérie qui donne à
la haute société de Besançon un air sombre et des façons prudes en har-
monie avec le caractère de cette ville" [*one of the queens of the holy con-
federacy that gives the high society of Besançon its somber air and its
prudish manners, which are in perfect harmony with the character of that
city*] (1:913), is a proud and devout (in the sense of *dévote*) woman, who
maintains her only daughter in a state of pious and arrogant ignorance.
The only literature the young Rosalie is allowed to study is "les *Lettres
édifiantes,* et des ouvrages sur la science héraldique" [*edifying texts and
works on the heraldric arts*] (923). In spite of her limited education,
Rosalie is possessed of a latent but indisputable intelligence that, because
of the circumstances of her upbringing and her family, can only manifest
itself as malicious and ultimately malfeasant. As Anne-Marie Meininger
pointed out, we can see in this character a precursor of Lizbeth Fischer
(Introduction, éd. Pléiade, 1:898); but as is almost always the case, Balzac
is more complicated than that one-to-one comparison implies. Rosalie has
more than one double in *La Comédie humaine,* for as much as she resembles *la cousine Bette,* she can also be considered a darker version of a
much different Balzacian heroine, Modeste Mignon.

   Superficially perhaps, Rosalie and Modeste have nothing in common, and it would seem that Balzac perceives them as being total oppo-
sites. Gauging their creator's feelings for them by their endings, as we did

with the princesse de Cadignan, we can deduce that Balzac had a great
deal of affection for Modeste. She is one of the few successful characters
of *La Comédie humaine,* as she ends up rich and happily married. By this
measure, it must be assumed that he intensely disliked Rosalie, who ends
up a bitter and grotesquely mutilated old maid. On closer examination,
however, a case can be made that the two *jeunes filles* represent two sides
of the same coin rather than opposite ends of a spectrum. Both are daughters of provincial nobility, both lead curiously if differently sheltered lives,
and both react strongly to literature. For Modeste, literature is dangerous
because she has read too much of it; for Rosalie, literature becomes almost
lethal—arguably leading her to a fate worse than death—because she has
not read enough. Both become fascinated, through literature, by men they
have never met, and both seek to arrive at their romantic goals through
epistolary fraud. A physical comparison is also revealing; Modeste is a
beautiful petite blonde, arguably the feminine physical type that Balzac
favored most heavily (think of Diane de Cadignan, Louise de Chaulieu,
Delphine de Nucingen, etc.). Rosalie, while also blonde, is a very different
type: "A dix-huit ans, Mlle de Watteville était une jeune fille frêle, mince,
plate, blonde, blanche, et de la dernière insignifiance" [*At 18, Mlle de
Watteville was a frail, skinny, flat, blonde, pale young woman, of the very
least significance*] (923). Rosalie can be considered a washed-out version
of Modeste, or, if we add twenty years and darken the tones, we have, as
Meininger suggested, a reasonable likeness of Bette.

    In view of the different fates the two girls find, it is also worth-
while to consider their beginnings, that is, their respective familial situations. Modeste grows into maturity in an essentially fatherless household,
her father having gone off to (re)make his fortune overseas. When she has
gotten herself into a compromising situation, however, her father returns
to save the day. As I said earlier, Charles Mignon, comte de la Bastie, can
be considered a sort of Balzacian superman: a member of the old nobility,
a survivor and hero of Napoleon's Russian campaign, a victorious and yet
still honorable player in the new capitalist economy of his time, and most
importantly here, a strong *paterfamilias.* He returns in the third act of
Modeste Mignon to take control of his wayward daughter and to ensure a
happy ending, not unlike the Orgon of Marivaux's *Jeux de l'amour et du
hasard. Modeste Mignon* follows a rather meandering path, but is ultimately a triumph of bourgeois morality. Rosalie's father is present in the

Watteville household, but remains a virtual nonentity. His subordination to his wife is represented in the atypical *mise-en-abyme* already discussed in chapter 3—"l'écusson [des Watteville] fut mise an abîme sur le vieil écusson des de Rupt" [*The arms of the Watteville family was placed 'en abime' on the old arms of the de Rupt family*] (913)—and also by the fact that, once married, the couple lives in the hôtel de Rupt, his wife's family home. As for the baronne de Watteville, she can be fairly said to incarnate much of what Balzac perceived as dangerous in women, especially in a domineering wife and mother; what Amélie Camusot is to the bourgeoisie, and Zélie Minoret-Levrault is to the lower classes, Mme de Watteville is to the *petite noblesse*. She is a hypocritical blend of rigid *bigoterie* on the one hand and petty vanity on the other, as she allows the absurd provincial dandy Amédée de Soulas to pose as her *cavalier servant* even as he schemes to win Rosalie's dowry. It is the baroness's short-sighted ideas about what is proper for a young girl—ideas represented by the limited reading material already mentioned—that create the moral monster that Rosalie becomes.

Rosalie's character is a composite of her family history and her mother's sheltering control. Rosalie, we are told, has the proud tenacity of the de Rupts and the "caractère décisif et l'audace romanesque" [*the decisive nature and romantic bravery*] of "le fameux Watteville" (924). Like Claire de Beauséant's mythic descent from the great medieval house of Burgundy, this latter reference is one of the bold blends of history and fiction that Balzac used both to realize his fictional world and to give his characters an added depth. The famous Watteville in question is a historical figure, a seventeenth-century renegade monk and soldier of fortune whose picaresque adventures—"beaucoup trop historiques pour être racontées" [*far too well-known in history to be told here*], according to the Narrator (913)—were recounted by Saint-Simon (Meininger, 9:1511, nb. 2). Rosalie is both very conscious and very proud of her dual ancestry that has given her a "caractère de fer" [*iron character*] (924). Like so many of Balzac's young, provincial nobles—Victurnien d'Esgrignon, Savinien de Portenduère, Emilie de Fontaine—Rosalie has an inflated and antiquated idea of her caste in general and her family in particular. Her contempt for Amédée de Soulas is partly a product of her native but underdeveloped intelligence, but also of her familial arrogance. In Rosalie's mind, Amédée's pretensions to her hand are an insult; she despises "ce gros comte joufflu . . . diseur de fleurettes, parlant d'élégance en face de la splendeur des anciens comtes de Rupt!" [*that fat, jowly count, spouting his pretty phrases, talking about elegance before the splendor of the ancient counts of the house of Rupt*] (930). She is also very proud of the "fameux Watteville," as she also calls him (987). The fact that Rosalie inherited the adventurer's decisive spirit—which completely bypassed her passive father—suggests that she, like her ancestor who repeatedly broke his holy vows, believes herself to be destined for great things, for more than what fate seems to have in store for her.

This appetite for life, which finds nothing to satisfy it in the *bien-pensant* society governed by her mother, makes Rosalie susceptible to what might seem exotic or extraordinary, to the stuff that novels are made of. As the Narrator tells us, there is a volcano hidden beneath Rosalie's placid exterior, undetected by those around her (924). If we consider Rosalie's age, "dix-huit ans, cet âge où les jeunes personnes sont facilement frappées par toutes les singularités" [*eighteen, that age when young girls are easily struck by anything out of the ordinary*] (923), along with the peculiarities of her character, we can understand why Rosalie is particularly vulnerable to stories and literature—like Mme de Rochefide in *Sarrasine,* the *jeune personne, amie du fantastique* of *L'Auberge rouge,* Modeste Mignon, or for that matter Emma Bovary. Unlike these characters, especially the last two, who are vulnerable because of an excessive exposure to literature, Rosalie suffers from a lack of exposure. Her desire for something new, extraordinary or romantic is that much greater for having been repressed. It is precisely because her life has been so ordered and controlled that, when something novel finally presents itself to her, it becomes larger and more important than it would be under normal circumstances, filling the vacuum all by itself. Rosalie becomes not only fascinated, but obsessed.

The new thing that falls into Rosalie's consciousness like a spark on dry tinder is a stranger in town, Albert Savaron. This Parisian lawyer has drawn the attention of the Watteville circle on himself by winning a case for the archdiocese against the city of Besançon, and by the curiosity he inspires by merely having chosen to live in Besançon. Ironically, it is Soulas who creates his own rival by seeking to make himself more interesting; the jowly little count tells the Wattevilles and their guests, "en affectant de rendre son récit quasi-romanesque," [*putting on airs in order to make his story novelesque*] about "*l'étranger*" (sic, 926). The name that the stranger has given himself, Albert Savaron, is close enough to the name in the title to let the reader know that it is in fact the same person, while different enough to create an enigma that will interest us. It is Rosalie, "très forte" in the "science héraldique" that her mother compelled her to study, who resolves the mystery for us, even while deepening it for herself: "Le nom de Savaron est fort célèbre [. . .] Les Savaron de Savarus sont une des plus vieilles, des plus nobles et plus riches familles de Belgique" [*The name of Savaron is quite famous. The Savaron de Savarus are one of the oldest, most noble, and richest families of Belgium*] (926). Soulas, perhaps in an attempt at dismissive irony, declares that if this Savaron "veut prendre les armes des Savaron de Savarus, il y mettra une barre." [*wants to take the arms of the Savaron de Savarus, he would put a bar on them.*] To the horror of her mother, Rosalie is quick to respond: "La barre est à la vérité signe de bâtardise; mais le bâtard d'un comte de Savarus est noble" [*The bar is in truth a sign of bastardy, but the bastard of a count de Savarus is noble*]. Mme de Watteville is scandalized by the very mention of illegitimacy, especially coming from her naive daughter in front of her own like-minded friends. For Rosalie, however, her head filled with antiquated concepts of heraldry and nobility, the mysterious stranger's possible illegitimacy means something entirely different. Because of her peculiar and very limited education, the question of "bâtardise" relates not to illicit sex, but only to that bar on a coat of arms.

By the time the dinner conversation has moved on from the subject of the mysterious stranger, Rosalie has already become fixated on him. She subtly schemes to learn more about Savaron, surreptitiously persuading her parents to build a belvedere in their garden from which she can gaze at Albert's window, and tricking her father into subscribing to the newspaper that the lawyer has established, just because it is his. It is in this publication that Rosalie stumbles on to the first piece of literature she has ever read, *L'Ambitieux par amour*, a short story attributed only to the initials "A. S." This publication is an event not only for Rosalie, but for all of Besançon; in this somber and pious provincial city, literature is a virtually unknown phenomenon; Nodier, Hugo, and other "gloires de la ville" are more or less ignored by their fellow Bisontins (920). The Narrator ironically highlights the exotic quality that this publication has for the locals by repeatedly referring to it as "la Nouvelle." We are also told that readers of *La Revue de l'Est,* even as little accustomed as they are to literature, find "cette première Nouvelle éclose dans la Comté" somewhat lacking: "selon les critiques du salon Chavoncourt, Albert aurait imité quelques-uns des écrivains modernes qui, faute d'invention" [*according to critics of the Chavoncourt salon, Albert had imitated some of those modern writers who, wanting of originality*] use their own lives as material for their prose (938). The gentle irony of these passages is directed not only at the Bisontins, but also for a select group of readers—Mme Hanska of course chief among them—who would have recognized Balzac's self-reference as one of those modern writers, we can also say that this irony is directed at the *nouvelle* and its author(s).

For Rosalie, there is no question of irony as she approaches the text. Indeed, she brings to it all the romantic reverence she feels for her idol, Albert. The Narrator warns us not to judge "l'effet que cette œuvre dut produire sur elle d'après des données ordinaires" [*the effect of this work was bound to produce on her according to ordinary standards*]; for Rosalie, *L'Ambitieux par amour:*

> ne pouvait point ne pas être un chef-d'œuvre pour une jeune personne livrant sa vierge intelligence, son cœur pur à un premier ouvrage de ce genre [. . .] Rosalie s'était fait, par intuition, une idée qui rehaussait singulièrement la valeur de cette Nouvelle. Elle espérait y trouver les sentiments et peut-être quelque chose de la vie d'Albert. Dès les premières pages, cette opinion prit chez elle une si grande consistance, qu'après avoir achevé ce fragment, elle eut la certitude de ne pas se tromper. (918)
>
> *could not fail to be a masterpiece for a young person giving up her virgin intelligence, her pure heart to a first work of this kind. Rosalie had, by intuition, created for herself an idea that singularly elevated the value of this Story. She hoped to find in it Albert's sentiments and perhaps something of his own life. From the first pages, this opinion became so strong within her that, after having read this fragment, she was certain that she was not mistaken.*

Following the strong language of this passage, we can say that the act of reading represents for Rosalie an emotional and intellectual loss of virginity. An intimacy is established that is as complete as it is completely one-sided. Savarus has indeed put his own life and his own sentiments into his *nouvelle,* but with the belief that this hidden message would be undetectable, except for one reader. Rosalie is able to identify Rodolphe as Albert precisely because of her very narrow education, just as the value and power of the text is enhanced precisely because it is the only fiction that Rosalie has ever read. By painting himself in purely romantic terms, in a purely romantic situation, Albert has unwittingly made himself the hero of the novel that Rosalie is composing in her mind and that she is attempting to make come true in her life. The image that Savarus projects for himself in the fiction he has based on his own life fits perfectly into what Rosalie longs for him to be.

As I mentioned earlier, this "Nouvelle" comes quite close to being the sort of narrated exposition that I said must be distinguished from embedded narratives. It comes at a point when experienced readers of Balzac are expecting *a retour en arrière,* and serves much the same purpose as these flashbacks do in other texts, filling in gaps in a character's history and clearing up enigmas presented in the beginning of a narrative. That said, I consider this an embedded narrative because the information we receive from it is fictionalized by Savarus. Reading between the lines with Rosalie, we know full well that Rodolphe is just a mask for Albert; we suspect that there is an aristocratic *Italienne* who loves him, etc., but the masks are there nonetheless. Also, the way that the information in the "Nouvelle" is communicated overshadows the importance of the information itself; that is, it is more important that Rosalie's obsession with Savarus deepens and turns to jealousy than that the reader learns that Savarus is sensitive and brilliant or that Francesca is beautiful, noble, etc. Finally, it is essential, for reasons of plot and character, that this narration is presented as a written, published (and thus public) story rather than as a story told orally. If Rosalie learned about Savarus's past in a conventional storytelling situation—from Amédée de Soulas, in her mother's salon—her interest in Savarus would become public knowledge; someone, at the very least the narrator who told her the story, would know what she knew, and that she knew it. Moreover, given the circumstances of Rosalie's life, it is doubtful that she would have heard the story alone, her mother would have been in the room with her, and would be alerted to Rosalie's unseemly interest in the stranger. The fact that the story of Albert and Francesca is published as fiction allows Rosalie to make her discovery in private, with-

out her mother knowing about her curiosity. The fact that the story is fictionalized allows Albert's history to remain a secret to everyone but
Rosalie—no one else has the special interest in the stranger that makes
Rosalie such a clairvoyant reader. Finally, the publication of the story
means that she can discover the truth about Albert without his being aware
of her interest in him. Most importantly, we must remember that literature
is a novelty to Rosalie, and, as the Narrator tells us, this new thing that is
literature is especially potent for the sheltered young girl. The almost
magical power of fiction increases the impact of Rodolphe's story and fuels Rosalie's obsession with Albert to new heights.

There is no question, either for Rosalie or for the actual reader
looking over her shoulder as she reads *L'Ambitieux par amour,* that Savarus is painting a self-portrait. His writing confirms all of Rosalie's hopeful
speculations about Albert Savaron's true identity. Rodolphe is described
as the "fils naturel d'un grand seigneur qui fut surpris par une mort
prématurée sans avoir pu faire de dispositions pour assurer des moyens
d'existence à une femme tendrement aimée et à Rodolphe" [*the illegitimate son of a great lord who was surprised by an early death without
having been able to make arrangements for the support of a tenderly loved
woman and Rodolphe*] (949). Savarus's intent may be to remind his intended narratee of his pedigree and of the reasons for his poverty, but his
unintended, hidden narratee, the only other person who can read between
the lines of the text and see the author behind the protagonists, sees in this
passage the affirmation of her own suspicions, that M. Savaron is actually
M. Savaron de Savarus, albeit with a bar across his arms. A bit further in
the same paragraph, the connection is made even more explicitly: "Né
d'une des plus charmantes Parisiennes et d'un homme remarquable de
l'aristocratie brabançonne" [*born of one the most charming of Parisiennes
and of a remarkable man from the Brabant aristocracy*]. The proud descendant of the ancient comtes de Rupt and the famous Watteville can thus
rest assured that her passion is justified.

It is not only Rodolphe's romantic lineage that encourages
Rosalie's attraction. It must be acknowledged that Albert (or for that matter, Balzac) is not shy about painting his literary self-portrait in the most
flattering shades. Our hero is blessed with "une excessive sensibilité" and
"la plus grande ardeur en toute chose" (940). His heart "à la fois si tendre
et si sensible, si violent et si bon" [*at once so tendre and so sensitive, so*

violent and so good] (941), and the passion he develops for the mysterious Miss Lovelace shows him to be a man far superior to the fat little "diseur de fleurettes" that Rosalie's mother wants her to marry. Love is not the only emotion that Rosalie develops while reading, however: "En achevant ce récit qu'elle dévora, Mlle de Watteville avait les joues en feu, la fièvre dans les veines; elle pleurait, mais de rage [. . .] elle était jalouse de Francesca Colonne" [*When she finished this story, that she had devoured, Mlle de Watteville had fire in her cheeks and fever in her veins; she was weeping, but with rage. . . she was jealous of Francesca Colonna*] (967). Although Rosalie is torn between her love for Albert and her conscience, her obsession eventually leads her to commit ever greater offenses as she becomes determined to win Albert for herself. She begins reading Albert's correspondence, which confirms for her that Savaron is indeed a Savarus—"Ah, j'en étais sûre, il est noble!" [*Ah! I was sure of it, he is noble!*] cries the triumphant heraldist (972)—and that he loves an Italian duchess. Rosalie eventually pushes her father into a lawsuit that she thinks will draw her and Albert together, or at least give her a chance to meet him face to face. Savarus refuses to help the baron, fearing that an overt alliance with the aristocratic Watteville faction will destroy his political ambitions in an electorate dominated by the bourgeoisie.

Rosalie, not surprisingly, takes the rejection personally. It is interesting to note that our heraldist couches her rage in expressions of wounded familial pride:

> Ah! j'aurai jeté mon père dans un procès! ah! j'aurai tant fait pour l'introduire ici! [. . .] ah! j'aurai commis des péchés mortels, et tu ne viendrais pas dans le salon de l'hôtel de Rupt, et je n'entendrais pas ta voix si riche? Tu mets des conditions à ton concours quand les Watteville et les Rupt le demandent!
>
> *Ah! I was ready to push my father into a lawsuit! Ah! I would have done anything to have him introduced into my house! I would have committed mortal sins, and you will not come to the salon of the hotel de Rupt, and I won't hear your voice so rich? You place conditions on your assistance when the Wattevilles and the Rupts ask for it!*

Rosalie vows victory and revenge:

maintenant je serais ta femme! [. . .] Oui, oui, regarde *ses* portraits, examine *ses* salons, *sa* chambre, les quatre faces de *sa* villa, les points de
vue de *ses* jardins. Tu attends *sa* statue! je *la* rendrai de marbre elle-
même pour toi! (992)
Now I will be your wife! Yes, yes, look at her *portraits, remember* her
salons, her *bedroom, the four sides of* her *villa, the views of* her *gar-
dens. You're waiting for* her *statue! I'll turn* her *into marble for you!*

Perhaps the most interesting thing about this passage is the way Rosalie
ironically uses the emphasis on pronouns that Savarus, in his correspondence uses to express reverence for Francesca, who is *elle* in Albert's letter to his friend Hannequin. The importance of this deceptively small
detail is that in a curious way it allies Rosalie with the brilliant and ruthless manipulator de Marsay, who uses this same technique to mock his
own youthful ardor for the duchess "Charlotte" in *Autre étude de femme.*
Savarus, who uses the technique in apparent romantic sincerity, is thus
implicitly compared to Lucien de Rubempré, whose talent and ambition
are not enough to compensate for his lack of resolve, and who writes very
sincere, and very mediocre, sonnets entitled *Elle.*

After manipulating virtually the entire city of Besançon, Rosalie
succeeds in sabotaging Savarus's electoral ambitions. Equally remarkable,
and far more vicious, is her success in turning Francesca into marble for
Albert. By blackmailing and bribing servants, Rosalie manages to place
herself in between Albert and Francesca—whose only contact is epistolary—by reading their correspondence. This is especially significant if we
consider the literary trope of lovers for whom letters take the place of
physical contact, Abélard and Héloïse being the archetype. By intercepting
the letters the two lovers intend only for each other, Rosalie goes beyond
mere voyeurism or stalking, and becomes the third party in a metaphorical
ménage à trois, of which the other two members are unaware. Eventually,
as she later confesses to the abbé de Grancey, she suppresses the letters,
effectively putting an end to Albert and Francesca's affair, again without
their knowing anything about it. Then, not content to let Francesca's love
wither due to benign neglect, she decides to actively kill it. Copying Albert's handwriting, she forges a letter in which Albert announces his engagement to Rosalie. Albert learns that he has been rejected at the same
time that he learns that Francesca's husband has finally died. In despair, he

runs after Francesca, who in turn flees from him, finally marrying the duc de Rhétoré. In despair, Savarus joins the cloistered monks of the Grande Chartreuse—*Aux cœurs blessés, ombre et silence.*

Rosalie continues her malicious ways even after Albert has cloistered himself. Her widowed mother having married Soulas—in an interesting twist on the frequent Balzacian motif involving mothers, daughters and lovers—Rosalie follows them to Paris for the sole purpose of inflicting a severe emotional wound on Francesca. Balzac, in his role as the vengeful god of his fictional world, in turn inflicts a terrible punishment on Rosalie: She loses an eye, an arm, and a leg in an explosion. She spends the rest of her life cloistered in her mountain retreat—her own *chartreuse*—at Les Rixey, the Watteville country property, giving an ironic symmetry to Albert and Rosalie's fates, another ironic echo of Abélard and Héloïse. What is most fascinating about this text, to my mind, is that Savarus's life is destroyed by someone he never meets. Mlle de Watteville is never more for him than a name, a vague impression of the girl he glimpses standing on the belvedere in her parents' garden. Rosalie's love and jealous revenge are inspired by an image that she constructs in her own mind, out of her own desires, and the impressions gleaned from the only work of fiction she will ever read in her life.

If the most interesting effects of *L'Ambitieux par amour* is, as I believe, the effect it has on Rosalie, there are other elements that make this embedded narrative worth a closer look. There are certain aspects of this *nouvelle* that are undetectable to Rosalie, and very probably to her fellow Bisontins, that are meant only for Francesca d'Argaiolo, but which the reader can appreciate as well. First of all is the pseudonym Albert gives to the fictional Francesca, Miss Lovelace. This name is used frequently in *La Comédie humaine,* almost always a reference to the rake of Richardson's *Clarissa Harlowe.* In this case, Balzac puts some distance between his usual usage of the name and this instance. Albert writes that Lovelace is the name of Richardson's well-known rake, but that it is also an old and respected English name. The mysterious lady's pedigree is thus established, but most important is the pronunciation guide provided in *L'Ambitieux par amour;* Lovelace, we are told, is pronounced *Loveless* (sic, 944). This pronunciation and spelling and all that it implies would be meaningless to the reader of this French text who was not acquainted with at least basic English. We can assume of course, that Francesca d'Argaiolo, like her [meta]fictional homologue, speaks English and receives the implied message, that she was without love before meeting Savarus. Extratextually, this same message could only be decoded by readers with at least this same basic familiarity with English, the same implied by the famous *"All is true!"* of *Le Père Goriot*. Of course, the most significant extratextual receiver of this message was Mme Hanska, a point that I mention only because it addresses, to some degree, Wayne Conner's assertion that the many fictional names of Eveline's textual alter ego are unrelated to her own (*"Albert Savarus* and 'L'Ambitieux par amour,' " 256).

A different case is presented by the recurring characters in the meta-*nouvelle*. The easy and superficial explanation for their presence is of course the linking of *Albert Savarus* to the rest of *La Comédie humaine,* but this purpose is achieved by the presence, however fleeting, of the duc de Rhétoré and Léopold Hannequin in the frame. In *L'Ambitieux par amour,* we find such recurring characters as the great Italian opera singers La Tinti and Genovese, the portraitist Schinner, and most significantly, Mme de Beauséant and Gaston de Neuil. This last connection is a curious one, for while it is perfectly logical—at least in Balzac's world—that Rodolphe and Francesca Colonna should find themselves in a villa near Claire de Beauséant's on Lake Geneva, Francesca d'Argaiolo's villa, where she and Albert declare their love for one another, is on Lake Constance, as Anthony Pugh pointed out (247). Wayne Conner, building on an argument made by André Wurmser, makes a strong case that what might seem like one of the minor oversights that are so common in *La Comédie humaine* is actually a deliberate and important detail. Conner proposes that Albert, who resembles Balzac in so many ways, also resembles him as a writer in that he uses "real" people as points of reference and comparison in his fiction; the fictional character Savarus uses Mme de Beauséant and Gaston in his metafictional text just as Balzac uses Talleyrand or Napoleon in his fiction, to blur the lines between the textual world and the real one. This strategy is interesting in and of itself, as Balzac's own characters become points of reference within his fictional world, but it also raises other questions.

Rodolphe is jealous of Gaston's happiness, for Francesca refuses to cuckold her husband even though she has already declared her love to the

Frenchman. Rodolphe expresses his envy as admiration, but his princess is considerably less impressed:

> « Ils sont heureux! dit Rodolphe avec un âpre accent, Claire de Beauséant, la dernière de la seule maison qui ait pu rivaliser avec la maison de France. . .
>
> —Oh!. . . elle vient d'une branche bâtarde, et encore par les femmes. . .
>
> —Enfin, elle est vicomtesse de Beauséant, et n'a pas. . .
>
> —Hésité!. . .n'est-ce pas? à s'enterrer avec M. Gaston de Neuil, dit la fille des Colonna. Elle n'est que française et je suis italienne, mon cher monsieur. » (965)
>
> *"They are happy!" said Rodolphe with a bitter accent, "Claire de Beauséant, the last descendant of the only house which could ever rival the royal house of France. . ."*
>
> *"Oh! She comes from a bastard branch, and by the women besides. . ."*
>
> *"In any case, she is the vicomtesse de Beauséant, and she didn't . . ."*
>
> *"Hesitate . . . isn't that it! To bury herself with M. Gaston de Neuil," said the daughter of the Colonna. "She is only a Frenchwoman, and I am Italian, my dear sir."*

The caustic reference to the illegitimacy of Claire's ancestry is intriguing, given Rodolphe's (and Albert's) own parentage. In the larger context, this passage reminds us how one story can be viewed from vastly different perspectives within *La Comédie humaine* itself. Mme de Beauséant is usually portrayed as a wholly sympathetic character, the symbol of romantic and tragic love, betrayed first by d'Ajuda-Pinto, then by Neuil; Savarus denigrates Claire de Beauséant—"la dernière fille de la quasi royale maison de Bourgogne" [the last daughter of the quasi-royal house of Burgundy] is Balzac's exaltedly romantic description of her in *Le Père Goriot* (263-64)—with the intent, of course, of flattering his own lover—by suggesting that she is less moral than Francesca.

Wayne Conner goes a step further in exploring the appearance of the protagonists of *La Femme abandonnée* in *Albert Savarus;* he points out a "poetic role" that these characters play in *Albert Savarus* which

demonstrates—yet again—that the interconnections between the different
texts of *La Comédie humaine* are both far more intricate and far more
subtle than is generally acknowledged. When Francesca is tricked into believing that Albert has betrayed her, the proud Florentine dismisses him
with the brief message: "Vous êtes libre, adieu" [*You are free, adieu*]
(1012). Most critics, fixated on the parallels between Albert/Francesca and
Balzac/Mme Hanska, point out that this was the phrase Eve used to dismiss Balzac when she heard some gossip about his philandering. Conner
points out the far more interesting fact that this is virtually the exact
phrase that Mme de Beauséant uses to "liberate" Gaston when he decides
to marry another woman ("*Albert Savarus,*" 258). Speaking very precisely,
the situation in *La femme abandonnée* is closer to the one in Albert Savarus than in real life. Since *La Femme abandonnée* dates from 1832, and
Mme Hanska's letter dates from 1842, immediately preceding the composition of Albert Savarus, perhaps what we have is in fact a case of art imi-
tating life that has imitated art. In any case, as Conner has illustrated, the
parallel with *La Femme abandonnée* gives this "brief Nueil-Beauséant
scene [. . .] a *predictive* value, suffusing with irony the Rodolphe-
Francesca interlude, and furnishing a refreshing example of the enrich-
ment made possible by the reappearing character technique" (258). Furthermore, this association also changes the sense of the words with which
Savarus closes his nouvelle: "Amoureux! Priez pour lui!" [*Lovers, pray
for him!*], becomes, in Conner's phrase, "less an exhortation than an epi-
taph" (259).

It is difficult, I admit, for a reader with even the most cursory
knowledge of the story of Balzac and Mme Hanska, to overlook the similarities between their love story and that of *Albert Savarus*. Once we have
looked beyond the autobiographical shadings of this text, however, we can
see how it is interesting in its own right, and not merely as a coded *roman
à clef*. Reading *Albert Savarus* as a part of *La Comédie humaine* is a
highly profitable enterprise, as is reading *L'Ambitieux par amour* as a part
of the fragment and as part of the whole. The embedded narrative serves
not only to ignite Rosalie's passionate jealousy, which becomes the engine
for the rest of the story, it also establishes the delicate intertextual connections that Conner demonstrated so well. Just as *L'Ambitieux par amour* is
a different text for Rosalie de Watteville than for her fellow Bisontins, so

too is it a different text for the alert reader, or rereader, of *La Comédie humaine,* than for Rosalie, or for Albert himself.

All of the embedded narratives discussed in this chapter have in common the fact that they advance the plot or—in the case of *Le Médecin de campagne*—the central theme of the larger work that they appear in, without being the most important element of that work. This is the key difference between the embedded narratives and those that I have designated as framed narratives. The dynamics between the object stories and the surrounding texts are similar in both cases; the two parts of the text are linked, whether by character, or subject matter, or some other element, but there is a difference of degree. Where framed narratives are complemented and supported by their frames, embedded narratives complement the texts they are inserted in.

It is also interesting to note that in all four of the cases discussed in this chapter, the embedded narratives are used with a subtlety that borders on deceptiveness on Balzac's part. In *La Muse du département*, the reader, like the characters, becomes so caught up in the storytelling, especially Lousteau's reconstruction of *Olympe,* that it is easy to miss the shrewdness revealed in La Baudraye's final, cryptic comment, which has as much predictive value as the stories of adultery. In *Le Médecin de campagne,* not only does the *veillée dans la grange* enliven the text, Balzac is in fact so successful in creating a lively, imaginative *récit,* that the reader is apt to overlook how well this seemingly most disparate fragment fits in with the rest of the novel. *In Les Secrets de la princesse de Cadignan,* the princess's performance is so skillful, and we are so well predisposed by the text to believe in her infallibility, that it is easy for us to miss, in the last few paragraphs, the revelation that all of Diane's machinations have been in vain; she finds love because of her flaws, not in spite of them. Finally, in *Albert Savarus*, it is not only the autobiographical elements of the text, but also the intricacy of the connection that cause us to overlook the fine thread that Balzac has subtly woven from the larger *Comédie humaine,* through the main narrative, and into the embedded narrative, thus drawing all three together.

The understated complexities of the three texts discussed in this chapter lead us to the final question that I will discuss in the conclusions; namely, whom can we trust? I will not be proposing any definitive answers to this question, since I find enough of a challenge merely in exposing, beneath the veneer of completeness (*complétude*) that covers the whole of the *Comédie humaine,* those faults and cracks that allow us to understand the instability of this seemingly fixed universe, and that permit us to see the movement of the *mobile romanesque.*

Conclusions

I
A Troubling Question: Whom Can We Trust?

THE FRAME/STORY CONFIGURATIONS IN BALZAC'S OEUVRE serve the double purpose of enclosing the object stories, and of opening the text to the reader. The distance between the authorial Narrator and the diegetic narrators and narratees offers us a point of entry into *La Comédie humaine*. From these points of entry, we move on to interpret the text, to make our own subjective judgments according to our knowledge of and assumptions about Balzac's fictional world. Studying these structures is just one way of demonstrating the intricacy of the whole text, of appreciating the complex interconnections of the fragments to the whole; it is just one way to illustrate the error of the widespread perception that Balzac is *le romancier qui dit tout*. There remains, however, one final question to be asked, a question that puts into doubt many of the subjective assertions made in this study: How reliable are the narrators of *La Comédie humaine*?

With a few exceptions, all of the analyses I have made are predicated on the assumption that the storytellers are telling the truth. And yet that same distance between the Narrator and the characters who tell and listen to the stories, the very element that allows us to enter into the text and to analyze it, undermines the certainty of those same analyses. Certain narrators have a credibility that comes from the larger text and from the Narrator, the ultimate authority within the text, but others are credible only because we allow them to be. For example, Derville's account of Gobseck's methods and power is credible to us because we see the old miser operating in other texts such as *Les Employés,* and because we see Mme de Restaud, in *Le Père Goriot,* in the same perilous financial position, caused by her affair with Maxime de Trailles, as in *Gobseck.* Bianchon, however, has only the credibility of his social and professional position—his *robe noire*—to make us believe the story of *La Grande Bretèche.* As readers of the whole, we know that Anastasie ruins herself for de Trailles, but the story of Mme de Merret might well be metafiction, invented by Bianchon to cause a shiver in the ladies around Mlle des Touches's table. This possibility reopens the question of exactly what Balzac meant in the doubly ambiguous closing sentence of *Autre étude de femme:* "quelques-unes d'entre elles avaient eu quasi-froid en entendant le dernier mot." Perhaps some of the women around the table thought Bianchon was telling the truth, while others believed that he was spinning a tale. In the latter case, their shiver might well be a willful response, their reward, so to speak, for having entered into a fictional contract with the narrator, just as we do whenever we read a work of fiction. The reaction of these women, their sensation of "quasi-froid," would depend on the degree to which they suspended their disbelief.

There is no question about Diane de Cadignan's credibility as a narrator—she has none. The Narrator very deliberately gives us the truth before Diane presents her *roman.* We are thus free to appreciate and evaluate her recitation for what it is: a carefully calculated lie, rich with double meanings for the reader, who is granted the favor of watching Diane's performance from the same Olympian viewpoint as the Narrator. Another narrator who we can say is less than wholly credible is de Marsay in *Autre étude de femme.* The pretense that the duchesse Charlotte is his first love is, like the discrepancy regarding his age, either a mistake on Balzac's part, or a deliberate and calculated lie. The textual clues in *Autre étude,* and the fact that de Marsay is such a duplicitous and devious character throughout *La Comédie humaine,* are strong evidence that what we have is a case of diegetic dishonesty rather than authorial oversight. The prime minister's discretion in not mentioning Paquita Valdès may be in part a courtesy to his father and other members of his singular family around the table, as Nicole Mozet suggested; even if that is true, however, there is no question that his silence is self-serving. De Marsay cannot tell the story of *La Fille aux yeux d'or,* for to do so is to reveal the secrets of the *Treize,* and thus the hidden, dark side of his own dual nature. The story of the duchess Charlotte is far more in keeping with the tone of the company present, while still casting its hero/narrator in a highly flattering light.

The reliability of several other character-narrators can be called into question for various reasons. The force of *Facino Cane* depends to a large extent on the uncertainty of both the narrating *je* and the reader as to whether the old man is mad or fantastic. In his study of *Sarrasine*, Ross Chambers makes a strong case that the narrator is lying, that this *je* makes up the story of obsession and castration in order to punish Mme de Rochefide for her flirtatiousness at the Lantys' ball. Chambers sees a "strong hint in the text that the narrator's discourse is not simply fictive in its rhetorical technique but that it is wholly fictional, in the sense that it produces not 'true' information but a fabulation" ("Seduction Denied," 85). Jealous not only of Mme de Rochefide's dancing with other men, but also of her infatuation with the portrait of Endymion, the narrator creates a "perverse" version of the kind of tale that he knows Mme de Rochefide likes, about "ces passions énergiques enfantées dans nos cœurs par les ravissantes femmes du Midi" [*those energetic passions inspired in our hearts by the ravishing women of the South*]. Of course, the ravishing woman from the South in this story is a monstrosity. This is also a tale in which a person is strongly attracted to a beautiful work of art—the castrato Zambinella— and is cruelly disappointed by the reality. Chambers argues that this is meant as a subtle reproach to the narratee for her impulsiveness, and a warning about the dangers of trusting appearances, especially the appearances of art. This second, more subtle connection seems lost on Mme de Rochefide who, for all her pensiveness, does not seem to go far beyond her extreme distaste for the story of castration. This teasing thrust is aimed at the readers; it is part sly and complicitous wink and partly a wry warning.

In a somewhat similar vein, Dorothy Kelly has maintained that *L'Auberge rouge* is a deceptive text, that the only reason to believe in Taillefer's guilt is the subjective interpretation that the narrating *je* gives to the banker's reactions to M. Herrmann's story ("Balzac's *L'Auberge rouge*"). Kelly thoroughly examines the text and points out that in addition to the narrator's suspicions, there are several other elements in the text that lead the reader to conclude that the banker is guilty; his debilitating headaches occur in the autumn, the same time as the murder in

Germany; his pain is compared to a sawing on his head, just as the murder victim was killed, etc. (39). But the essential point of Kelly's analysis is that we readers never know for certain—beyond a reasonable doubt, as it were—that Taillefer is guilty of the murder, or for that matter that Prosper Magnan is innocent. "The text points to Taillefer's guilt, without ever stating it definitively" (40). The entire text, and all of our assumptions about guilt and innocence, are built around "an empty signifier, around the lack of a confirmed murderer" (39). This same empty signifier forms the basis for all of the narrator's angst-filled reflections on the morality of accepting Victorine and her fortune. Thus the text, when read in this light, is not only ambiguous but highly ironic, as the narrator's scruples are based in large part on his somewhat arrogant and perhaps misguided faith in his own powers of perception. The reader, following the narrator as our familiarity with the norms of fiction compels us to do, is thus led down the same, possibly mistaken, path.

While both of these interpretations are interesting and strongly argued, in the end I do not find either of them wholly convincing. To begin with *L'Auberge rouge,* Kelly's analysis stands up well with regard to the text as a fragment, even makes it considerably more interesting, but it does not hold when *L'Auberge rouge* is taken as a part of the whole. Taillefer's guilt is confirmed for us by Vautrin in *Le Père Goriot;* the larger text confirms the suspicions of the narrating *je,* and thus those of the reader who believes him. With regard to *Sarrasine,* my objection is more subjective, based on my personal reaction to the text. One element that supports Chambers's arguments is the weakness of the narrator's reaction to Mme de Rochefide's breaking of their implied contract: "Ah! Vous savez punir!" [*Ah! You know how to punish*!]. A stronger reaction would imply greater, more sincere surprise. As it stands, one could argue, following Chambers, that Mme de Rochefide's reaction was exactly the one the narrator sought to provoke in the *femme-enfant* whom he wanted to punish for inconstancy. However in the end, I am dissuaded from this argument by the lack of any indication from the narrator as diegetic narrator—that is, speaking directly to the reader—that his story is false, that his motivation for narrating is to take revenge on Béatrix. Also, the frame-text complements the object story too well, I think, for us to believe that Balzac's intention was to trick the reader. The strength of the double strand of the romantic and the fantastic running from frame to object story suggests to me that Balzac wanted to give the object story greater credibility, not less. These elements are reported to us by the narrator, but do not in any way seem to be invented by him; that is, the allusions to romantic and fantastic images such as pirates and vampires, the rumors that are said to circulate through Paris about the Lantys, the old man, and the origin of their fortune, the seemingly supernatural physical sensation of cold that Mme de Rochefide experiences near the old man. All of these elements act upon the reader's imagination, creating in our minds an atmosphere that lends itself to suspending disbelief, preparing us to believe that what we are about to read is 'true' rather than a fabulation. Finally, for the reader of *La Comédie humaine*, La Zambinella is a manifestation of an image that haunts Balzac's text and world in many different forms, a grotesquely realistic incarnation of the androgyne that we see in so many forms, from the philosopically fantastic (Séraphita) to the romantically ordinary (*filles manquées* such as Lucien de Rubempré and beautiful masculine characters like Marguerite Claës and Laurence de Cing-Cygne). This familiar if sometimes bizarre image tends to suggest that the story of the sculptor and the castrato could have happened in Balzac's created world.

The fact that I disagree with these interpretations, even though they result from attitudes about and approaches to the text that are similar to my own, illustrates how important that subjective Balzacian baggage is to the act of reading *La Comédie humaine*, how important the reader is as a producer rather than a mere consumer of text. The fact that different parts of Balzac's work give rise to varied and valid interpretations merely confirms that this supposedly complete text is not "plein" or "lisible," to return to Barthes's terminology. Dällenbach's "Leerstellen" are to be found throughout *La Comédie humaine*, perceived in different places and filled in differently by individual readers. As I have maintained from the beginning, this supposedly monolithic text is unstable and wide open to the reader, if we know how to find the points of entry.

Several of the character narrators are posed in front of spaces—textual faults—that are not so immediately apparent as the ones behind Diane de Cadignan or Facino Cane. In these two cases, as with Chambers's interpretation of *Sarrasine*, it is a black and white question of truth or falsehood; more often, it is a more subtle question of shading and perception. *Honorine* offers a good starting point. By his own admission, Maurice de l'Hostal is not an objective narrator; he is in love with his patron's estranged wife, the subject of his story. His emotional connection to Honorine necessarily colors his telling of her story; her beauty, grace, intelligence, etc., may be overly emphasized if not actually exaggerated. The way her virtues are brought to the fore tends to overshadow her own share of culpability in the ruin of her marriage, which is further mitigated by her exquisite repentance. We cannot ascribe this exculpation of an adulterous woman to Balzac alone, to his sympathy for one of his *mal mariées*. That Balzac's views on the subject of marriage and adultery were quite complicated is evident even if we consider only the text of *La Comédie humaine,* without recourse to Balzac's biography or his non-fiction writings. I have already mentioned Honorine's resemblance to Béatrix de Rochefide, an adulteress who is viewed with far less sympathy than Honorine, even though she too is the victim of an unhappy marriage. We should also remember Mme de Sérisy and Caroline de Bellefeuille, the unfaithful women who bring misery to the comte Octave's *mal-mariés* brethren, Sérisy and Grandville, the latter also being an adulterer. The sympathy the reader feels for Honorine is of course one facet of Balzac's own complicated views, but it is most directly the result of Maurice de L'Hostal's narration.

Honorine also offers an excellent opportunity to examine the effects of a biased narratee. As I discussed in the second chapter, it is in part Camille Maupin's authority that draws the reader to share her conclusion that Octave is somehow responsible for his wife's suffering and death, a conclusion that both strengthens and is strengthened by the sympathy generated by Maurice's telling of the story. If we were to read the object story only, we would probably not arrive at this conclusion on our own; rather we would see this tragedy as the result of a cruel and arbitrary fate, for which no individual can bear responsibility. Again, I believe that it is Félicité's identification with and sympathy for Honorine that leads her to this harsh judgment; neither Balzac nor the reader is necessarily compelled to share it. Camille is just one of the narratees whose reaction should inspire some caution on the part of the reader. Daniel d'Arthez is already in love with Diane when she attempts to rewrite her past in his mind. If the brilliant writer is temporarily blinded by the force of her performance, it is his prejudices in favor of the princess that cause him to ignore the clarity of his retrospective perceptions. For the narratees of *La Comédie humaine,* listening is not a passive activity, and they are rarely neutral receivers of information.

Just as Camille Maupin is predisposed to be sympathetic to the story of Honorine, Béatrix de Rochefide seems, as I said earlier, to be vulnerable to stories in general. For various reasons of temperament and environment, she is especially susceptible to the stories she hears in *Sarrasine* and in *Un Prince de la bohème*. Béatrix's spiritual cousin, the provincial *bas-bleu* Dinah de La Baudraye, also seems to be vulnerable to stories, seduced as she is by Lousteau's narrative performance in *La Muse du département*, and then seeing herself reflected in Claudine when she hears Nathan tell his story to Béatrix. In both of these opposing cases, it is Dinah's feelings about Lousteau that determine her reaction to the stories she hears. In the earlier scene, it is because of her fascination with this exotic creature—a Parisian writer—that she falls into his recreation of *Olympe*. In *Un Prince de la bohème,* it is her growing disenchantment with the reality she has come to see behind the image that causes her to see herself reflected in the figure of an aging, humiliated ex-prostitute who abandons all dignity for an unworthy lover. Finally, we should remember the multiple narratees in *Autre étude de femme,* "où chacun entend ce qui se dit." The intellectual and social sophistication of these characters gives them a special capacity for listening; they are connoisseurs, especially able to appreciate conversation and storytelling. The reader, flattered to be included in the select company gathered around the table, aspires to the same capacity for *entendement* as Félicité's guests and is thus inclined to share in the general approbation that greets each recitation, and finally in the stunned and respectful silence that follows *La Grande Bretèche*.

On the other side of the spectrum are those narratees who are, in different ways and for different reasons, ill-suited to act as narratees. Textual narratees are often less than perfect receivers of the stories directed to them. The vicomtesse de Grandlieu offers one example of such a poorly equipped receiver in *Gobseck,* as does, in a different way, her brother, who falls asleep halfway through Derville's story. In *La Peau de chagrin,* Raphaël's friend Émile falls asleep (passes out, really) in the middle of the story of Foedora. As with the Matifats falling asleep in the middle of Bixiou's *roman à tiroirs* in *La Maison Nucingen,* these dozing narratees are intended partly for comic effect, but suggest something more profound as well. The comte de Born's practical absence from the storytelling situation emphasizes the authority of his sister, who is the real object of Derville's anecdotal pleading on behalf of Ernest de Restaud. In the case of Emile, his unconsciousness is perfectly logical, given that Valentin chooses the aftermath of the drunken orgy as his moment for storytelling, but it has another purpose as well. The narration thus becomes a soliloquy, emphasizing Raphaël's solitude in the midst of the Parisian crowd, as he tells his story to a roomful of sleeping revelers and courtesans. A certain intimacy is thus established between Raphaël and the reader, the lone recipient of his story, who thus understands him as no one else can.

There are several other characters whose relationship to the story told—whether that be the motivation of a narrator or the reaction of a narratee—can be challenged and explored. One good example is the anonymous couple in the frame of *Une Passion dans le désert*. If we follow the comparison of this text to *Sarrasine,* especially the implied exchange of story for sex, we can ask ourselves why the narrator would invent such a bizarre story—presuming he never met the old soldier who supposedly related it to him—if his intention is to seduce his narratee. If we accept the notion that these two have already become lovers before the scene at the menagerie that opens the text, that their relationship is more advanced than that of the Mme de Rochefide and her suitor, then that stronger bond would permit the narrator to be more daring, more provocative in his choice of material. His intention is not to inform her in order to earn compensation, but to tease and amuse her. The narratee, more sophisticated than Mme de Rochefide, more secure in herself with regard to her lover, feels free to respond in kind, sardonically calling the tale a "plaidoyer en faveur des bêtes." Their shared joke will hopefully lead to other shared sensations.

Juliette Frølich has proposed a complex and fascinating reading of this ambiguous ending in her article "'Le phénomène oral': L'impact du conte dans le récit bref de Balzac." Frølich suggests that the narratee has perceived the tale to be an invention, part of a romantic game her lover is playing. The emphases that Frølich adds to the passage concerned help clarify her reading of the narratee's reaction: "Eh! Bien, me dit-elle, j'ai lu votre plaidoyer en faveur des *bêtes;* mais comment deux *personnes* si bien faites pour se comprendre ont-elles fini?" [*Well, I've read your plea on behalf of beasts, but how did two people so well made to understand each other end up?*]. Frølich proposes that the implicit association of "bêtes" and "personnes" is a "lapsus révélateur" that reveals that the young woman has concluded that the passion in the desert is a fiction meant to inspire a passion in Paris. She is mistaken, however, for her interlocuter is quite sincere and does not understand what his partner is implying by her questions about the story. Again, Frølich's emphases clarify the misunderstanding:

> —Ah! Voilà!. . . . Elles ont fini comme finissent toutes les grandes passions, *par un malentendu!* On croit de part et d'autre à quelque trahison, l'on ne s'explique point par fierté, l'on se brouille par entêtement.
>
> —Et quelquefois dans les plus beaux moments, dit-elle; un regard, une exclamation suffisent. *Eh! bien alors, achevez l'histoire?*
>
> —C'est horriblement difficile, mais vous comprendrez ce que m'avait déjà confié le vieux grognard, quand en finissant sa bouteille de Champagne, *il s'est écrié : "Je ne sais pas quel mal je lui ai fait, mais [. . .]*
>
> *"Well, voilà! They ended up like all great passions, with a misunderstanding! On both sides, there is the suspicion of betrayal, pride prevents explanation, stubbornness causes a rupture.*
>
> *"And sometimes in the most beautiful moments," she said, "a look, an exclamation will suffice. So, shall we complete the story?"*
>
> *"Its terribly difficult, but you will understand what the old soldier confided to me, when he finished his bottle of Champagne, he cried, 'I don't know what I did to her, but . . ."*

Following Frølich's reading, this exchange becomes a *dialogue de sourds.* We can almost hear the uncomprehending narratee's frustration with her equally (but differently) uncomprehending narrator's inability to understand exactly how she would like to finish the story. Just as the passion in the desert came to an abrupt end, so too will the passion in Paris, because of a *malentendu* (Frølich, 188). The sketchiness of the identity of the couple, who are anonymous in every sense of the word, allows us, even requires us, to fill in the blanks of the text, and allows us to do so in any way we wish.

Less vague but perhaps just as open to the reader is the narrative structure of *Z. Marcas.* The more "Balzacian" the reader of this text, the more familiar he is with not only *La Comédie humaine* but also Balzac's biography, political views, etc, the more weight he is likely to give to the portrait of Marcas as presented by Charles Rabourdin. We know that the views expressed in the text on the gerontocracy of the July Monarchy coincide with Balzac's, we recognize the elements of self-portrait in the character of Marcas, and so we are inclined to accept our young narrator's appraisal of his neighbor's genius, to give some credence to the implied argument that the abandonment and death of Marcas is a tragic loss for France. For the reader of the fragment alone, however, the text becomes much more ambiguous, as with Dorothy Kelly's reading of *L'Auberge rouge*. Both Charles and his friend Juste are very young, impressionable, and romantic. It is not difficult to imagine that their youthful intellects are more easily impressed by the discourse of their neighbor. We need only think of how many young people believe themselves to have found the Great Truths of the Human Condition in the work of Karl Marx, Ayn Rand, or for that matter Jerry Garcia.

Children of their time, Juste and Charles are undoubtedly attracted by the figure of the impoverished and unrecognized genius living in a lonely garret. In Balzac's pragmatic and politicized fictional world, it is logical that their Chatterton should have a genius for politics rather than poetry. However cynical and disillusioned they may be, they are too young for their disenchantment to be complete. Ready to believe in something or someone, they are overwhelmed by the story and the ideas of their new, older friend. We readers, with a bit of distance from both Charles and his anonymous friend who relates the tale to us, are not necessarily obliged to share their unqualified admiration.

The reading I suggest here is less a break with the traditional interpretation of this text than an extension of it, for I am not proposing that Marcas is a fraud, or that the government so darkly portrayed in the text is any more competent or trustworthy than Marcas claims it to be. Rather I am suggesting that the cynicism of this text can be extended to cover even the brief dream that Charles and Juste have of their friend's ability to change and improve the government and society. Marcas's brief return to power is thus not even a last ephemeral hope, but rather one more pointless attempt at salvation by a government that "chang[e] de ministres comme un malade change de place dans son lit [*changes ministers like a sick man changes place in the bed*]" as Marcas himself puts it (8:851). As a political doctor, Marcas may be an excellent diagnostician, but perhaps he has no more of a cure than anyone else. His return to power is merely one more move of the dying man; the difference is that we learn his story not from an objective point of view, but doubly filtered through the youthful enthusiasm and subsequent discouragement of Charles Rabourdin and his friends.

II
La Comédie humaine:
Unfinished, Unfinishable

As we read *La Comédie humaine,* it is easy to come to trust the veneer of *complétude* that covers the text. Even those of us who believe strongly—as I obviously do—that the text is richer and more complicated than is generally recognized, come to count on the text to fill in its own gaps, to "bouch[er] les interstices" found in and between the texts with information found in other fragments (Dällenbach, "Du fragment au cosmos," 427). But if we hope to appreciate the true worth of this work of art, we must always be prepared to challenge the text, to question the authority of the Narrator or narrators. Returning once more to Butor's essential analogy of this text as a *mobile romanesque,* we must never forget that the whole of *La Comédie humaine* is greater than the sum of its parts. In addition to the great blocks of text that make up the principal, and most visible, parts of the mobile, there are also the countless threads that bind these parts together, in incredibly complicated patterns, to form an unstable whole. Again, the recurring characters are only the most obvious connections between the textual parts, and we must be constantly vigilant if we hope to detect the more obscure connections that run behind, beneath, parallel and sometimes even counter to the ones that stand out so clearly.

The last part of the mobile that we must consider is the most abstract, the motion. Motion comes from the reader's engagement with the text(s); it is as we understand the instability of the text that we see how a situation that seems quite innocent can actually be deeply ironic, how a seemingly anodyne remark can be rich with double meaning if we know more about a character or situation than is provided in the text-fragment immediately concerned. This motion is also perhaps the most subjective

aspect of reading *La Comédie humaine,* closely linked as it is to our own
judgments about the true nature and importance of characters and motifs.
Paradoxically, our increased familiarity with the patterns of Balzac's
world and the idiosyncrasies of his thinking, as revealed through his writing, increases the instability of the text; rereading and continued exploration of the fictional world raises more questions than it answers, leading us
further and deeper into the textual labyrinth. The reader who has read
through Balzac's text(s) once has not finished reading *La Comédie humaine.* Indeed, I have come to believe that his text is unfinishable for the
reader, just as it was for the writer.

That Balzac never finished *La Comédie humaine* is a matter of re-
cord. At the time of his death, several important texts were left incomplete, such as *Les Paysans* and *Les Petits bourgeois,* and several others
were never more than titles or rather vaguely sketched ideas. What is less
widely recognized is that Balzac never could have finished *La Comédie
humaine.* The open-endedness of this work was inherent in Balzac's underlying literary project, the textual recreation of an entire society. As
Balzac said in his *avant-propos* of 1842, the ultimate goal was to paint
every species of the social animal, both the male and the female (1:8-9).
As each new character required both a history and a story, as each of those
histories inevitably introduced new characters, et cetera, ad infinitum.
Permanently eliminating any possible closure to this massive text was the
fact that the expansion of Balzac's fictional world had become a self-
perpetuating process; as Anthony Pugh said: "There can be no doubt [. . .]
that Balzac was often inspired by his own fiction to develop new possibilities, to ask 'what happened next?' or, more significantly, 'what had
happened previously?' " (*Balzac's Recurring Characters,* 461). This auto-
inspiration virtually ensured that Balzac could never have brought an end
to his own world; its growth only stopped because of the creator's death.

If *La Comédie humaine* was unfinishable for its writer, I believe it
is equally unfinishable for the reader, in a different way, and for different
reasons. Certainly, we are working with a finite text, which we can read
through given the time and the desire, but the reader who has read through
the text(s) once has not finished *La Comédie humaine.* It is as we reread
that we come to truly understand the complexity of this fictional world.
Once we have established a certain familiarity with the text, we can return
to it, not only with knowledge of the recurring characters, we are also

armed with our familiarity of the idiosyncrasies of Balzac's world, and—last but certainly not least—a certain degree of informed imagination. It is at this moment that we begin to detect that intangible movement of the mobile, the instability of the world portrayed, the openings in the text itself. As Dinah de La Baudraye observed, "on ne relit une œuvre que pour les détails" [*we only reread a work for the details*]. Details that in a first (or even second reading) seemed barely significant have ever greater resonance in our minds, undermining our conclusions and assumptions and raising new questions, leading us back into this endless labyrinth of text. All the factors that complicate the storytelling situations, that make narrators more eloquent than they know themselves to be, that make narratees active players in the transmission of the stories they seem to merely listen to, these factors set the textual mobile in motion, bring life to the *chaomos*.

This is the wonderful paradox of *La Comédie humaine:* the more information we have, the less certain we become. This supposedly monolithic text, "plein" and "lisible," is actually destabilized by the very details that create that deceptive veneer of *complétude;* the text grows more complex, not clearer, the more we explore it. We read *La Comédie humaine* as consumers of text, when we reread, we produce within it. Balzac never finished *La Comédie humaine,* and I believe that we readers never will either.

Bibliography

Balzac, Honoré de. *La Comédie humaine.* 12 volumes, Paris: Gallimard, Bibliothèque de la Pléiade, 1976-81. Ed. Pierre-Georges Castex, et al.

——. *Splendeurs et misères des courtisanes.* Paris: Garnier-Flammarion, 1968.

Barbéris, Pierre. *Le Monde de Balzac.* Paris: Arthaud, 1973.

Barthes, Roland. *S/Z.* Paris: Seuil, 1970.

Baudry, Jean. "George Sand, Balzac et *Honorine.*" *Année balzacienne* (1988): 395-98.

Bowman, Frank. *French Romanticism.* Baltimore: The Johns Hopkins University Press, 1990.

Butor, Michel. *Répertoire.* Paris: Editions de minuit, 1960.

Chambers, Ross. "Gossip and the Novel: Knowing Narrative and Narrative Knowing in Balzac, Madame de Lafayette, and Proust." *Australian Journal of French Studies* 23: 2 (May-August 1986): 212-33.

——. "Seduction Denied: Sarrasine and the Impact of Art." *French Forum* 5 (1980): 218-36.

Chatman, Seymour. *Story and Discourse: Narrative Structure in Fiction and Film.* Ithaca: Cornell University Press, 1980.

Citron, Pierre. *Dans Balzac.* Paris: Seuil, 1986.

Conner, J. Wayne. "Frame and Story in Balzac." *L'Esprit créateur* 7 (Spring 1967): 45-54.

——. "*Albert Savarus* and 'l'Ambitieux par amour.'" *Symposium* 37:4 (Winter 1983): 251-60.

Dällenbach, Lucien "Du Fragment au cosmos (*La Comédie humaine* et l'opération de lecture I)." *Poétique* 40 (1979): 420-31.

————. "Le tout en morceaux (*La Comédie humaine* et l'opération de lecture II)." *Poétique* 42 (1980): 156-69.

————. *La Canne de Balzac*. Paris: J. Corti, 1996.

Diderot, Denis. *Jacques le fataliste et son maître*. Paris: Garnier-Flammarion, 1970.

Fischler, Alexander. "Duplication and *Comédie morale* in Balzac's *Les Secrets de la princesse de Cadignan*." *Studies in Romanticism* 24 (1985): 257-66.

Fortassier, Rose. *Les Mondains de "La Comédie humaine": Etudes historique et psycho-ogique*. Paris: Klincksieck, 1976.

————. "Balzac et Laclos: Echos des *Liaisons dangereuses* dans *La Comédie humaine*." *Année balzacienne* (1976): 277-81.

Frappier-Mazur, Lucienne. "Lecture d'un texte illisible: *Autre étude de femme* et le modèle de la conversation." *MLN* 98 (1983): 712-27.

Frølich, Juliette: " 'Le phénomène oral': L'impact du conte dans le récit bref de Balzac." *Année balzacienne* (1985): 175-89.

Genette, Gérard. *Figures: Essais*. Paris: Seuil, 1966.

————. *Figures II*. Paris: Seuil, 1969.

————. *Figures III*. Paris: Seuil, 1972.

Guyon, Bernard. *La Création littéraire chez Balzac: La genès du "Médecin de campagne."* Paris: Colin, 1951.

Heathcote, Owen. "Balzac's Go-Between: The Case of *Honorine*." *Nineteenth-Century French Studies* 22: 1-2 (Fall-Winter 1993-94): 61-76.

————. "Balzac at the Crossroads: The Emplotment of Terror in *Une ténébreuse affaire*." In *The Play of Terror in Nineteenth-Century France*. John T. Booker and Allan H. Pasco, eds. Newark: University of Delaware Press (1997): 130-46.

Kelly, Dorothy: "Balzac's *L'Auberge rouge:* On Reading an Ambiguous Text." *Symposium* 36: 1 (Spring 1982): 30-44.

Lastinger, Michael. "Narration et 'point de vue' dans deux romans de Balzac." *Année balzacienne* (1988): 271-90.

LeRoy Ladurie, Emmanuel. "Introduction" to *Le Médecin de Campagne*. Paris: Folio, 1974.

Maingueneau, Dominique. "Polyphonie" in *Eléments de linguistique pour le texte littéraire*. Paris: Dunod, 1995: 69-83.

Marceau, Félicien. *Les personnages de La Comédie humaine.* Paris: Gallimard, 1977.

Mazet, Léo. "Récit(s) dans le récit: l'échange du récit chez Balzac." *Année balzacienne* (1976): 129-61.

Michel, Arlette. *Le Mariage et l'amour dans l'œuvre romanesque d'Honoré de Balzac* (4 vols.). Paris: Champion, 1976.

Mortimer, Armine Kotin. "*La Maison Nucingen,* ou le récit financier." *Romanic Review* 69 (1978): 60-71.

————. "Problems of Closure in Balzac's Short Stories." *French Forum* 10 (1985): 20-39.

————. "Second Stories" in *Short Story Theory at a Crossroads.* Susan Lohafer and Jo Ellyn Clarey, eds. Baton Rouge: Louisiana State University Press (1989): 276-98.

————. "Balzac: Tenebrous Affairs and Necessary Explications" In *The Play of Terror in Nineteenth-Century France.* John T. Booker and Allan H. Pasco, eds. Newark: University of Delaware Press (1997): 234-55.

Mozet, Nicole. *Balzac au pluriel.* Paris: Presses Universitaires Françaises, 1990.

Paris, Jean. *Balzac.* Paris: Balland, 1986.

Pacqueteau, François. "Idéologies et formes dans *Le Médecin de campagne.*" *Année balzacienne* (1970): 155-73.

Pasco, Allan. *Balzacian Montage: Configuring the Comédie humaine.* Toronto: University of Toronto Press, 1991.

————. "Balzac's Gobseck and Image Structure," in *Novel Configurations: A Study of French Literature.* Birmingham: Summa Publications, 1987.

Picon, Gaëton. *Balzac par lui-même.* Paris: Seuil, 1956.

Pierrot, Roger. *Honoré de Balzac.* Paris: Fayard, 1994.

Prince, Gerald. "Introduction à l'étude du narrataire." *Poétique* 14 (1973): 178-96.

————. *Dictionary of Narratology.* Lincoln: University of Nebraska Press. 1987.

Proust, Marcel. *Contre Sainte-Beuve.* Paris: Gallimard, Bibliothèque de la Pléiade, 1971.

Pugh, Anthony. *Balzac's Recurring Characters.* Toronto: University of Toronto Press, 1974.

————. "Note sur l'épilogue de *Un Prince de la Bohème.*" *Année balzacienne* (1968): 357-61.

Robb, Graham. *Balzac: A Biography.* New York: Will Norton, 1994.

Seylaz, Jean-Luc. "Réflexions sur *Gobseck.*" *Etudes litteraires* 1 (1968): 295-310.

Simons, Madeleine A. "Le Génie au féminin ou les paradoxes de la princesse de Cadignan." *Année balzacienne* (1988): 347-66.

Slatka, Denis. "Sémiologie et grammaire du nom propre dans *Un Prince de la Bohème,*" in *Balzac: L'invention du roman.* Claude Duchet and Jacques Neefs, eds. Paris: Belfond: 235-55.

Stendhal. *Le Rouge et le noir.* Paris: Garnier-Flammarion, 1964.

Talbot, Emile J. "Pleasure/Time or Egoism/Love: Rereading *La Peau de chagrin.*" *Nineteenth-Century French Studies* 11 (1982): 72-82.

Thompson, Marcia June. "Narrators and Narratees: A Study of Inner Narratives in the Comédie humaine." Dissertation, University of California at Santa Barbara, 1988.

Todorov, Tzvetzan. *Introduction à la littérature fantastique.* Paris: Seuil, 1970.

Vercollier, Claudine. "Le lieu du récit dans les nouvelles encadrées de Balzac." *Année balzacienne* (1981): 225-34.

Wurmser, André. *La Comédie inhumaine.* Paris: Gallimard, 1970.

Zélicourt, Gaston de. *Le Monde de "La Comédie humaine."* Paris: Seghers, 1979.

Index